The
Great Haydn Quartets

The
Great Haydn Quartets

Their Interpretation

Hans Keller

J. M. Dent
London

Music examples set by Tabitha Collingbourne

Printed and bound in Great Britain by
Butler & Tanner Ltd, Frome and London
for
J. M. Dent
The Orion Publishing Group
Orion House
5 Upper St Martin's Lane
London WC2H 9EA

British Library Cataloguing-in-Publication Data

A catalogue record for this book is available
from the British Library

ISBN 0 460 86107 7

Contents

Preface
The string quartet in general and the Haydn quartets in particular

What is more, it is an honest preface, in that it is being written well before a word of the body of the book goes down on paper. On the other hand, it is, in the main, chronologically that the present chapter precedes the rest of the book; musically, my introductory throughts are so much part and parcel of the book's substance that I hope the reader will remember specific observations from the Preface when the centre of his attention, his creative concentration, is an equally specific, overpowering moment in one of the great Haydn quartets.

In the course of a life in which not a week (or, to be absolutely precise, only one week[1]) has passed without active preoccupation with a great string quartet which, if it was not by Haydn, invariably led my thoughts back to its sources, its inspirations, its anticipations in the great Haydn quartets, I have had to cope with countless sneers and slightly fewer countless compliments – normally an easy task, because either category of reactions against or to my thought has left me equally untouched. As a matter of fact, I only remember two compliments which deeply touched me, and since both of them addressed themselves to that central part of my mind for which the great string quartet is identical with life itself, they may be of some relevance in the present context.

Both of them happened behind my back – which increased their value for me. The first occasion was a string-quartet session in my mid-teens when, without prior warning and at a moment's notice, I had to take the second-fiddle part in Haydn's C major Quartet, Op.64, No.1, under the leadership of my teacher, Oskar Adler (who, generations before, had been Schoenberg's first teacher and quartet leader), and with Franz Schmidt playing the cello in what was a regular ensemble, whose second violinist was not available in that particular half-hour. With Schmidt facing me at a yard's distance, I was so nervous that I was extremely grateful to Haydn not only for the opening 8 bars' rest, but also for the first 1½ bars of the restatement of the first movement's theme, i.e. their octave unison with the first violin, behind which I could hide my nervousness.

At the same time, the prospect of the third movement's first variation virtually paralysed me, and when I actually came to play the theme in this

---

[1]The week I was imprisoned by the Nazis.

variation, my bow trembled to such an extent that I thought Schmidt would now simply terminate the session, and suggest that one should wait for the return of the regular second fiddler. Somehow or other, I finished the entire quartet – not to my satisfaction. I could only hope that behind my back, Adler would tell Schmidt that normally my understanding of quartet-playing in general, and of the second violin's unique problems in particular, was in far clearer evidence. All the greater was my surprise, therefore, when a few days later, Adler quoted Schmidt's reaction: 'I can't tell you what is going to become of this young musician, but one thing I *can* tell you: the world will know of him.' It has taken me a little time to discover that as a teacher (and Schmidt was one, outstandingly so), you can hear right through a player's nervousness.

The reason why Schmidt's compliment touched me deeply was, simply, that he had heard what I wished to convey, and the textural means by which I wished to convey it, despite what was, in the circumstances, their physical inadequacy. The second compliment, many decades later, came from a composer, too. When Benjamin Britten passed a student on to me who was in the process of writing a string quartet, he told him that 'Hans Keller knows more about the string quartet, and understands it better, than anybody alive, composers and players included.' The reason why this particular compliment touched me yet more deeply was that Britten and I had had far-reaching discussions about the string quartet, especially his own Second, and that I now felt sure that my marginally critical message had got across – as indeed, many years later, his Third Quartet showed: in my opinion, he dedicated it to me only because its first movement deals, in a highly original way, with structural and textural problems I had raised decades before.

All of which is simply to say that from both the composing and the playing point of view the string quartet is a secret science – if by a 'secret' we mean, not something that shouldn't be told, but something that can't. It is impossible for any outstanding instrumentalist who is not a string and quartet player to understand a quartet player's string quartet in all its intended dimensions; likewise, it is impossible for a composer, however great, to write an intrinsic string quartet if he is not himself a quartet player: the quartets of Brahms, Schumann, Debussy, Ravel, and, yes, Bartók are more than adequate evidence. It is true, however, that, paradoxically, Bartók created a new quartet sound just because the intrinsic string quartet was unknown to him; as a string player, he could not have introduced his textural innovations.

For the fact is that the intrinsic string quartet as realized by Haydn, Mozart, Beethoven, Schubert, Mendelssohn, one Smetana quartet (No.1), one Dvořák quartet (the E flat), Hindemith, and Schoenberg is addressed, in the first place, to the player; the listener is a more or less welcome eavesdropper – more so in proportion as he is capable of identifying with the player. Through the balance and blend he wishes him to achieve, the composer can say more to the player than to the mere listener; in fact, the fundamental difference between balance and blend can only be wholly realized mentally if one is capable of realizing it physically – of turning it into reality. It is, in other words, parts that are balanced against each other, whereas, prototypically, the notes of a chord are blended with each other. Needless to add, there are textural junctures in a well-developed string quartet which demand simultaneous balance and blend in varying proportions; obviously, such subtleties have to be produced in order to be fully comprehended.

One can go further, therefore, and say, without any desire to be paradoxical, that the only difference between a string quartet (or a Mozartian or Schubertian or Mendelssohnian string quintet) and a symphony is that the quartet (or quintet) is more symphonic: symphonic thought is at its purest in the quartet, which does not have to enlist the help of sound effects, however elevated, in order to hold the listener's attention, for the player's attention is held in any case. And since the intrinsic quartet is primarily addressed to him, to the player through the player, through conversation between the players, its ideal acoustic conditions are indeed those of the chamber; the so-called 'projection' of tone does not play any role in its intended realization.

Even amongst the greatest quartet composers' works, to be sure, there are occasional exceptions – quasi-orchestral textures which, however inspired and masterly, will always strike the true quartet player as ultimately unsatisfactory, marginally inadequate, not fully and subtly expressive. Haydn's single exception is the outer movements of the 'Emperor' (Op.76, No.3), Mozart's is, complexly, the last movement of his last quartet (K.590 in F major), Beethoven's, more than complexly, the Grand Fugue[2] (Op.133), Schubert's, the Quartet Movement, Mendelssohn's, the outer movements of his D major quartet, Schoenberg's, his single-movement First Quartet (actually his second).

Every true quartet, on the other hand, inevitably loses refinement when it is transplanted into the concert hall and addressed to an audience. But though the gramophone record with its repeatability represents our age's most potent anti-musical force, counteracting as it does the indispensable singularity and spontaneity of any performance that is entitled to call itself musical, it is on a record or a tape that one can reproduce true quartet sound for the eavesdropping non-player: in my years as radio producer, I used to tell quartets about to broadcast not to project, but to play (if they still could) as if they were at home, and leave the rest to me. I then took the studio manager into the studio, placed him next to the viola, texturally the ideal position preferred by all great string-playing composers (Haydn, Mozart,[3] Beethoven, Schubert, Mendelssohn, Hindemith, Schoenberg), let him listen to the quartet's practice for about twenty minutes, and instructed him to reproduce the sound, the

---

[2] There is no justification for the phoney German title, *Grosse Fuge*, which wasn't Beethoven's. There is an amazing English compulsion to use non-existent German titles: *Quartettsatz* is another example – the translation, not of the movement's title, but of its German description.

[3] When they played the Mozart quintets together, Haydn and Mozart played the two violas, alternating between first and second after each movement.

balance and blend he had now heard: the result was often barely distinguishable from the sound one would have heard had one played the viola oneself.

Speaking personally, the quartet texture's fate in the concert hall was one
of the decisive reasons why I never wanted to become a public player – though
in my early years in this country I had to be one if I wanted to stay alive; in
fact, at that stage I was a member of two public quartets, playing the viola in
one of them. It was at that time that the highly imaginative first violinist of
what was to become one of the world's leading quartets suddenly surprised
me, in an artist's room, with an invitation – after we had played Elgar's
Introduction and Allegro for string quartet and string orchestra: 'I want to
found a quartet; will you join?' My 'No!' ensued after a second's hesitation
that felt like an hour's.

The great and not so great composers did not, alas, say 'No!' when the
concert hall invited the string quartet to join its performing stars – and in due
course, the classical quartet's expressive range and finesse were reduced, if not
altogether lost: the former eavesdropper had become the primary recipient.
Yet, even in modern times, we still encounter the occasional great composer
in full possession of the string quartet's secret, as his quartet textures show:
with the exception of the First, Schoenberg's string quartets (not forgetting
his greatest, which is the String Trio!), for instance, are as chamber-conscious
as Haydn's – even though they try, intermittently, to have it both ways, like
the greatest public quartet players.

Haydn, too, wrote for the concert hall in London – without, however,
sacrificing the tiniest particle of the quartet's expressive range: there simply
was no later quartet composer capable of having it both ways as consistently,
and as variedly. Nor indeed is this the only respect in which he can be
regarded, if a comprehensible simplification be permitted, as the first and last
quartet composer altogether. Musicological readers will object for a start that
he wasn't the first. Musician readers, on the other hand, will agree that so far
as the art – as distinct from the craft – of string-quartet writing is concerned,
he was not only the first, but actually turned what seemed an unpromising
medium into what was to become the most expressive form of Western
instrumental composition – and it became that in his own hands, too! What,
then, had been unpromising about it? The symptoms of this lack of promise
are still palpable; it has resulted in the problems of the second violin, which
are so grave that in my lifetime, and on an international scale, there have never
been more than two or three outstanding second fiddlers per generation.

For we must not forget that while the first violin is a soprano instrument,
the second is, too, whereas the tenor part is taken by an alto instrument. As a
result, the string quartet, although it seems a contrapuntal medium to
everybody not in possession of its secret science, has never been able to
develop a truly well-sounding polyphonic texture, and the secret of good
quartet-writing contains the answer to the question of how to get round the
polyphonic problem without landing in sheer or too emphatic homophony.

True, when Haydn came in, a Viennese quartet tradition had established itself which indulged in the fugal finale as a matter of tedious course: there is not a single such quartet whose musical weight has enabled it to survive, or whose texture gives one the remotest inkling of the string quartet's extreme potentialities in terms of subtlety of sound. Characteristically enough, as soon – or rather, as late – as Haydn had attained his mastery of the medium (he had reached middle age), he turned the fugal quartet finale from what had become a chronic failure into a unique, and uniquely variable creative event: what he created in Op.20 was no less than *the* paradigm for all great quartet fugues by Mozart and Beethoven; significantly and indeed amusingly, it was only he himself who subsequently refused to follow his own prototype – on a single later occasion, to wit, in the F♯ minor Quartet's (Op.50, No.4's) finale, which is a monothematic fugue. In Op.20, to the contrary, the C major fugue (No.2's) is on no fewer than four subjects, while the F minor (No.5's, in his very own key) is a double and the A major (No.6's) a triple fugue, thus ensuring the necessary textural variety which both Mozart and Beethoven accepted as an indispensable model. In the exceptional case of that demanding F♯ minor fugue, textural contrasts are brought about by other means; besides, there is multiple evidence that the work as a whole had firmly decided to make interpretative life jolly difficult for the players, however realistically so. The very choice of key imposes a life sentence of more or less well concealed insecurity upon quartet-playing humanity: let us not forget that the entire history of the string quartet boasts a mere four major works that have set up home in that tortuous, indeed torturous tonality, whose proximity of kin to A major would have made it more popular amongst composers if it had been less unpopular amongst players – and, what is less, only one of the remaining three F♯ minor quartets is a comparably supreme masterpiece. Though Reger's Fifth (Op.121) and Tippett's Second must not, of course, be underrated, the only quartet in that key which, like Haydn's, is in possession of its genre's secret science constitutes, in fact, a critical climax in the history of composition: it is Schoenberg's last tonal – indeed, intermittently atonal – work, his Second Quartet.

And why, or rather, how, can Haydn be described as the last quartet composer altogether? On a conservative count, he wrote 45 profound and profoundly different, absolutely flawless, consistently original master quartets, each a violent, multi-dimensional contrast to any of the others: *pace* the ultimate metaphysical discoveries of Beethoven's late quartets, which great quartet composer's output in the medium can begin to compare with Haydn's comprehensive testament? Though from any naturally musical point of view, every string player ought to know the 45 at least as well as every responsible pianist knows the '48', we still find string players all over the place who mention the great Haydn symphonies and his great quartets in the same breath, unaware of the immeasurably weightier and subtler substance any of the master quartets evinces when heard next to a comparable master symphony. What I have said about the stronger, purer symphonism of the quartets is easily demonstrable, in that the symphonies never show the structural and textural complexities of the quartets; as a matter of fact, what, in a symphony, will be a straightforward homophonic accompaniment will readily turn into far more meaningful and proportionately more unpredictable subordinate parts in a comparable quartet, with the result that the ensuing texture, neither homophonic nor contrapuntal, throws up combinations of the two styles for which no name has yet been found: outside the intrinsic string quartet, these combinations simply do not exist, and inside it, those who hear the secret clearly don't worry about technical terms for its various aspects – though it must be admitted that from the standpoint of composition-teaching, a neologism for the characteristic string quartet's homophonic polyphony would not come amiss. Come to think of it, 'homophonic polyphony' might do: those who can conjure up the sound of it will immediately know what it means, and those who can't have not yet earned themselves the right to verbalize what is not part of their musical experience, anyway. For the rest, even H.C. Robbins Landon, one of the world's few musical musicologists and the author of the monumental *Symphonies of Josef Haydn*,[4] unreservedly accepts my comparative evaluation of the quartets and symphonies.

One grand illusion, in any case, has to be destroyed at the outset of any sound-conscious investigation of the string quartet – a piece of textbook wisdom conveyed to many a student, composer or instrumentalist, by many a so-called expert: that in the string quartet, there are 'four equal parts'. Of many a lousy quartet, this textural definition is, of course, perfectly true, at least so far as the composer's confused intentions are concerned, but as soon as you turn to the master quartet in general and the 45 in particular, you realize that, on the contrary, there isn't a single leaderless juncture or stage – an all-important, clearly audible fact, this, from the playing point of view. It inevitably implies that likewise, there isn't a single interpretative problem that can be solved in committee: either whoever leads at a given point makes his solution – ideally, everybody's solution – convincingly and persuasively clear through his playing, his phrasing, his tone production and tone modulation, or there just won't be any solution, and what will be heard instead will be the most inartistic sound imaginable – a compromise.

Not for a moment should it be assumed that those 45 are, in any way, an arbitrary selection, and that my 'conservative count' opens up the possibility of there being a greater number of great Haydn quartets. In fact, amongst those who know their Haydn quartets because they understand them both as structures and from the standpoint of their quartet-writing, there cannot be the remotest doubt about whether any given work is amongst Haydn's sublime achievements or not – even though amongst musicologists and critics whose understanding is limited in either dimension, you will not be able to

---

[4] London, 1955. Cf. also, amongst many other writings on the composer, his *Haydn Symphonies*, London, 1966, and *Haydn: Chronicle and Works*, i–v, London, 1976–80.

find the clear-cut, decided diagnostic attitude of the initiates. The 'conserva-tive count', then, has merely two implications. For one thing, it does not include the final fragment (Op.103), which we shall only touch upon at the end of the present book. But though those middle movements of what would have become a D minor quartet[5] might well have taken their place in a great work, it never came to be written, whence it cannot, realistically, be included amongst Haydn's greatest quartets: we don't know anything about its outer movements.

For another thing, a musically conscientious classification has to exclude, from the works evincing simultaneous, ultimate originality and mastery, the B♭ work from Op.33 (No.4); it is a multiply interesting quartet in all conscience and, of course, forms part of an otherwise great *opus*. However, not only does it evince textural shortcomings, but its melodic invention is often surprisingly unoriginal, at times downright conventional. Equally surprising is what is, at best, its harmonic routine mastery which, I submit, disqualifies it from membership of the group composed of works of con-sistent, towering genius, even though a perspicacious musician might well be able to divine the stature of its composer in view of the work's all too rare imaginative moments.

It has, unfortunately, to be admitted that by playing the B♭ quartet as often and as importantly as any of the other quartets from Op.33, many a famous quartet enjoying a reputation it has fostered for its Haydn specialism – on our age of inartistic specialization more anon! – proves its utter ignorance and incomprehension of what matters in a great quartet and what doesn't: an essential part of what does matter could not, of course, be arranged, reinstru-mentated for a different combination, whereas a disturbing proportion of this B♭ work easily could; in places, it might even gain. We are justified, then, in ignoring Op.33, No.4, if only because its playing ought to be discouraged until the master works are known inside out.

As for those Haydn specialists, there cannot, musically speaking, be any such person as a 'Haydn specialist' who knows all about the Haydn quartets and little about Mozart's or Beethoven's or Schubert's or Mendelssohn's or Schoenberg's: a profound insight into the Haydn quartet will inevitably engender equally deep preoccupation with their progeny, with all later quartets of genius, be they by Mozart, the successful lover of Haydn's quartet-writing, or by its unsuccessful lover, Brahms.[6] Artistically speaking, one can go so far as to say that all specialism is phoney – a submission which, in view of our age's pseudo-professional prejudices, our preface will have to substantiate a little more closely in a few pages' time.

[5] Inanely, my edition of Eulenburg's pocket scores entitles the movements 'Quartet in B♭ major': the distinguished firm must, at that stage, have employed an editor who was musically illiterate.
[6] To be absolutely fair, there are traces of Brahms' love of Haydn's quartets throughout the A minor quartet, and in the middle movements of the C minor and B♭.

The Op.17 quartets, in their turn, are loved and played by many specialist quartets, though they are neither sufficiently substantial as music nor sufficiently unproblematic as quartets to be attempted by any except those who have acquired a thorough knowledge of Haydn's true masterpieces, all of them. As, in a lifetime, I have met only three such musicians it would be unrealistic to go into Op.17's interpretation, the more so since these quartets do not in any respect foreshadow what was to come. Yet again, one can't simply say that it is Op.20 that marks the sudden, late, and sustained explosion of Haydn's genius – not without qualification. For one thing, the aforementioned B♭ work was to come, definitely not a work of manifest genius. For another, there is a single earlier work which, without the slightest hesitation, has to be included in the initiate's master class – as decidedly as the *Seven Words* (Op.51) have to be excluded from it: like the early divertimentos (*Opera* 1, 2 and 3), they aren't really quartet textures at all, for obvious reasons.

But far from being obvious, the reasons why suddenly, in the D minor work from Op.9, we get a consistent, deeply moving preview of Haydn's quartet genius which compels us to accept it in our Haydn repertory cannot, to my knowledge, be traced. Few are the psychologists who are honest enough, sufficiently self-knowing, to confess that so far as the penetration of the mystery of genius is concerned, of that *ingenium* that puzzled even the civilized rather than cultured Romans, we have made depressingly little progress – though Freud, major (if utterly unmusical) genius himself, was certainly among them when he remarked that in the face of art, psycho-analysis had to 'lay down its arms' (a charming, metaphorical admission, incidentally, of the aggressive nature of psycho-dynamic research, particularly where it is unconscious safes that have to be blown!). We for our part have to be honest enough to stress that there are riveting questions to which we don't known the answer; the abrupt, isolated lack of inspiration in Op.33, No.4 is one of them, the equally sudden, equally lonely flood of inspiration in Op.9, No.4 another – almost unbearably intriguing upon one's conscience. None of Op.9's other five quartets deserves study; they are immeasurably, and bafflingly, more primitive than is the D minor.

In our reluctant march backwards, the less said about the early divertimento 'quartets', a dozen-and-a-half of them (*Opera* 1, 2 and 3), the better, though Jens Peter Larsen, in his *New Grove* article on Haydn,[7] devotes quite a bit of wordy thoughtlessness, as well as his only music example from a quartet, to the negligible Op.1, No.1.[8]

The other year's sensationalizing and dramatic disclosure that some of these prenatal works, i.e. Op.3, or at least part of it, were not by Haydn but by Roman Hofstetter bored those of us to death who had always been aware

[7] Republished in book form (London, 1982), on which I have written at some length in the *Haydn Yearbook*, Vol.XIV (Cardiff, 1983).

[8] Op.1, No.5, incidentally, is a symphony, and Op.2, Nos.3 and 5 are sextets with horns.

that musically speaking, none of the eighteen was, anyway: in no conceivable sense characteristic quartets, and indeed not intended as such, they far antedate the emergence of Haydn's mastery as well as his genius. In the early days of the Third Programme, they were broadcast with musicological enthusiasm – and there their function ended.

About the authenticity of the so-called quartets of Op.3 I have, rather amusingly, always had my doubts in any case – on purely and demonstrably musical grounds. Rather paradoxically, though, my doubts concerned the single movement whose melodic invention could have been the embryonic Haydn's inspiration – the well-known, so-called Serenade in C major from the F major Quartet, Op.3, No.5 – a beautifully unfolding, lavishly extended (72-bar) melody. What I couldn't credit Haydn with were the mutes. It wasn't only that I couldn't hear any reason for them; far more importantly, I have always been clearly aware of the undesirable, levelling, de-characterizing effect of mutes on an intrinsic string quartet's tonal personality: not even the as yet unborn quartet composer, I felt, would have sunk to such aural insensitivity. In view of its accompanimental pizzicatos, of course, the texture of the Serenade is not tangibly undesirable; at the same time, there is no acoustic evidence of the desirability of the muted melody, the tone modulation of whose phrasing can be far more clearly and movingly defined *senza sordini*.

This is the moment to draw attention to a simple, important acoustic fact of which astonishingly few quartet players (not to speak of listening quartet lovers) are clearly and concretely conscious. The mute imposed upon a string quartet produces, strictly speaking, an invalid quartet sound: robbed of essential overtones, the player is no longer able to produce and modulate his tone to the extent required by a quartet texture which has to differentiate more delicately than any comparable choral instrumentation. Neither here nor anywhere else in this book am I theorizing; what I am advancing is simple, historical fact: with a single, explicable exception, *there is no great quartet, no insider's quartet or string quintet, in which any instrument or movement or section, however short, is muted.* The sole exception occurred, admittedly, at the very centre of the great quartet's or string quintet's literature: it is the slow movement of Mozart's G minor Quintet.

Why did Mozart for once change his, as well as every other past and future great quartet composer's, mind? Because this was the only occasion on which he, or any other great quartet composer, needed two successive adagios – the slow movement proper and the slow introduction to the last, between which he had to establish palpable contrast despite their identical tempo character – a contrast, therefore, which could not content itself with the structural dimension, but had to penetrate the sheer sound of either movement: the immediate impression either texture made had to be sharply contrasted. It was, I suggest, for this reason that, uniquely, he decided on the muted slow-movement adagio as opposed to the unmuted adagio that introduces the finale – and, needless to add, he turned the slow movement's texture into one whose balances and blends could, exceptionally, tolerate mutes; only Mozart has proved himself capable of such a feat.

The resulting contrast is, as we all know, quite overwhelming – the more so since the respective textures themselves do not share any essential element. But this single textural sensation apart, no mute can be found in any master quartet or quintet – an elementary fact which has not, to date, given rise to any comment, has not even been noted: a measure, this, of the pitiably low level of literally all investigations into the nature of the string quartet (or any particular master's quartets).

More than a word is necessary, at this particular stage, on our book's prospective addressee. Superficially, its desirable readers, as well as those to whom it isn't addressed, fall into neatly distinguishable, mutually exclusive categories – but any such simple-minded classification would be grossly misleading: it would lead not only prospective readers and non-readers, but also the author himself astray, for unless he knows his potential audience at least as well as he would if he were giving a lecture, not only will he select wrong points for discussion or discuss points of secondary importance at the expense of what, for at least some of his readers, is all-important, but he will not formulate his observations in what, for his readers, are the clearest, most effective possible terms.

A superficial, misleading classification would place the professional quartet player right at the centre, the amateur player on a concentric circle at a safe distance from the centre, and the inactive eavesdropper on the most peripheral concentric circle, where he would be invited to deepen his under-standing purely passively, without, that is, being able to participate in the actual shaping of musical thought.

Human nature, especially its musical side, is both simpler and more complicated than that: the interplay between natural musicality and environ-mental determinants of either comprehension or incomprehension produces the most astonishing differences between individual inhabitants, active or passive, of our musical world. I speak, yet again, without any theoretical prejudices, quite empirically, when I say that on the one hand, there are leading (read: misleading) quartet players whose esoteric insight into the quartet is nil, despite all the practical experience they have accumulated; whereas on the other hand, there are not only amateur players, but even mere listeners, whose knowledge of the string quartet is by no means exoteric only. In the case of these sheer listeners, I seem to be contradicting myself when I argue that complete, comprehensive insight into the nature of the string quartet is confined to its players, but though I haven't encountered any mere listener yet whose understanding of the quartet could possibly be regarded as comprehensive, I have come upon more than one whose insight seemed, unquestionably, superior to many a player's; on closer inspection, such personalities invariably disclose an exceptional capacity for identifica-tion with the player's attitude; maybe sensitively balanced recordings have helped these people on the way towards their entirely passive esotericism!

All of which is to say that while this book does not address itself to those professionals, however successful, from whom nature has withheld any ability, manifest or latent, to dive into the quartet's depths, its potential readers certainly do include a variety of amateur types, passive as well as active, whom nature and environment have, as it were, capacitated towards becoming initiates; I'd go so far as to claim that my observations and suggestions are designed to turn a gifted amateur's insight from latent into manifest understanding of at least some of the initiate's areas and layers of comprehension – and I still speak purely experientially, on the basis of what I have observed has happened to certain listeners who consistently attended my coaching sessions with both leading quartets and aspiring youngsters about to form a quartet. In other words, it isn't I, it is the reader, from whichever category of musicality he hails, who must be the ultimate judge of whether this book is for him or not – nor will he find judgment difficult on whether he is on my wavelength: a few paragraphs read in a bookshop will show him whether my approach fascinates or bores him; there won't, or shouldn't, be anything in between, no occasional or intermittent, half-hearted and – curse of the age! – half-minded interest. For the interest this text demands and will receive from the naturally gifted reader remembers its Latin roots: the reader either *inter-est*, participates, gets right in between the notes, motifs, phrases, and sentences, or he will please go away, reduce my royalties and increase the book's reality; those who remain will remember that this third person singular, *interest*, also means 'it matters'.

The reason why I assert the simple alternative between total interest and equally continual boredom with such certitude and seeming arrogance is that once again, I am confining myself to my experience of the effect my coaching has had on outsiders, apparent or real. Since this book is not going to theorize at any stage, since its every observation is going to flow from my practical, teaching or coaching or advisory experience, since every problem it is going to discuss will be a problem, real or, more often, seeming, which I have actively encountered, with which I have been specifically presented, I am able to foresee the only possible reactions to my proposed solutions: after – or rather, before – all, I've seen them.

Heaven protect this book, then, from a specialist readership; if it will be found consistently to oppose one particular pseudo-artistic attitude, it is that of specialism in all its dimensions. A chest surgeon will be a better chest surgeon for having concentrated on, or even confined himself to, chest surgery throughout his surgical life: the scientific specialist, whether practical or theoretical, is a realistic phenomenon, whereas artistic specialization is phenomenally unrealistic, for the obvious reason that – again practically as well as theoretically – wider artistic insight means deeper insight, and deeper insight ineluctably widens your understanding; a virtuous circle, this, of a kind with which those thinkers who discovered and named the *circulus vitiosus* should have confronted it, in order to avoid the paranoic implication that all circles are vicious. Let me, therefore, introduce the virtuous circle as a logical complementary concept, for which I propose the technical term *circulus virtutis*. As for the factual nature of my submission about scientific *v.* artistic specialism, can the reader recall a single great scientist or doctor who had not specialized, *or a single artist who had*?

Like the professional opera producer, for instance, the professional viola player – violist in the States and even, by now, in this country's more reckless linguistic regions – is the product of our senile century's inferiority feelings (in the main entirely justified), and of the resultant urge towards well-fortified, emphatic specialization. My parents and many trustworthy musicians of their generation saw, and some of them even played in, Mahler's productions of the classical and romantic operas which, dominated as they were by his musical structuring of the work in question, yet in no way oblivious of the need for lively acting, were unanimously held to have been far more exciting, consistent, and indeed dramatic than anything seen subsequently. In Mahler's time, the opera producer simply did not exist: all Mahler (or, for that matter, Wagner) had at his disposal for the purpose of realizing his own theatrical intentions was what we would nowadays call a stage manager with no re-creative will of his own.

The viola player was equally, wholly unknown to the nineteenth and early twentieth centuries; his nounlessness should have made aspiring 'violists' ponder both their own musical non-existence and the fact that as violists, one would logically expect them to be performers on the viol. And this is where, for natural musicians who, as a matter of inescapable course, are viola-playing violinists, *circulus virtutis* comes in with a well-blended bang, again both musically and practically: the width of their instrumental experience deepens their characterization of and differentiation between, violin tone on the one hand and viola tone on the other, and sharpens their bowing techniques for the respective instrument, while their increased awareness of these contrasting characters widens their aural outlook on the range of musical colour and of the means of tone production and tone modulation.

From our own, quartet-playing point of view, a concrete understanding of the utter unmusicality of what is, nowadays, an officially legitimized brand of specialism – you are either a fiddler or a viola player, and de-specialization is bad for you – is of fundamental importance. Wherever possible – at the Summer School of Music in Dartington, at the Yehudi Menuhin School, at the Guildhall School of Music and elsewhere (even, strictly in private, amongst some of the world's so-called leading quartets) – I have successfully forced players (all but physical force is quite often required) to change over from one instrument to the other; in fact, in this particular respect I have never yet failed once, though wellnigh invariably I am promised certain failure by my prospective victims.

That our musical civilization (which has replaced our unspecialist culture) is gradually becoming one big, deaf, obsessional neurosis can be gathered not only from the usual argument, supported by many a teacher, 'The change-over will spoil my intonation', but even more so from the fact that my equally usual reply, 'In that case, don't ever move into the higher positions on your own instrument, but turn yourself into a first-position specialist, for the difference in finger-distance between them and the first position is greater than that between violin and viola', is regularly received as if it were a stunningly surprising, major revelation.

I can say without hesitation or reservation that the few truly great viola players I have heard in my life, those who produced the almost forgotten, characteristic viola tone rather than playing the fiddle on the viola, were all violinists with a personal, deep-cutting experience of the extreme unalikeness of the two instruments' characters – Oskar Adler and Arnold Rosé among them. Our technique-conscious youngest generation might usefully be reminded that men like Adler or Arnold Rosé or Carl Flesch or Paul Hindemith or Arnold Schoenberg still played both instruments as a matter of natural course, without making a fuss about it – Adler, Rosé and Flesch indeed at the virtuoso level. As for Schoenberg's *Pierrot lunaire*, which is intrinsic chamber music, you have to change to and fro between the two instruments at the shortest possible notice – as he himself did when playing quartets in his mid-teens. But some of our highly professional, modern specialists labour under the anti-musical illusion that he wanted two players for the job! So far have we regressed that the illusion is, in fact, quite often realized in public.

Carl Flesch played *Harold in Italy* in several concerts, and as a boy, I still saw Rosé get up from his leader's desk in the Vienna Philharmonic, pick up the viola from the open case that lay to attention on the floor next to his left foot, and play the *Concertante* with Huberman – immeasurably more impressively, more characteristically in tone colour, than any viola specialist I have heard since.

Mozart's work, incidentally, is an unambiguous pointer to the character of the viola. In it, Rosé's very personal viola-tone, as opposed to his equally individualistic, but brilliantly 'leading' violin- and quartet-tone, was breathtakingly contained, emphatically unbrilliant outside the virtuoso passages: how did the *Concertante* enable him to be contained on the one hand, and brilliant on the other? It is, we must remember, the only viola concerto by a great composer, for the great composers, every single one of them, were acutely alive to the fact that the viola was not a solo instrument, even though some modern makers have tried to de-characterize and thus turn it into one.

Why and how, then, did Mozart decide on this exceptional composition? He employed a *scordatura* on the instrument he, as a player, preferred to the violin, and his use of the device has been misunderstood throughout the history of performance: most virtuoso performers think that by turning the viola into a transposing instrument and letting it play in D major, he wanted to make things easier for the player – and in order to prove their own virtuosity, they proceed to ignore his easement, his technical disentanglement which, in compositorial reality, is inseperable from the intended sound of the work, for two reasons.

First, by covering, indeed containing the sound of the violin through its having to play in E♭ and, at the same time, liberating the viola's sound through its playing, in effect, in D major, he moves the contrasting personalities of the two instruments more closely towards each other, thus enabling them to indulge not only in interplay, but in taking on each other's roles throughout the three movements. Secondly, by making the violin's E♭ technique a little more burdensome and the viola's D major technique that much more flowing, he takes a further step in turning what normally are antipodean siblings into near-identical twins: he does not rest content with adjusting the sound of the respective instrumental characters, but actually integrates the sound of their execution, too.

To any violin-playing viola player who has grown up in the string quartet (which, invariably, sharply defines the character of the viola), the *Concertante*'s means of turning the viola, for the duration of the work, into a seeming solo instrument are instinctively obvious – and realistically, every quartet player of any of the upper three parts must be both violin-playing viola player and viola-playing fiddler; it is unfortunate enough that with two exceptions known to me, none of us can play all four parts. The two exceptions were Hindemith (whose intensely characteristic, deeply moving viola tone I was still able to hear) and Schoenberg, who, to begin with, played only the viola and the violin in his quartet sessions. One day in his mid-teens, however, he announced to his staggered friends: 'Tonight we're playing Beethoven C minor, and I'll play the cello.' He had, the day before, bought himself a cheap cello at Vienna's second-district flea market (*Tandelmarkt*) and proposed to practise all day, in preparation for the event which, nevertheless, his pals previewed with a certain amount of trepidation: how would he cope with Ex.1 – the development section's F major version of the second subject high up on the A-string?

Ex.1

Why did he choose this particular work?

In the evening, the reconstituted quartet assembled under its usual leader, Oskar Adler (who, generations later, became my leader – and the greatest chamber musician I have ever encountered). Everybody held his breath from the first movement's double-bar, but nobody noticed Schoenberg's special preparations: on a stool behind him, he had placed his viola, and in bars 102–3, ten bars before the solo, he grabbed it and played the theme on it with consummate skill – if not quite in the tonal character required.

Instrumental specialization apart, there are two, negatively complementary types of specialists against whom this book is directed to the extent of my harbouring the hope that they'll never move anywhere near it. One is the musicological expert – on Haydn, or on the Haydn string quartets, or on the string quartet and its history – who has never played a note of what he is talking about.

The other type of specialist who is the present book's enemy No.1 is the unthinking player who prides himself on 'just being a player', and who has never thought, but only felt music – who, in fact, feels thought to be the foe of feeling, whereas in musical reality, there is no feeling that cannot be articulately thought. It all depends, of course, on what we mean by musical thought: you can think *about* music, which is what musicologists and critics and, alas, most teachers do, and you can *think music*, which is what this book will encourage its readers to do. It is thought *about* music which is the real foe of musical thought; at the present stage in the history of interpretation, it has, to a mortally dangerous extent, replaced transitive musical thinking – the capacity to think music in the same natural, spontaneous way the 'normal' (unmusical) human being thinks pictures, words, concepts, terms: the laws of musical logic are best followed without the intervention of the very different laws of conceptual thought.

My book is a book, of course: it cannot consist of expositions of my new, wordless method of musical analysis, called 'functional analysis' (though in a decade or two, it will be possible to write such a wordless book, consisting of music alone, on the present subject). But my words will adopt the opposite course of logical action to that usually taken in books about music: they will, throughout, try to serve their master, to wit, musical logic, rather than impose verbal logic on musical thought processes.

My preface is reluctantly drawing to a close, and I'm very conscious of the motives behind, even the rational reasons for, my hesitation – of which I propose to make a meal, in the hope of destroying the indestructible: prejudices at the very centre of the spirit of our times. Let me give a musical example of such indestructibility – one which is far removed from the prejudices I myself am frantically trying to crush or, at the very least, upset, but which is at the same time extremely relevant to my case, in view of its very maximum of indestructibility.

In his book on *Harmony* (*Harmonielehre*[9]), Schoenberg devotes his very first chapter, entitled 'Theory or System of Presentation', to the clear, simple, unambiguous fact that the book cannot in any sense be considered to contain, or consist of, a theory; the chapter's short, central paragraph is worth quoting in full:

To hell with all those theories if, invariably, they only serve to put a

[9] Vienna, 1911. Third and last edition: Vienna, 1922.

stop to the development of art; and if anything positive they achieve
consists, at most, in helping those who in any case are going to compose
badly towards acquiring that ability speedily.
(My translation, more accurate than the – admittedly largely competent
– published one, of which more below.)

He finishes the chapter with the exclamation that he would be proud if he
could say that in his book, he had 'taken from composition pupils a bad
aesthetics and given them, instead, a good course in craft'. In our terms, his
Harmony thinks harmony instead of thinking, theorizing, *about* harmony. In
fact, there is no claim the entire work makes more strongly than his almost
threatening assertion that it is anti-theoretical. However, in this age of
thinking about instead of thinking music, anything Schoenberg wrote in
words rather than notes has to be theory, whether he likes it or not – so how
did the English, or rather American translator of the book, Roy E. Carter,
start his job, what title did he give the book? *Theory of Harmony*[10] – the one
thing Schoenberg said and said again it was not!

Similarly, I emphasize and reiterate that the present book is not by a
specialist on Haydn, or the string quartet, or the Haydn quartets. Throughout my life, I have wrongly been known as a specialist, though amusingly
enough, my specialism has been subjected to drastic variations. Apart from
the just-listed specialities, I have been described as a Mozart specialist, a
Beethoven specialist, a Mendelssohn specialist, a Britten specialist, a Schoenberg specialist, a 12-tone specialist, a New Music specialist, a chamber music
specialist . . .

Yet it is precisely as important, as crucial, to realize that the present work
is not an act of specialization as it is not to read Schoenberg's *Harmony* as a
'Theory of Harmony'. What I am trying to help towards is the most fundamental, general, comprehensive approach to the whole realm of the string
quartet and, beyond that, to the interpretation of symphonic thought at its
subtlest and purest.

Now, it might be suggested that so far as consistently natural excellence,
profound musical greatness, and unfailing textural mastery are concerned,
Haydn's only serious rivals, the interpretation of whose quartets could be
studied towards the selfsame purpose, are Mozart and Beethoven. But
Mozart's great quartets are far more alike in their basic structural approach
than Haydn's, and the development they represent is such that, if we are
honest, we do not even always find it easy to say, on purely musical grounds,
which is the earlier and which the later. It is in the spheres of the piano
concerto and the string quintet that Mozart's instrumental music is at its most
original and varied, that it develops most intensely from work to work. A
never-asked question arises here with elemental force: without Haydn's
stimulation, would Mozart have made the quartet (and quintet) one of his
central creative areas at all? Before Haydn's inspiration came in, his quartets

[10] London, 1978. The translation is based on the third edition.

and quintets were, as Mozart's works, downright pitiable – mere occasional pieces – with two partial exceptions: the first two movements of K.156 in G major and the first movement of K.157 in C major.

As for Beethoven, possibly humanity's greatest mind altogether, his quartets are a special case. For one thing, his great quartets – unlike Haydn, he didn't write any 'celebrated' quartets, or, if you like, only celebrated ones – are, of course, far fewer than Haydn's, and therefore give a far less detailed and complete picture of his spiritual development. For another, while his evolution as a quartet composer eventually carried him into spheres of unheard-of – in fact, unheard – expression where nobody, with the possible exception of Schoenberg, has been able to follow, let alone join him, it was inevitable that on the way, he had to sacrifice classical perfection to the extent of discovering the beauty of ugliness in general, and of an ugly quartet sound in particular: the unrelieved four-part writing of bars 418ff. from Op.130's second finale, or of bars 143ff. from Op.135's finale, *fortissimos* and all, are outstanding, elementally expressive examples of the ultimate mastery thus attained – both, significantly enough, from the very end of his life, for Op.130's second finale was the last piece of music he wrote before he died.

In point of fact, a certain (very certain, acutely imagined) kind of imperfection, of both instrumental and sheer acoustic strain, became part and parcel of the creative act. This is not, of course, a criticism; the obverse, rather. It does mean, however, that at his sublimest, Beethoven is sometimes at his most problematic: in the case of one famous, discarded finale – Op.130's first – he burst the bounds of the string quartet altogether, and can only be heard without aural frustration in Furtwängler's self-conducted, string-orchestral arrangement.

Needless to add, you get the occasional problematic Haydn quartet, too; we have mentioned the F♯ minor Quartet. But with Haydn, any problems are incidental, not essential to his highest achievements. In sum, I have yet to hear a quartet solve the intrinsic problems of Beethoven's most towering creations without a firm grounding in Haydn; all those ensembles which specialize in Beethoven's quartets are as suspect as those which specialize in Haydn's.

After I have torn virtually everybody else to shreds, I might well finally be asked what my own credentials for the task before me are, not in terms of Franz Schmidt's prophecy or Benjamin Britten's comparison between myself and everybody else, but in straightforward, exclusively factual terms.

Having grown up in the string quartet from an early age and thus recognized it fairly early on as, potentially, our profoundest instrumental form, and having continually played quartets, in private from my childhood, and in public from my late teens until well into my thirties, I can say that I have a complete knowledge of the important (and far too great a part of the unimportant) literature which, by now, I have been able to examine from every conceivable standpoint – not only as a player and listener, that is, but as a teacher (also a teacher of composition), coach, or adviser on the widest possible scale, of world-famous ensembles on the one hand, of toddlers on the other, and of every possible group in between, quite especially embryonic quartets about to be born with my assistance. As an analyst, 'critic', 'music-ologist' and lecturer (the quotation marks surround quotations of other writers' descriptions of myself), I have, I hope, given sustained public proof of that part of my insight which can be verbalized, while my functional analyses of many Haydn quartets have given equally public proof of my wordless insight.

The only really important question about myself, however, I cannot answer: what has my teaching achieved? The answer is up to the reader, after he has heard such groups as have been through my school (and haven't regressed too far since – though arguably, I should blame myself for any such regression, however far behind my back it may have happened).

Meanwhile, my credentials are, perhaps, confirmed by those composers who have felt the need to dedicate quartets to me: amongst the works dedicated to me, it is string quartets that assume pride of place, in that almost all composers with whom I have been in prolonged, technical touch, pupils included, chose to honour me with quartets – among them Benjamin Frankel and Benjamin Britten, with their last works in the medium.

As for the technique of reading the present book, as will already have been noticed, its footnotes are not an integral, thematic part of the text, and can therefore be read at leisure – perhaps on re-reading whichever chapter the involved reader wishes to examine more closely.

Op.9, No.4, in D minor
(Hoboken III: 22)

Where in our overflowing, largely superfluous literature on music and its history can one find the simple, crucially informative statement that Haydn's first quartet in the minor mode is the first great string quartet in the history of music? But then, where can one find awareness of the fact? When I joined the BBC in 1959, I was soon put in charge of chamber music, where I found that none of the quartets broadcasting for the BBC, native or foreign, had played the work or knew of its stature. I immediately acquainted as many ensembles with it as I could, coaching quite a few of them at least to the stage where their interpretations evinced no climaxes of incomprehensibility; when I left the BBC twenty years later, the work had become the most-played early Haydn quartet, though it remains his least known, least played, least discussed great quartet. It therefore has to receive special and detailed attention which, in the circumstances, cannot possibly be considered disproportionate.

An early quartet? Haydn's genius thus exploded for the first time at the age at which Mozart died;[1] the quartet antedates his almost unbroken flow of gigantic masterpieces, which started with Op.20, by 2 or 3 years.

It is the first of his three D minor quartets (if we exclude the Introduction to the *Seven Words* and the final fragment), probably the first of Op.9's six and, of course, the first real Haydn quartet. Is the fact that his genius first exploded in the minor significant? Once again, we have to have the courage to be lost for an answer, though it is certainly remarkable that without exception, all great composers' favourite or eminently personal keys are minor modes – two of them in the case of Mozart, i.e. not only G minor (the key of his only great original quintet in the minor mode), but also D minor itself (the key of his only great quartet in the minor mode). Moreover if we look at the totality of Haydn's quartets in the minor mode (eight of them if we except the – 'Rider' – Op.74, No.3 – for reasons to be advanced in their proper context), we discover the equally certain fact that each stands out even amongst his great quartets, in view of the wide variety and deep intensity of its innovation. And

---

[1] And Mozart himself was, as a genius, a late developer too, considering his precocious talent, which made things so easy for him that there was no need for his genius (as distinct from Schubert's or Mendelssohn's) to emerge before the age of 19, when he wrote his fiddle concertos instead of following his father's command to practise the violin.

especially the first movement's D minor mood, together with its rhythmic and harmonic build-up, makes one feel very concretely that Mozart must have known this work when he wrote his great minor-mode quartet – in which case Mozart's very own D minor developed under the influence of Haydn's! In which case again the influence was reciprocal, for by the time we reach the 'Fifths' (Op.76, No.2), there is no doubt about the influence of Mozart's D minor Quartet on Haydn's last complete quartet in that key! On the fate of Haydn's very own F minor and its influence on Mozart, on the other hand, we shall reflect when we come to discuss the first of Haydn's two F minor Quartets – Op.20, No.5. Meanwhile, we have to admit that there does not seem to be any positive historical evidence for Mozart's knowledge of Haydn's first D minor Quartet: the first extant Haydn quartet parts bearing notes from Mozart's hand are some from Op.17. But the musical evidence is strong and specific; besides, since Haydn (second violin) and Mozart (viola) played quartets together, there is historical likelihood anyhow.

On the whole, the present quartet is not very difficult to play, and is suitable (though not the most suitable) for initiation into the very greatest masterpieces, especially in the lower parts. (The most suitable initiation is the next D minor Quartet, Op.42.) There is the one or the other awkward spot, but nothing that cannot be mastered by less than masters. The leading part is brilliant without being as difficult as it sounds. All the quick movements are, of course, in the best-lying tonality of D (minor and major) and Haydn makes the most of it. Like the first movement, the slow movement and indeed the finale are in sonata form: Haydn wouldn't have been Haydn if he hadn't started the long line of his great quartets with a vertibale sonata festival, for like Beethoven and unlike Mozart, he was a developmental composer; his passion for harmonic adventure, key constrasts and development in the technical sense equalled Mozart's passion for tonal economy, thematic contrasts and melodic invention, i.e. statement as opposed to development.

Like three other opening movements of the otherwise boring set, the present work's *Allegro moderato* evinces what, for short, we might call 'Boccherini metre' – the kind of weighty tempo character, that is, which induces the somnolent, quasi-orchestral lower-part player, even though he may not be slow-witted, to mistake half a bar for a whole one during rest- or also minim-time: yes, one has even heard it happen on the platform and in the recording studio, i.e. in situations in which the real quartet player should know, texturally as well as structurally, how the movement goes.

It is indeed essential to have a clear, mentally sounding picture of the tempo character from the outset if a well-defined growth of the theme's rhythmic structure is to be achieved – which may seem elementary but, empirically speaking, isn't.

In the characterization of this principal subject, care must be taken not to accent the semiquaver upbeat (de-accentuated in Ex.2 with the help of

Schoenberg's symbolology[2]) at the end of the second bar and in the ensuing imitations. The figure does indeed play a fundamental role throughout the movement – including, of course, its development, and if it is misphrased, everything is lost. Yet nothing is easier than to phrase it wrongly, for whenever one newly enters, especially with short notes introducing a new character, an accent will readily slip in on the entry, and the danger is obviously tripled when one imitates *a tre* (bars 3–4). The most natural, constructively meaningful way to avoid the danger – *mere avoidance never communicates*, since its sound doesn't tell the listener what it is that is being avoided – is to play the figure as a contrasting variation, but still a rhythmic variation, of the model (x) and its echo (x^1) in bar 2; it will be noted that the relationship between the model and its echo is retained in its outline, but varied and developed into antecedent and consequent motifs.

For the purpose of a crystal-clear definition of the movement's rhythmic structure, two conditions have to be met, one in the leading part, the other in its accompaniment. So far as the theme's antecedent is concerned, this phrase moves up to the middle of the second bar, which should be the first main accent in performance, as if a new bar did in fact start before my (Schoenbergian) accent (Ex.2):

Ex.2

The second, accompanimental condition has to counter what, from the phrasing point of view, I have experienced as the first movement's greatest – and most obvious – danger, yet one which even outstanding quartets do not always escape: a wrong accent on the first of three accompanimental quavers that follow a quaver rest on the strong beat – especially, needless to add, where they are marked *forte*. In classical music, forte means *forte level*, not a dynamic explosion as soon as one sees an '*f*'. One cannot warn too forcibly: this type of accompanimental pattern occurs throughout classical literature (as indeed it does in the first movement of Mozart's aforementioned (second) quartet in the same key) and beyond, and even in the highest playing circles there are still too few people who realize that the first of several equal notes on the same pitch will ineluctably sound strongest unless one does something about it. It is an elementary interpretative point in all conscience – but one which remains unheeded by the majority of the world's (mis)leading quartets.

What, in an ordinary eighteenth-century composer, would have remained a case of unresolved and hence vague ambiguity, is presently utilized by the rhythmic structure: on the basis of the 'Boccherini metre', the structure yields asymmetry which is as well-determined as it meaningfully contradicts expectation – an important consideration, this, for the performer, who has to build up the Boccherini metre's expectations in order comprehensibly to contradict them. Nobody, that is to say, would find anything wrong with the four-bar phrase of Ex.3:

Ex.3

It is, I submit, the implied background (persuasively to be implied by the players!) against which Haydn establishes his foreground tension (Ex.4).

Nor does the extreme articulation with which the overlapping restatement of the theme is thus introduced remain without consequences. The wonderfully contrived paradox – cadence and new beginning overlap, yet the latter is sharply thrown into relief against what precedes it! – discloses its solution in the recapitulation, where this new beginning is the only one: by way of recapitulatory compression, the restatement has turned into a single statement, the first six bars of the piece having been condensed into it, suppressed into the background, never to appear again. The performance has to be as two-dimensional as the composition; admittedly, the background implica-

Ex.4

tions, the sum total of expectations, can look after themselves – once they are as clearly felt, experienced, and hence defined, as the course of foreground events which contradict these expectations and so establish musical meaning.

Another case of violent compression, which suddenly intensifies the structure after the broad beginning and the first subject's twice repeated closing gesture, is the so-miscalled bridge passage,[3] the modulatory transition which is in fact effectuated in a mere two bars, with the climax again exploiting the Boccherini metre – in the middle of the bar (Ex.5):

Ex.5

As a result, transitional feeling flows over, pointedly has to flow over in performance, into the opening stage of the second subject, which therefore must not be allowed ever to settle down despite its well-established relative major key. For by the time it would have settled down (or has done so in the suppressed background), i.e after the general pause, thematic definition leaves no doubt about the fact that we are approaching the main cadential stage, the end of the exposition: *we have to be heard to have played the second subject that never happened*. In the circumstances, the archaizing triplets that abound

[3] In good music there are no bridge passages – sections whose function it is to bridge a gap, for the simple reason that there are no gaps; good music is continuous meaning.

at the second-subject stage lose their conventionality: the structure is too overpoweringly new, and when played with improvisatory imagination rather than mechanically as a bowing display, the triplets can be made to convey that very newness. At the end of the exposition, with codetta feeling having already been rife, equilibrium has to be re-established by way of the formal codetta, which is as short as the transition (Ex.5), i.e. two bars, while structural variety will be ensured through its three-crotchet upbeat between the two violins, which, of course, will have to be felt to be a summarizing augmentation of previous three-quaver upbeats at both the first- and the second-subject stage.

But perhaps the subtlest point will have to be made at the lead-back, which is based on the transition, even though it is three bars long instead of two. The feeling of delay thus engendered balances the parallel delay before the restatement of the theme in the exposition (Ex.4), while the fact that the sequence here composed would normally turn the lead-back into a four-bar phrase produces a feeling of drastic abridgement, to which the leader will give expression through his imaginative agogics in the four-semiquaver upbeat to the recapitulation – perhaps by an infinitesimal and, as it were, almost well-resisted hesitation: since, ideally, he'll do it differently each time the movement is played, the viola and, quite especially, the cello will have to concentrate on his interpretation to the extent of being able to forehear it.

For the rest, my analysis reminds us that – as I have often pointed out in other concrete contexts – all well-composed extensions hide compressions and make them palatable: meaningful composition itself is compression. The second subject in the recapitulation is as drastically compressed as the first, and in the same way: only its second stage is used – not, of course, without variation.

As for the work's ready playability, the first movement's demisemi-quavers need not be feared: they flow 'like oil' (as Mozart used to say), and even the high passage at the end of the second subject will be found to lie comfortably once you are safely up there: normal fifth position, and hence the same fingering as in the third, where the passage recurs in the recapitulation.

In that respect – and only in that respect! – as of old, the minuet comes second: we must never forget that highly developed structures often revert back to early, primitive stages of their formal background, as when not only Beethoven's Ninth, but even Schoenberg's revolutionary single-movement First Chamber Symphony reaches the scherzo stage before that of the slow movement, or when Schoenberg's Third String Quartet reverses the subjects' order in the first movement's recapitulation. Nor is there any reason why we shouldn't describe Haydn's minuet itself as a highly developed structure: even it is more developmental in the middle than many a renowned development section I would not care to mention without giving offence to those who think that developments are confined to sonata forms – or, for that matter, that sonata structures are confined to sonata forms. Like literally every other great minuet, with the sole exception of the minuet from *Don Giovanni* (the only great minuet that has to be danced to), the movement must not be played as a minuet, but rather against, very much against, the background of a well-subdued minuet rhythm; bar accents all the way would be deadly. The harmonic evolution is quite shattering: no sooner have we arrived in the relative major than we are forced to concede that we shall not be allowed to end the first part there in the traditional manner. On the contrary, we are pulled back to the tonic, D minor, and just as we are about to lose our bearings, having been pulled away from the tonic with one string and to the tonic with another, just as we are about to remind Haydn that both pulls must now be shown to be meaningful if we are not to get lost altogether, he presents us with the most unexpected, most logical solution – for musical as opposed to conceptual logic derives alternative, contradictory solutions from the same premises. Haydn's solution, simple as it is, needed the inspiration of a genius: he drives us into A minor, which is both away from the tonic and back to it at the same time. For immediately after the double bar, the dominant function of the last-reached key is disclosed to the naked ear; in fact, via the dominant seventh, back we slip into D minor within a bar, with the result that the miniature development unfolds, to begin with, in the tonic! Not, however, that the section renounces its essential modulatory function: needless to say, it modulates at the point where, by then, we least expect it to, drawing us further away from the tonic than we have ever been (and thus fulfilling a development's central task), into the relative major's subdominant, in fact – which, because of the subdominant region's relaxing function, produces a feeling of repose despite the tension caused by the unexpected, far-reaching modulation as such. But the relaxation behind the tension is necessary at this late stage in the structural arch; indeed, since there has been so much D minor in the middle, the stage is later than it would be otherwise, and a mere four bars are enough to confirm the tonic at the end. Their *pianissimo* has to be a real contrast to the preceding *piano*, nor should it be achieved passively and negatively, by playing as unloudly as possible: as we have remarked before, avoidance does not communicate. A firm, expressively understating, subtly shaded *pianissimo* is required, with the cello's and viola's D's being just as subtly balanced against the violins' cadential phrases, and blended with each other.

Before I proceed to the *Trio*, let me make one point of investigative principle absolutely clear. My fairly detailed analytic remarks about such quartets as have hardly received any analytic attention – and to my knowledge, the present D minor Quartet has received none! – are not intended as academic exercises; on the contrary, they are designed to articulate the players' own experience of the music, perhaps half-conscious and ill-defined, in the hope that once their own instinctive reactions are clear to them, clearly present in their minds, logical, meaningful phrasings will follow as a matter of spontaneous course: my teaching and coaching experience has taught me that ultimately, all fruitful artistic teaching aims at self-education, by way of clarifying the student's own artistic understanding and the intentions that flow from it.

Superficially, the *Trio* is 'as of old' too, in that it is indeed a string trio – for two violins, though! The question has been asked, by more than one clever outsider, why the second fiddle can't play the first's lower part, with the viola playing the second's line. The answer, one of sonority, is twofold. For one thing, since the *Trio* is in the tonic major, the double-stoppings create a fuller sound through overtonal support on the same instrument than two instruments could. For another, the harmonic blend is perfect just because the viola, which would add a new colour, is left out of it. If the reader doesn't believe me, let him try it the other way, and if he doesn't hear the difference, let him give up quartet-playing as well as perusal of this volume. Haydn's sound-consciousness prompted him to create an absolutely continuous 3-part texture, apart from the respective parts' first, and last two, beats which, in the textural circumstances, thus produce a major contrast; and his genius made a virtue of the string quartet's basic problem – the second fiddle. But then, it is genius's wont to turn insoluble problems into unproblematic solutions: Beethoven did that even with his deafness, which not only sharpened his inner ear, but made him wholly independent of contemporary sound-ideals. For the rest, we shall encounter continuous 4-part textures both in the next work (Op.20, No.1) and in another D minor Quartet, at a much later stage (Op.42); in the composing hands of outsiders, such quartet textures invariably become thick, anti-quartetlike, but, again, we shall hear how Haydn replaces an insoluble problem with an ideal sound-picture that has nothing to solve.

The major-mode *Trio* modulates to the dominant just as the minor-mode principal section had modulated to the dominant minor, and with the same motif too, which thus draws our attention to the unifying parallelism! This is the first time, then, that the dominant (major) is reached in the movement, and again as in the principal section, the tonic is immediately resumed: whatever the individual player's phrasing preferences, the shapes of these central parallels will have to evince striking similarities if the eavesdropper is to have his money's worth.

A fleeting reference to the subdominant (G major) serves as a remote but distinct reflection, at the identical structural juncture, of the principal section's turn to B♭ major (the relative major's subdominant). It remains to be said that technically, the double-stoppings throughout the *Trio* are about the easiest of their continuous kind in the entire literature.

I have, in passing, mentioned repose. In the whole history of symphonic thought, there are only 2½ composers capable of a sustainedly reposeful *adagio*. The first is Haydn (the source of every single compositorial (innovation right up to the present day), the last Beethoven (certainly not Mozart), and the part-timer is Bruckner who, over large stretches of his *adagios* and assuredly in their actual themes, recaptures Beethoven's capacity for repose. The present *adagio cantabile* is Haydn's first profound exploration of this field of emotional, or rather spiritual stillness, the key being, of course, the submediant, the relative major's subdominant – that of the reposeful moment in the minuet: B♭ major. Heavy playing must be avoided at all costs: more often than not, I have heard the movement in ³/₈ as it were, with a leaden accent on every available triplet; in the inner parts in particular, a continuous flow has to be maintained, which requires quite especial attention where they move together, i.e. most of the time.

The exposition shows Haydn's characteristic combination of forms – in this instance a marriage of sonata and variation, which introduces a new variation of sonata form; Haydn was, in fact, the only composer who invented new forms single-handed; we shall have to deal with all of them in the course of this book. But variations of established forms were introduced by other composers too. Beethoven, for instance, in the first movement of the second of his three F major Quartets, Op.59, No.1, dropped the exposition's repeat, though he did, for the duration of its opening 4-bar phrase, return to the first subject in the tonic at the end of the exposition, thus building a mental bridge between the expected repeat and the actually ensuing development – a formal variation which proved so vital that it survived right up to the first movement of Schoenberg's last tonal – in fact, partly atonal – composition, his Second String Quartet in F sharp minor, which we have already been able to mention.

In the history of composition, before a repeat is dropped it usually is replaced with a variation of what would have been repeated – and this is precisely what Haydn introduced in the present *adagio*: a varied repeat of the exposition, an innovation which itself was to show intense formal potency, not only in the first movement of the classical concerto, but in the combination of sonata, variation, and the concerto's first-movement form that is the finale of Beethoven's Ninth. The interpretation has to go with this large-scale contradiction of expectation and point the variation rather than the restating elements, which form the variation's framework.

As in the first movement, it is again a restatement, here the variation of the first subject, that opens the recapitulation. But where the exposition turned to the dominant, the recapitulation balances with a fleeting turn to the subdominant, which deepens the movement's repose. In fact, balancing relaxation, ever-increased repose, is continued to the end: while the first subject was recapitulated in its varied form, its restatement, what there is of a thematic second subject is recapitulated in its original form. In its turn, the performance will have to be marked by ever-increased relaxation, in which a little climax leading to the *forte* before the coda will have to be accommodated – the more so since this *forte* is a mere preparation for what, I suggest, is an indispensable little first-violin cadenza 4 bars from the end. Ideally, the leader should genuinely improvise, thus inventing a different cadenza each time the work is played – as Mendelssohn did at each rehearsal of Beethoven's G major Concerto, improvising, again, an utterly new one at the actual concert.

I have been able to stimulate youngsters into imaginative improvisations at such crucial cadential points; nothing sounds more stupid, more vapid, more contradictory, than what normally happens, quite officially, at this stage in the movement, to wit, nothing: like good boys, leaders adhere to the first half-bar's metre which, without a cadenza, is senseless, and proceed to a just as senselessly protracted trill under the pause. In musical reality, it is at this point that the leader's capacity for improvisation will show whether he is at all entitled to play string quartets, in whose interpretation improvisation must, continually, play an essential part; it is in intrinsic string quartets, more than anywhere else, more even than in *concertante* music, that the reality of performance depends on its being the tail-end of composition.

The coda can only be played as an answer to the cadenza. Since it corresponds to the 3-bar codetta, however, it would be more accurate to say that the movement achieves its conclusion without a coda – an achievement indeed which the young as well as the mature Mozart was to remember, amongst other works, in his own string quartets: the slow movement of his only truly original early quartet, K.156 in G, is without coda, as is, virtually, the first movement of the A major Quartet he dedicated to Haydn – a work which seems to have impressed Beethoven above all other Mozart quartets. In the present instance, it has to be remembered, of course, that what precedes the coda, i.e. the new climax with its cadenza, functions as a pre-coda that facilitates the coda-less end: no such easements are to be found in any of the coda-less Mozart movements. As an innovatory genius, we cannot possibly place Mozart above Haydn, but as a successful formal perfectionist, we can – while Haydn outshines Mozart as an innovator, as indeed does Beethoven, or Wagner, or Schoenberg.

As altogether the greatest and most characteristic master of monothematic sonata structures, too, Haydn ought to be far more deeply and clearly experienced – above all, by quartet players. If the slow movement of the present work is near-monothematic, the finale is almost wholly so; in fact, the opening of the second subject is identical with the opening of the first. Mozart's irresistable urge to go one better produced the structure of the first movement of his great Clarinet Trio, wherein the opening of the second subject is identical with, wait for it, the concluding cadence of the first!

The large-scale purpose of Haydn's own motivic identity soon becomes apparent: recalling the first movement's structural compression, the lead-back slips straight into the recapitulation of the second subject, pretending, with good reason, that it is the first; the interpreter, needless to add, has to play Haydn's highly creative game – for it is only thus that Haydn is able to make the *presto* as fast structurally as it is temporally, and it is only the very greatest composers that are alive to the need for structural tempo.

Finally, though the fifth-position passage in the finale (again repeated in the third position in the recapitulation) is slightly stickier than that in the first movement, it is nothing to write home about by registered mail: this particular bowing across the strings must have been encountered in studies, if it was ever attempted at all.

Op.20, No.1, in E flat major
(Hoboken III:31)

With what we know and H.C. Robbins Landon accepts as the first work of Op.20 – early editions show vastly different sequences – we reach the starting-point of a wellnigh unbroken line of towering, ever-contrasing works of genius – broken only by the B♭ Quartet from Op.33 and the *Seven Words*. And Haydn reached his 40th birthday in the year in which he wrote these works, three of which (Nos. 1,2, and 5) still explore Boccherini metre (see p.20) in their opening movements, rolling two bars into one and, in fact, at times stressing the middle of the bar more strongly than its beginning; while merely two of them (Nos. 1 and 3) are without the finale fugues which not only our Preface apotheosizes (see p. 5); as we have explained, Mozart's and Beethoven's quartet fugues do, too. But Boccherini metre and final fugues apart, none of these six quartets has any essential creative characteristic in common with any other or indeed with anything else: a miracle that is to extend over three decades has begun – one that no other composer has been able to repeat, though Beethoven did re-create it on a different level, with fewer masterpieces, more metaphysics, and a still wider and further-reaching development to his credit.

One notes with dismay that at least the first three works of this *opus* are not as well known, nor as frequently played, as their stature demands, hence they will have to be examined, like Op.9, No.4 was, in considerable, conscientious detail; at the same time, one is delighted to find that two great composers, at any rate, knew at least the E♭ Quartet inside out – Mozart and Brahms. My evidence for Mozart's knowledge is musical, for Brahms' circumstantial. Mozart's own E♭ Quartet, that is to say, the one he dedicated to Haydn, contains a slow movement in A♭ that is so closely modelled, texturally as well as structurally, on the present Quartet's slow A♭ movement that, paradoxically, I would suggest the better-known and more often played Mozart movement as a preparation for the Haydn movement, not only because most players will already have taken this preparatory step without suspecting that a great, indeed perfect Mozart movement could ever serve as a preparation for something else, but also because the Haydn movement's textural complexity and finesse is yet greater and – dare I say it? – profounder than the Mozart movement's; after all, for the duration of this *Andante con moto*, Mozart turned himself into the creator of a piece that paid homage to its model.[1]

As for Op.20's first movements, Haydn's thirty-year-long lesson on what to do instead of sonata form while retaining sonata form in the background now begins in earnest – a lesson which came to prove potent, decisive even, right up to Schoenberg.

The first subject of the opening *allegro moderato* is constructed with unprecedented motivic economy, and so foreshadows the intense thematicism of the entire movement. In fact, the only sharply characterized motif in the principal part of the theme, the movement's basic motif, is shown – as BM – in Ex. 6. At the same time, there are three contrasting motifs – one on the

Ex.6

same note (Ex.7(*a*)), but accompanied by a scalic motif (Ex.7(*b*)), one a scale itself (Ex.8), and the third a cadential figure, again in conjunct motion (end of Ex.8). On closer aural inspection, indispensable from the interpretative

Ex.7

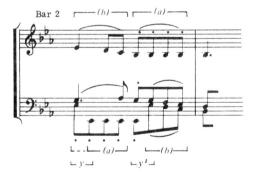

[1] In the finale of the second quartet he dedicated to Haydn, on the other hand, he seems to have wanted to outdo the finale of the dedicatee's Op.33, No.5. Did he react against his presumption when he came to write the A♭ movement?

Ex.8

standpoint (or rather, motion-point!), the theme does in fact prove scalic throughout – if, that is, we confine ourselves to its basic line (Ex.9a), which gives us an imperative clue to the phrasing, so readily and indeed frequently spoilt by grossly illogical accents on the notes marked in Ex.9b with Schoenberg's de-accentuation sign.

Ex.9

(a)

(b)

Ex.10

But it is only the top line that confines itself to the scale. The complementary triad appears as a thematic bass, a top line at the bottom as it were, emerging as it does in a solo fanfare that links antecedent and consequent (Ex.10).

How, one may well ask, does this surprising contrast, this wholly unprepared, seemingly unmotivated trumpet call, hang together with the theme itself? Why does it feel so natural, notwithstanding the circumstance that there is little motivic connection with its surroundings, the only common element being the third marked '*x*' in Ex.9b, whose harmony and rhythm could hardly be more different?

The answer points to a constructive principle which Haydn introduced into symphonic thought, and for which even the late Beethoven owed him the deepest gratitude. I call it the *principle of complementation*: it is precisely because Haydn here works more by complementation than by way of underlying identity that our feelings of unity and of expectation contradicted are equally strong: the theme's scale is complemented by the fanfare's triad – and what there is of a triadic undercurrent in the main part of the theme; Ex.11a furnishes itself a perfect complement to the basic line of the fanfare (Ex.11b), on the basis of what I have called 'the creative *principle of reversed antecedents and consequents*'.[2] If you whistle Exs.11a and b in reverse order, with b in the necessary augmentation, you will hear that this principle is responsible for the basic contrast of the movement, all the more so since the descending octave (see *y* in Exs.6,7 and 9), one of the movement's building-stones, is now traversed in the opposite direction (y^1 in Ex.10, also in Exs.7 and 8), only to land in its descending version once more (*y* in Ex.10).

Ex.11

(a)   **(b)**

As for Haydn's principle of complementation radiating as far as the late Beethoven, let me just give a single and pure example: in the first movement of the B flat Quartet, Op.130, the sub-thematic integration of the opening *Adagio ma non troppo* and the body of the first movement, the *Allegro*, is solely achieved by way of complementary intervals.

From the playing point of view, now that the cellist is, I hope, aware of the nature of his feelings of both contrast and unity, he will enunciate the contrast with single-minded conviction, alive to the fact that the experience of unity follows as a matter of ineluctable course, so long as he looks after the continuity of his mitigated fanfare – mitigated by Haydn's *legato* which does not reappear in any conventional edition, but which emphasizes both unity and continuity. Ideally, the leader's overlapping *g'* as well as the viola's concurrent *e♭*, two octaves above the cello's, will turn the latter's continuity at its near end into child's play: whereas first violin and viola have to achieve a perfect blend, the cello's intervening E♭ has to be just as perfectly balanced against it – a helpful example, this, of simultaneous blend and balance, and of the necessary differentiation between the two, which is more easily played than talked about.

The consequent moves straight on to the dominant, where the antecedent

---

[2] 'The Chamber Music' in *The Mozart Companion* (ed. H.C. Robbins Landon and Donald Mitchell), London, 1956, p.104.

is repeated – too soon to be true. There is no question, in other words, of the second-subject stage having yet been reached; indeed, we are – in Tovey's terminology – *on* rather than *in* the dominant. But it's early even to be *on* it: Haydn balances his thematic economy with an almost immediate, tightening key contrast which cannot help invading the first-subject stage with second-subject implications, second-subject feeling. Accordingly, the first subject's tonality has to be reassured within a half-bar, wherein the dominant version returns to the home key and to a variation of the home phrase (Ex.12):

Ex.12

Where, in the D minor Quartet from Op.9, transitional feeling has flowed over into the second subject (see p. 23), the second subject here filters back into the first – another structural invention of which, amongst many other movements, the aforementioned first of Beethoven's late B♭ Quartet[3] avails itself.

For the rest, these two opposite procedures produce the same long-range result: the second-subject stage proper is delayed until, intriguingly, it is too late, so that the second-subject theme assumes codetta character. Yet more intriguingly, it wasn't so much in his 'Haydn Quartets' that Mozart took up this structural 'confusion': in them, he wanted to show Haydn what *he* could do about sonata form. But in the first movement of the first quartet after the Haydn Quartets, of what is known in German-speaking countries as the 'Hoffmeister'[4] Quartet, i.e. the first of his two great D major quarters, he accepted Haydn's structural suggestion with profound passion, as the second subject (Ex.13) shows, none the less overwhelming for its relegation to the area of the codetta.

Back to our present movement's second-subject theme: before it settles down, there are, in fact, four bars which adopt the first D minor Quartet's structural approach too, in that the dominant key is now established while its theme, as yet, is not: for the theme, see Ex.14 which, incidentally, tries to forestall another frequent phrasing mistake; it will easily be noted that interpretatively and *mutatis mutandis*, the same considerations apply here as in the

---

[3] His only other B♭ Quartet – Op.18, No.6 – is early and surprisingly uninfluenced by Haydn. In fact, it seems to me that Haydn's influence is concentrated on, if not confined to, the mature Beethoven; the young Beethoven may have harboured too much ambivalence towards his teacher!

[4] Not to be confused with Roman Hofstetter: see p.8.

Ex.13

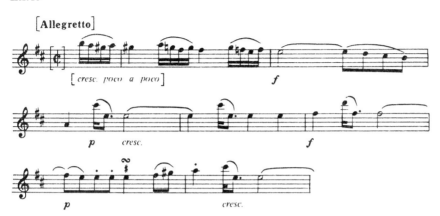

Ex.14

case of the semiquaver upbeat (Ex.2, p.21) in Haydn's first D minor Quartet.

As a result of this adoption of the earlier masterpiece's structural approach, when the new theme eventually arrives, it is even more of a codetta than the delayed second subject in the first movement of that other work, nor does a formal codetta follow it, as it does there: what we are here confronted with is, therefore, a second-subject theme composed against the firm formal background of a codetta. At the same time, we have to remind ourselves that the revolutionary Haydn's postponements of second subjects are as nothing compared to the conservative Mozart's – who, significantly, did go the whole hog in a Haydn Quartet, to wit, the 'Hunt', whose first movement postpones its second subject until you firmly expect its opposite, i.e. development – until after the double-bar!

The false recapitulation in the development of the present movement, far from being a superficial joke, subtly balances the insistent return of the first phrase in the first subject, where the consequent starts like the antecedent, and the middle section 'on' the dominant is not markedly different from the antecedent either. I hope it is not necessary to stress that there has to be all the difference in the structural world between the phrasing of the false recapitulation and that of the true one – and all the similarity at the same time, against which the contrasting differences will stand out! The interpretative imagination should have two of its greatest moments at these junctures, identifying with the composer to the point of participating, as it were, in the composition.

Throughout Op.20, Haydn alternates between having the minuet second and having it third: we sometimes tend to forget how close, chronologically speaking, he was to the old order of movements – because historically, musically speaking, he himself was so new, quite especially with his anti-minuets, which the consequent of the present minuet's theme explains far more clearly than words could possibly do: to all intents and purposes, its first two bars are a $^6/_4$-bar, which is all too frequently destroyed by a minuet-like performance. The antecedent is, of course, more neatly divided into two 2-bar phrases, and though the *forte* on the first beat shown in all editions I know but one is not Haydn's, there is no doubt that he meant the *forte* antecedent and the *piano* consequent to be juxtaposed: the *piano* on the consequent's upbeat to its '$^6/_4$' upbeat phrase would not otherwise make sense. Only, as the editors of the authentic edition[5] logically suggest, the *forte* starts with the *piece*, whose antecedent proceeds at *forte* level. The aim of the antecedent remains its very last and top note – the ab″, a circumstance emphasized, in bars 3–4, by the unprecedented absence of slurs in the second violin and cello and of a tie in the viola.

The contrast between antecedent and consequent could not, in fact, be more drastic: the disjunct antecedent with its first accent in the fourth bar storms; the conjunct consequent with its corresponding first accent in the seventh bar calms. This balancing juxtaposition must be realized as decidedly as at all possible not only by the leader, but also, empathetically, by the lower parts; it is even possible to take the antecedent slightly faster than the basic tempo, and the consequent a little more slowly, though as flowingly as the '$^6/_4$' bar suggests, with the result that the basic tempo itself does not establish itself until after the double-bar – a fact of which the listener must be made aware before it! However, ideally one shouldn't even suggest such temporal liberties: as soon as one articulates them, they tend to become exaggerated – and once again I am not hypothesizing, but speaking from bitter coaching experience, quite especially, ironically enough, in the highest playing circles; youthful, inexperienced players tend to take this message far more spontaneously, with instinctive understanding.

[5] *Urtext-Ausgabe*, ed. Reginald Barret-Ayres and H.C. Robbins Landon, Vienna, 1981. The present writer will be responsible for the as yet unpublished authentic editions of the Haydn quartets.

As in the D minor Quartet, the *Trio*, whose unchanged key throws its extreme contrasts into relief (a circumstance we shall again encounter in the fourth and last works of the set), is in actual 3 parts, and both violins are again engaged, but the bass, this time, is the cello: would that Dvořák had written his *Terzetto* for this combination! As it is, the otherwise beautiful music for two violins and viola always gives you the feeling that the cellist hasn't turned up for a quartet session, for the viola is as little bottom as it is top. Where our *Trio* isn't in three parts any more, it isn't really the trio any longer: the leadback to the principal section has been reached, which is why this second part is constructed without repeat.

One reason why the aforementioned Mozart movement is, paradoxically, a wonderful introduction to the *Affetuoso e sostenuto* is Mozart's ⁶/₈: Haydn's ³/₈ need not in fact be taken all that literally either, except where it is stressed by *sforzatos*, which Haydn marks *forz.* each time; their very presence shows, on the most superficial level, how Haydn wants the texture to flow when they aren't there. The *mezza voce* direction is certainly Haydn's; it does not mean an affectedly passive and lifeless *piano* such as one often hears in this type of textural context, but the kind of repressed, contained tone which is only possible in a string quartet. The blend must of course be treated with extreme caution in a well-written movement of this exceptional sort, where an instrument which does not as such blend well with the rest will easily show up.

What exceptional sort precisely? One which only succeeds in a composing insider's master hands; otherwise and invariably, it fails abysmally – the brim-full quartet texture unrelieved even by rests. We shall encounter it again on later, equally exceptional occasions. In the present movement, it is only interrupted, admittedly by way of extreme contrast, by the first violin's little solo cadenzas, which serve to articulate a structure that is Haydn at his most characteristic: a compressed sonata which is even more economical thematically than the first movement; 'mono-motivic' would be the only possible description.

In textural respects, too, the movement's Mozartian offspring serves as a considerate, none too radical, downright tender preparation for its interpretative mastery, for Mozart does not evince Haydn's zest for an extreme texture: in his own 4-part writing, he does allow himself various kinds of relief after the unrelieved opening sentence – a mere $4\frac{5}{6}$ bars, to be exact; for the dotted-semiquaver upbeat of the sentence's concluding cadence is, likewise by way of extreme contrast and for the purpose of structural articulation, for the first violin alone.

Two crucial points of phrasing arise in the somewhat simpler *presto* finale. One is the viola's and cello's restatement of the opening, whose *forte* means again *forte* level, not an inadvertently accented upbeat; indeed, the main beat of the structure is not reached until the next bar – and this, of course, goes for the opening phrase itself too. Players may be interested to know that the universally printed *forte* is not even Haydn's own (nor is the opening *piano*), though the editors of the authentic edition assume that he just forgot to notate this *piano-forte* contrast, which he did mark in the recapitulation: I think both the player-reader and I would have recommended likewise.

Secondly, there are the syncopations. It is astonishing how many players who manage what seem the most complex modern rhythms with superficial ease prove incapable of realizing this texture naturally, until one draws their attention to its basic requirements. (*Mutatis mutandis*, a similar observation could be made about quite a few conductors who do not seem to have much difficulty in solving contemporary intricacies.) Everybody must hear everybody in this passage, so that when it eventually flows, the leader will have a chance to shape his line without anxiety; the whole quartet will then be prepared for the coda of the opening movement of Haydn's third D minor Quartet, the 'Fifths' (Op.76, No.2), of which more at a later stage (pp.212ff.) in our investigations.

These syncopations form the transition in what is again a highly original sonata movement with just a touch of a rondo implication – not by way of one of the more conventional sonato-rondo forms, but as a result of a fleeting reversion to the first subject in the tonic at the beginning of the development. (When we come to examine the first movement of the G major Quartet, Op.33, No.5 (pp.75ff.), we shall hear to our amazement how such a tonical reversion – to be sure, to the tonic minor in that instance – can have an altogether different function which does not remotely recall rondo form.) Thematic economy continues to reign supreme; in fact, the second subject is scarcely more than an inversion of the first, meeting again the demands of complementation and indeed revealing the principle of reversed and postponed antecedents and consequents (Ex.15) which we diagnosed in the first movement:

Ex.15

And where smaller great composers confine themselves to varying their recapitulations in view of what has happened in the development, Haydn does not let his first, unofficial development – the transition – go without consequences either: stabilized texturally as well as harmonically, the syncopations reappear in the second subject; the interpretation will ensure that they are heard to do so.

Op.20, No.2, in C major
(Hoboken III:32)

Musically, it must remain incomprehensible that the first three quartets of the set have not received the analytic and evaluative attention they require; proportionately, they are receiving a disproportionate amount of attention in the context of this volume – an approach we have already justified. For the first time since Op.3, No.3 (which probably isn't by Haydn anyway: see p.8), the composer here adopts what was to become the classical order of the movements, the *adagio* preceding the minuet into which it runs; precisely the same innovatory step, pregnant with future, even distant future significance, was going to be taken in precisely the same keys in Op.54, No.2 (see p.120), likewise what I call a 'homotonal' work, all of whose movements share a single tonic. Just because Haydn is more adventurous in his excursions into remote keys than Mozart, he sometimes needs a rigid tonal framework in order to contain them; unlike Mozart and like Haydn, whose developmental, modulatory creative character he produced twinlike, Beethoven in his turn was to indulge in passionate tonal and harmonic contrast within homotonal frameworks. Within the world of the string quartet, we get Beethoven's first homotonal experiment as early as his C minor Quartet (Op.18, No.4 – significantly in his most personal key). Haydn's first homotonal masterpiece is, of course, the present work. He had last attempted homotonality in two works from Op.17 – No.1 in E major and No.5 in G major. The two attempts had been equally unsuccessful.

It is generally held that the increasing weight of the slow movement was responsible for the establishment of its new position after the first. The proposition is totally meaningless: why unbalance a structure by having most of its weight in its earlier half? The weightiest slow movement in all Beethoven symphonies is that of the Ninth, where it comes after the scherzo! The demonstrable truth is exactly the reverse: it was the increasing substance of the dance movement and especially the finale that produced the need for transposing the slow movement.

The opening movement is still in Boccherini metre (see p.20) which, however, is utilized even more subtly than in the case of the E♭ Quartet. The rhythmic structure marked x in Ex.16, and consisting of two rhythmic motifs, exploits the Boccherini metre's ambiguity in the development where, as

Ex.16

opposed to the exposition's half-bar to half-bar, it covers the distance from bar-line to bar-line (*x* in Ex.17):

Ex.17

As for the interpretation of the opening, normal string trio, it is, texturally, easier than that of the ensuing, abnormal string trio, once the theme has, like the E♭ Quartet's, modulated to the dominant: the viola is not a natural bass, but Haydn is immeasurably more careful here than Dvořák in his thus-scored *Terzetto* (see also p.37), with the result that all that's needed is the viola's clear consciousness of its exceptional bass role; Haydn has provided the necessary notes whose colour makes the role manageable. The cellist should not be afraid of an agogical approach to his opening solo – by which the leader will, for once, have to be subsequently led, employing less rubato, though in proportion as by now we've heard and know the tune. As for these modulatory themes themselves, these early departures from the tonic, we note that Mozart never indulges in them, and that Haydn himself feels them to be daring enough to let them follow an exceptionally low level of opening tension: cf. the first movements of Op.33, Nos 2, 3 and 5.

The development, on the other hand, is the second fiddle's finest minute. Neither exhibitionism nor timidity (the symptom of its repression) will do in the semiquavers, which are no mere accompaniment: the viola part is. They need a flexible and calm *forte*. The insider Haydn has calculated, inwardly heard, the texture marvellously: cello and first violin stand out far more easily than the inexperienced musician might assume from the printed page, and the second-violin part isn't half as difficult as it sounds – *the* virtuoso background, as it were, as if a soloist in a concerto 'accompanied' the orchestra, overcoming all the difficulties that aren't there: the part lies ideally throughout its thirteen bars, which feel like twenty-six owing to the Boccherini metre and its *moderato* tempo: either Boccherini metre so far encountered has, at least, been an *Allegro moderato*.

The scoring of the work is utterly new – characteristically, in two opposite respects. On the one hand, that is, the contrasting opening string trios are a sign of Haydn's awareness of the multiplicity of textural contrasts, of contrasting ensembles within the string quartet: they serve him to develop the *genre*'s unequalled expressiveness and its capacity for differentiations; on the other hand, the richness of the instrumentation foreshadows the texture of the 'Emperor' Quartet, Op.76, No.3 (p.216), likewise in C major (or 'in C', in view of its C minor finale) – a key whose overtonal reinforcement through the open strings of the tonic triad, and of the bottom and top of the dominant triad, makes it possible for this approach to result in natural physical reality. As a matter of fact, Haydn wrote more master quartets – seven! – in C major than in any other key.

And to C major we return almost guiltily after the early excursion into, or on to the dominant even as we did in the E♭ Quartet's first movement: in both cases, the basic theme is once again used in order to re-confirm the tonic. In either case, too, the second-subject stage is kept fluid enough for the firmly established dominant to assume codetta character (Ex.18), so that the subsidiary theme really falls, or rather raises itself, between the stools of the principal subject and the closing section: thus does Haydn, as opposed to the Mozart who is not preoccupied with out-Haydning Haydn (cf. pp.34f), insist on continuous development – and not solely in the extra-technical sense of the term!

Ex.18

It is this gradual evolution which the interpreter's intuition and intellect have to heed – not at the same time, but, preferably, successively, with intuition calling not only the tune, but also its subordinate parts and accompaniments. The first-violin part of the opening string trio has, unforgivably, been described as a 'counter-subject', and many a well-read, badly-intuiting second violinist has played it as one, whereas any well-intuiting child recognizes it as a subordinate part: I still speak, exclusively, from experience.

At the tune's dominant stage, the second fiddler must support its new, more extrovert character, even though his relation to the first violin is precisely the same as his relation to the cello at the beginning: the dominant key and the higher register suffice to re-characterize, but also frequently tempt the second fiddler to overdo it. The first violin remains the main part, and it, too, must not forget the *dolce* it has inherited from the cello, notwithstanding the newly obtaining spirit of exhileration. When all's played and done, we are no further yet than the mere restatement; the movement, the extra-technical development, has only just started.

It is the *Adagio*'s tonic minor that makes the work homotonal, as indeed are Op.20's Nos.3 – 5; as in the case of Haydn's minuets in second place, it is Haydn's newness, here the newness of his homotonality – its counterbalancing his harmonic adventurousness – which makes us forget how close he lived to the old instrumental forms – the homotonal suite in particular.

The semiquaver accompaniment of the slow movement has proved its most difficult aspect, although it shouldn't (Haydn and Mozart would have said, couldn't) be. I was not an admirer of the Carmirelli Quartet's Haydn, but one thing they did splendidly, though it wasn't their invention: they – above all and outstandingly, the leader – played this kind of accompaniment up and down on the upper half of the bow, describing a little curve in the process, almost a semicircle – rather than running, in the orthodox fashion, strictly parallel to the bridge. Actually, this kind of bowing was quite usual towards the end of the last century, but vanished with the modern development and musical decline of technique.[1] When I coached quartets at the Summer School of Music in Dartington at the time the Carmirelli Quartet gave recitals there, one or two of my students, now members of leading quartets, were, fortunately, most impressed by the sound the Carmirellis thus produced, and I only had to say 'Carmirelli bowing!' in the case of an accompaniment like the present one in order to hear the most sensitive accompanimental sound ensue.

The movement starts with an 'old-fashioned' unison, like the rhetorical orchestral part of an *opera seria*'s accompanied recitative, but it would be disastrous for the players to pretend that they are an orchestra: the tone should never be forced. The restatement of the theme in the cello, now harmonized in the upper parts in the shape of the aforementioned accompaniment, should really start *piano*, and the *crescendo* does *not* begin where it is printed, i.e. at the very opening of bar 7, but naturally and logically a little later. In the following transition, the leader should be free to develop his fantasy; where the others join in, they must not only be heard to result from, but anticipate what his fancy is going to tell him and them. By now it is clear that the structure of the movement will indeed be that of a fantasy, freer than any comparable movement in the classical era except for one or two of Haydn's own – of which more at later stages in our investigations. After the eventual re-restatement of the theme in the dominant minor, recapitulatory to the extent of the cello being again accompanied by upper-part harmonization, what will prove the strongest possible contrast is prepared by a *pianissimo* tutti of a bar and a bit, which communicates intense anticipation. The contrast itself is one of style, material, texture and, of course, harmonic level. Tonality, that is, stabilizes, and a lyrical, aria-like melody unfolds in the first violin, the quasi-human voice being accompanied by the other three, instrumental instruments.

[1] Cf. my 'Violin Technique: Its Modern Development and Musical Decline', in Dominic Gill (ed.), *The Book of the Violin*, London, 1984, pp.145ff.

The first antecedent and consequent of the tune, covering its first four bars (Ex.19), may seem a conventional eighteenth-century idea, a tag almost, used,

Ex.19

amongst others, by Mozart for the theme of his simple, late C major Piano Sonata for beginners (K.545). But the specific turns of the tune's phrases, its accompaniment, and the contrast it forms to the preceding, modified ternary section, render it immediately and deeply moving – even before it grows into the most unexpectedly extended melodic structure, twelve bars in all, and long and eventful bars they are too. The phrasing will have to be *semplice* rather than sentimental, naive rather than conventional – which is supposed to direct rather than limit or inhibit the player's imagination and its resultant agogics.

For a natural, unspoilt musician, the articulation ought, in fact, to be easy, whereas the most difficult part here is the viola's: it has to be unobtrusive, continuously adjustable, contrasting the slurred triplets with the detached *leggiero* ones without a self-conscious *spiccato* whose self-centredness would immediately produce rigidity. I have in fact heard amateurs play this passage much better *on* the string than some professionals, professionally conscious of their *spiccato*, play it off it. I am not implying, of course, that the triplets need or should be played on the string – though it may be fruitful to remember that that was, no doubt, the way Mozart played them when he and Dittersdorf and Haydn made music together.

Anybody who thinks that after this seeming middle section we are going to return to the basic C minor theme is in for a violent shock, however gently expressed. As a matter of fact, we aren't returning anywhere, be it theme or key. Instead, the development, which every properly brought up person would expect in the middle of the movement if anywhere at all, comes at the end. Introduced by another of those free passages for the leader, a cadenza in fact, and by a brief 'tutti' which combines elements from both preceding sections, the second violin takes over the solo part with Ex.19 in F minor, Haydn's most personal key which, in three quartets' time, we shall encounter as overpowering, homotonal home key. And true to the concluding stage's developmental (that is, modulatory) style, one of the movement's many unison transitions now carries us to E♭ major, the tonic's relative major, wherein Ex.19 was first heard and is now heard again, though still in the second violin. The structure, then, is slightly tightening up in order to give at least some indication that the slow movement is coming to an end – if end it can be called: more modulation leads via A♭ major and its relative minor (Haydn's own close relative) to the dominant of C minor and, within the movement, no further. What's this? A binary form?

When people go to sleep at my lectures, I invariably wake them up with the spontaneous thought that there is no such thing as binary form, since everything has a beginning, a middle and an end. I have earned untold sums with hour-long, practical proofs of this revelation, whose very life-blood our present Haydn *adagio* seems to threaten. Or does it? Haydn doesn't put the development at the end without thinking of the consequences. If you want the development at the end, you've got to have the end elsewhere: at the beginning of the next movement, that is to say – which, sure enough, follows *attacca*. It is here that, at long last, the harmonic structure returns to the tonic and resolves, Picardy-like, in the major mode (Exx.20a and 20b).

This is one of Haydn's most original minuets (an observation I shall probably make another 40-odd times). The textural contrasts are extreme: at the beginning, we get five parts, later two. And when the texture is full, it's *piano*; when it's thin, it's *forte*. The effect, if the players do not (as so often happens) thoughtlessly ignore Haydn's dynamics, is truly overwhelming.

The rhythmic structure of the basic antecedent (Ex.20a) is in itself most anti-minuet-like: the minuet rhythm is used as a remote background against

Ex.20(a)

which rhythms are thrown into relief which a modern composer would have notated thus:

Ex.20(b)

At the same time, it has to be remembered that this whole antecedent, $6\frac{2}{3}$ bars of it (Ex.20a) or $4\frac{5}{6}$ of mine (Ex.20b), is one single upbeat phrase towards its last note (bar 6 in Ex.20a, bar 5 in Ex.20b); intermediate accents should be of the very slightest. Otherwise, the melody is cut to pieces; without a crystal-clear realization of this rhythmic structure, the movement has no chance of survival. The accent in bar 6 of Ex.20a or bar 5 of our re-barred Ex.20b really and simply means that the temptation to stress any previous beats should be far-sightedly resisted. Players will note, incidentally, that Haydn does not place the accent on the melodic note, but only in the accompaniment, including the leader's self-accompaniment, thus avoiding exaggeration and preserving further continuity.

In the tonic minor trio – don't worry, cello: the solo comes out however discreetly you play it, the softer, the better – there is a subtle reminder of the last time we were in C minor, i.e. in the *adagio*: the conjunct unison descent evokes the spirit (and the notes) of the slow movement's 'tuttis' in no uncertain terms. And the disjunct unison in the second part of the trio, too, harks back to corresponding passages (and tonalities) in the *adagio*.

The finale is the first great fugue in the history of the string quartet. '*Sic fuget amicus amicum*' Haydn wrote over it, but if the players don't remember the *sempre sotto voce* right up to the *piano* that introduces the eventual *forte* 34 bars from the end, *amicus* will rather sound like a hefty full-back chasing a fleet-footed winger and employing a late tackle or two while the referee is looking the other way. If, on the other hand, the very necessary dynamic shadings are continuously kept within the limits prescribed by the composer, yet remain equally continuously alive, the ensuing sound will be magnificent, and Haydn's unfailing subtleties of textural treatment will come to the fore. In short, what must be avoided is a row on the one hand and a phoney *sempre misterioso* whisper on the other.

By way of final encouragement, it may be added that this fugue is easier than the one which closes Haydn's first F minor Quartet, Op.20, No.5 (see p.60), for which it is a wonderfully detailed preparation. The A major one that concludes the set (see p.63) is its most difficult fugue, and the F♯ minor one in Op.50, No.4 (see pp.99f.) is the most difficult altogether.

Op.20, No.3, in G minor
(Hoboken III:33)

Rather surprisingly, this is Haydn's only great G minor quartet; for we shall see that the 'Rider' (Op.74, No.3), always described as being in G minor, must be considered to be 'in G'. But then, even his most personal, private and favourite key, F minor, is confined to two great quartet appearances! The only other keys which he confined to two master quartets are A major and B minor, while E major and, yes, F♯ minor celebrate a single inspired appearance each. But the case of G minor is particularly interesting – not so much because of Mozart's characteristic handling of this, his own most personal key, but because Haydn's sole G minor quartet appears at the beginning of the inspired part of his quartet life, at whose other end what there is of a tonical G minor in 'The Rider' is remarkably unaffected by Mozart's G minor: it is as if, upon hearing Mozart poking fun at his F minor (of which there is voluminous evidence in *Così* as well as in *Figaro*), Haydn, the less aggressive of the two, had unconsciously decided to take his revenge a little less actively – by simply ignoring G minor as a full-blown home key for quartets altogether, together with its Mozartian implications. That can't have been all that easy in the context of their mutually stimulating relationship, and perhaps his virtual avoidance of a tonical G minor in the many years between these two quartets at either end of his mastery of the medium is in itself a reaction to, or rather against, Mozart's mock tragedies in F minor. For the rest, Op.20, No.3 is one of the set's four homotonal quartets, and one of its three which feature the minuet second – in the old order.

There is another great composer whom the interpreter might fruitfully consider in the context of Haydn's G minor quartet – Brahms: it is one of the Op.20 works whose autograph the Viennese *Gesellschaft der Musikfreunde* received from his estate, and conceivably one which stimulated him as creatively as Haydn stimulated Mozart who, according to the evidence collected by Vincent Novello,[1] openly acknowledged that Haydn had played an essential role in the formation and development of his style. The irregular rhythmic structures of this G minor Quartet's first movement not only look into the most distant future, and by no means merely Haydn's own, but are often also of such complexity that many of Brahms's own anti-symmetries sound simple in comparison, while others, especially in his three string quartets, seem to have been directly inspired by Haydn's first movement. What a pity that Haydn's quartet-writing didn't inspire Brahms to comparable textures in outer movements!

The theme itself (Ex.21) is already an overpowering 4 + 3 build-up; the

Ex.21

three-bar phrase (*b* in Ex.21) will have to be played with a conviction that is proportionate to its unpredictability after the four-bar antecedent (*a* in Ex.21). It is the consequent's second bar, i.e. the background structure's inaudible, but none the less tangible bar 6, which the foreground omits, suppresses so naturally that the continuity across the suppressed bar, from bar 5 to bar 6 of Ex.21, could not carry stronger melodic logic – just because at the beginning of bar 6, the disjunct motion arrives at its climax, to be followed by two motifs in conjunct motion which are separated by a retrograde version of bar 5's leaps. Never mind about the sixth now being minor: the harmonic context leaves the ear in no doubt about the reality of the retrograde version, which a sensitive interpretation will be able to confirm in its phrasing, despite the fact that the leap is not now between two *staccato* notes; on the contrary, the different articulation will help the player towards realizing this last leap as

[1] Rosemary Hughes (ed.), *A Mozart Pilgrimage: Being the Travel Diaries of Vincent and Mary Novello in the year 1829*, transcribed and compiled by Nerina Medici di Nariguando, London, 1975.

a variation on bar 5's leaps. The last leap is, in fact, between two phrases (which viola and cello help to separate), where previously it wasn't. The consequent (*b* in Ex.21), in short (very short!), must take the shape of a firmly and persuasively decided answer: for once, the usual metaphorical, 'technical' description of antecedent and consequent as 'question and answer' is not altogether out of place.

The octave-unison 'aside' (*y* in Ex.22) on the relative major's dominant (which introduces the second subject of what is one of Haydn's characteristic monothematic sonata forms) should be played with all the subtle imagination

Ex.22

that is needed for this kind of thing. What kind of thing? In order to facilitate the verbal answer (the whistling of examples of 'this kind of thing' would be immeasurably easier), let us vary the metaphor and call it an off-stage effect: an element in its required witty interpretation will be the pseudo-interjection as which the phrase will be played – as if it didn't belong, only to prove its central relevance in the further course of the structure. Inasmuch as it is played with *knowing* wit, its future uses, no fewer than eight of them, i.e. its enormous structural importance, will be paradoxically implied, together with the pretence that it doesn't belong.

For the purpose of readier interpretative insight, we had better list the eight occasions chronologically.

1. In the second subject that follows it immediately, the phrase is stressedly de-characterized, or – attention, first violin! – *lyrically* re-charac-terized, to form an upbeat phrase (Ex.23):

Ex.23

2. Retaining the couple of quavers after the opening semiquavers, but not yet resuming its original character, it marks the main articulation point *within* the second subject (Ex.24), first on the relative major's dominant, and then on its implied tonic minor – of all keys at this stage!

As a firm basis for this harmonic implication, Ex.24's *fortissimo* will have to be played with emphatic rhythmic definition – conceivably at a marginally slower pace, 'holding it' as it were.

Ex.24

3. To lead in the codetta, it makes its sole appearance with a triplet upbeat (Ex.25):

Ex.25

4. And at last, in order to mark the compressed codetta (whose start it turns into a double start), it resumes much of its original character, even though the upbeating four semiquavers are cut down to two, with an incisively compressive effect, to which the octave-unison performers have to be intensely alive (Ex.26):

Ex.26

5. Logically, it is as an intervention in the development section, designed to draw attention to contrasting sections based on the identical (opening) phrase, that the phrase does appear, for the first time, in its original form (y in Ex.22), which we need not re-quote.

6. The stage has thus been reached where the phrase's function reverts to its early use within a section rather than between sections. In fact, it is now allowed to speak in the middle of a thought, which then has to be resumed by way of partial repetition: from a witty intervention it turns into jocular interference – on the way to the lead-back, where it first appears in the same shape as Ex.25, except that it finishes on a crotchet; while four bars later, in the same context, it is cut down to its smallest possible size, serving as a renewed, now most subdued disturbance, whose interpretation will need a clear idea of what, in human intercourse, would be described as subtle rudeness (Ex.27):

Ex.27

A quartet without a leader who has a subtle, intrinsically musical, imaginative sense of fun is utterly lost in these places: many are the players who've never been heard again, at any rate for the rest of the movement.

7. The next appearance parallels Ex.24 in the relevant spot in the recapitulation – though it is not, of (Haydnian) course, identical.

8. And now, with the recapitulatory parallel to Ex.26, the phrase emerges, for the first time, in the tonic: what we have described as much of its original character is, for the first time, minorized (pardon my verb). This must needs be the last appearance. It remains to draw attention to the refined blend of this as well as the other unison sounds: it is achieved by Haydn having it, characteristically, both ways in that the upper three play in unison – and in octave unison with the cello.

It takes the movement a mere 26 bars to get up to the second-subject stage which, on the other hand, is substantially extended: there are another 66 bars until the double-bar! The freest fancy begins to flow after Ex.24 and before Ex.25 – in a quasi-improvisation on the leader's A-string. It all happens as we think that the exposition's main events are past, since we are evidently drawing to its close, and 'it all' is a deeply inspired piece of what Reger or Schoenberg would have called 'musical prose' – a natural consequence of the movement's basic and all-pervasive asymmetry.

Its interpretation might be facilitated by a reminder of how a modern composer would have written it, Ex.28a being Haydn's metric background, Ex.28b the re-barred, metric foreground:

Ex.28

Haydn wants the first violin to keep to the A-string ('sempre una *corda*' are his words), not primarily because of its colour, but because the two parallel *glissandos* involved are part of his melody: we labour under one of our performing age's most unmusical illusions to think that the Classical playing style was free of *portamentos*, or freer than the Romantic style. In fact, for the first time in the present book, we are facing a psychological obstacle in the way of a musically authentic performance: these slides have to be executed without the usual contemporary inhibitions about *glissandos* in the so-called Classical style (the correct term is *portamentos*, but apart from Flesch nobody uses it).

The playing of this – often ruthlessly, metrically misrepresented – passage must be both tender and capricious, and graceful to boot. The *glissandos* from *c″* to *g″* will have to be fine, yet yearning *diminuendos*, which will achieve the necessary gracefulness, while the so-called *staccato* dots – yes, Haydn's own – must result in charming persuasiveness: the mechanically sprightly fashion in which they are normally realized goes against the very essence of these quasi-improvisatory thoughts. They will, therefore, be played on rather than off the string, so that their expression can be constantly varied and they never assume the type of contemporary characterlessness which is best described as utility *grazioso*: if I am right, I must get the very readers who are guilty of it to agree with my description upon reflection, for it is concerned not only with the effect, but with their own motives, which must be almost as conscious as they are shallow.

The rich, ultra-Haydnian development is about as long as the second-subject stage (69 bars including the lead-back); for the purpose of experiencing and lucidly defining the variety of its rhythmic structures, the original, fundamental 7-bar sentence should be kept at the back of both the music and hence one's mind. The radical thematic economy of the entire movement shows that Haydn has reached, in this respect, the centrally characteristic area of his maturity; the second subject, for instance, begins with the same bar, in fact the very same notes, as the first – reinterpreted in B♭ major. Again and again, we shall encounter this approach – or rather, inventive variations of it – in later masterpieces.

We have noted that as of old but with brand-new structural intentions behind it, the minuet (see also Op.20, No.1, p.36) comes second. It is as original as the opening movement, and both it and the *Finale* maintain the work's rhythmic approach, the minuet with its 5 + 5 structure. The basic unit, that is to say, is a compressed 5-bar phrase, composed of 3 + 2, whose crucial bar is the fourth: in order to clarify the rhythmic situation, a slight hesitation is indicated at this climactic stage, registering as it were the compression which the asymmetrical structure signifies.

The relative major is just touched upon before the double-bar – only to be abandoned in favour of an unforeheard D minor which, in interpretation, must be given its full news value without being rubbed in. Immediately after the double-bar, we reach a complete understanding of the reason why D minor was touched upon before: now we do plunge into the relative major which, anon, is confirmed by its own dominant – and which then duly serves itself to confirm the unexpected E♭ major that precedes the return of the principal section's principal section. What a harmonic scheme! If 'scheme' is indeed the word: the inspired and intense harmonic invention whose every progression has Haydn's name written all over it could hardly be less schematic. It is the *harmonic* build-up which has to be played *con amore*; people all too often play across it, thinking of a crude minuet character which isn't there. I suggest it is literally true to say that no title has even done so much harm to great movements as *'menuetto'*.

Seeming tonal finality is reached *before*, not *in* the coda which, on the dramatic (yet soothing) contrary, turns the G minor chord into a G major one – not, heaven beware, Picardy-like, but as the dominant of C minor, with which what had seemed a G minor piece presages the advent, a whole era later, of 'progressive' (or rather, as I'd here call it, 'regressive') tonality.[2] But never, before or after this quartet, did homotonality receive such a jolt – a soothing jolt, I repeat: we have, after all, moved in a reposeful subdominant direction. An emotionally comprehensive interpretation will be able to produce a soothing shock effect – which, of course, the players will have to have experienced in the first place.

The *Trio* is in the relative major's subdominant (the most frequent slow-movement key in a classical work in the minor mode) – or, feeling it in continuity, i.e. from the point of view of the minuet's last key, simply in the relative (E♭) major, which has been anticipated in the minuet's miniature development section. It has to be played with flowing freedom, and there is no need for the second fiddler to think that his solo is his last grand statement before he dies. We can hear him anyway, and the first violin has to remain clearly audible (which is not to say that it ought to scan or play *espressivo*). The violins mustn't forget, in any case, that the leader comes to land on the second violin's melody notes more than once – significantly, yet with conceding caution, one can only hope. The first part ends in the dominant, which is the second main key, the relative major, of the work, and of the forehearable part of the minuet. Then, in quick succession, we are driven, developmentally, through F minor and E♭ major to – C minor and its dominant again, so that the *Trio* finishes in the same harmonic field as the minuet, with the result that the beginning of the minuet, when it returns, produces quite a tonal shock: the last thing you expect after the G major chord is G minor, since the G major chord has had dominant function. Yet, total tonal disintegration is avoided by this chordal metamorphosis (we observed the precise opposite, G minor changing into the dominant of C minor, at the

---

[2] At the same time, this is by no means the end of Haydn's prophetic story about progressive tonality: when we come to discuss his two B minor quartets, we shall actually hear not a preview but a downright transplantation of the nineteenth century into the eighteenth.

end of the minuet), while the identical tonal disruptions at the end of the trio and the minuet confirm each other.

The *Poco Adagio* in the tonic (G) major, completes the paradoxical treatment of the triad on G: it turns the chord of G major at the end of the minuet into the unexpected key of G major, where C minor is expected. The cello's semiquaver declamation after the resumption of the first 4-bar phrase should be natural rather than – as is often heard – emphatically rhetorical: the cello has to turn into a first violin, as it were, rather than compulsively enjoying its protracted moment of glory.

The structure is as freely inventive as a consistently inspired improvisation – consistently inspired and hence without the trimmings, and hence again as logical, indeed as strict as it is free. The strictness of the fantasy emerges as soon as one realizes that despite the loose, sometimes almost recitativic shapes, it ultimately falls into – or, if you like, out of – a sonata scheme: the dominant level is, in fact, more stable than in many a Haydn movement where the thematic entities are more formally defined. Can we please ensure the repeat, which all editions I know except for the *Urtext-Ausgabe* omit? Haydn does put a double-bar with dots at the end of the exposition. The development's modulations, melodically generated, are overpowering; and since the opening, principal theme forms their basic material and has introduced the development in the dominant anyway, it is omitted from the recapitulation; the earliest, most outstanding and masterly successor to this innovatory structural device will be found in the first movement of Mozart's second D major fiddle Concerto – a mere three years later.

The *Finale, Allegro molto*, retains the fanciful character of the work but, despite the minor mode, introduces an element of playfulness: where previously there was both witty and jocular behaviour, profound and pure wit now gains the upper hand – a flexible emotional attitude which the players have to add to their sence of fun. Much is made of the dialogue between the instruments, some of which really only concerns the players and nobody else: from the audience's point of view, first and second violins could (and, perhaps, should?) reverse roles in bars 11–12: compare bars 1–2. The utmost care must be taken to de-accent the first violin's upbeat phrase – especially the dangerous *staccato* note – in bar 1 and, of course, in all its recurrences, in the different instruments, throughout the movement, right to the very end (cello). Thematically, the second subject is, once again, the same as the first; in fact, this time the notes are not reinterpreted as in the opening movement, but simply transposed, thus stressing the simpler mood and matter of the piece. The movement is fast, very fast, but never faster than it can be phrased. Slow existence is not just better than, but something entirely different from, non-existence, however well concealed by pseudo-existence.

Op.20, No.4, in D major
(Hoboken III:34)

For reasons which are beyond my comprehension, the D major quartet has found itself in some editions of 'celebrated' Haydn quartets. In most cases, the reasons for such celebration are obvious: it is the relatively symmetrical structure of its themes which will always enable a Haydn quartet to gain access to the bogus category of famed works. But asymmetry abounds in the present quartet – though not in the slow, variation movement (his first!), which starts with a 4-bar antecedent and a 4-bar consequent: it may well be that this movement, and this theme in particular, has rescued the work from oblivion.

In respect of its thematic material, its keys, and indeed its dynamics, unprecedented economy is the work's basic motive; in fact, the first bar's unobtrusive basic motif in octave unison is the source of the first movement's entire complex structure. The unusual tempo marking, *Allegro di molto*, has to be understood as a description, not merely of speed, but above all of character: the first four bars are a single, accentless upbeat phrase aiming at bar 5; the same is true of the consequent. The often-heard stresses on the first and/or second bar destroy the movement from the outset.

As for the work's key economy, not only is this the third homotonal masterpiece, but the slow movement in the tonic minor renounces the contrast of a major-mode variation; however, whenever Haydn decides to do without a conventional contrast (as indeed the contrast between the successive movements' tonalities), it is in order to establish a firm framework for unheard-of contrasts of his own invention. As a matter of fact, this variation movement can be considered a further, and entirely new, union of variation and sonata (cf. the slow movement of Op.9, No.4, p.27). What starts as the recapitulatory, fourth variation develops into what has wrongly been described, by a Radio 3 announcer, as 'a fantastically free coda'. No, a coda is a concluding section that confirms finality, whereas what the fourth variation develops is exactly the opposite – a stage of inconclusive instability, unprecedented in the movement; one could call it a 'developmental variation', but for the fact that a classical variation is tonally stable, a restatement of the theme from the standpoint of its rhythmic and harmonic structure, and thus the very opposite of a development with its necessary modulatory instability: it is polar opposites that Haydn marries in this utterly original structure, against the background of the expected coda which the Radio 3 announcer pushed into the foreground. In short, the expectation of final and total stability is contradicted by a type of instability, i.e. modulatory destabilization of the home key, unknown to variation from as such. But a developmental concluding stage we have encountered on one previous occasion – in the slow movement of Op.20, No.2 (see p.43).

In the interpretation of the movement, there are strong objections to the slur the editors of the authentic edition (*Urtext-Ausgabe*) suggest over the theme's entire second bar; I in my turn suggest that they simply put it there because Haydn notated it in the aforementioned recapitulatory variation, thereby for once committing what I regard as any editor's original sin, to wit, the standardization of expression marks, on the wrong assumption that a great composer always wants the same things to be played in the same way, whereas in creative truth, all meaningful composition is alteration. In the case of the present theme (Ex.29), bar 2 is a rhythmic contradiction of bar 1, of

Ex.29

whose rhythmic pattern it is the retrograde version – a contradiction which does not yet make itself felt in the sequential continuation which is bar 2's first beat and should, of course, still be slurred: it is only with the ensuing crotchet that the melodic friction arises, that rhythmic opposition is established – and as well-defined contradictor, this crotchet has to be articulated against what preceded it. By the time of the recapitulation, on the other hand, the other side of the picture, the melodic continuity, has to be thrown into relief; not only is the melody known by now, but the variations have justified, substantiated, legitimized what was the opposing crotchet, explained its melodic context, so that it can, indeed must, now take its natural place in the melodic flow. In the first variation, the second fiddler has to turn into a leader with a decisive personality, thus proving that while there are many outstanding leaders who would make indifferent second violinists, every outstanding second fiddler has to have a dual personality, be able to turn himself into a characterful first violinist at a quaver's notice – the upbeat quaver's of the first variation.

There are quite a few leading cellists in this world who bear a lifelong grudge against fate in general and first fiddlers in particular, because they don't lead a string quartet. Others, especially in this self-conscious age, react against this grudge by way of a sophisticated musicality with a capital M, with the result that they play their solos with precious restraint. It must be emphasized, therefore, that the cello solo that is the second variation of this *Un poco adagio e affetuoso* wasn't marked *piano* by Haydn, but by all subsequent editors known to me, including those of the authentic edition (who do, of course, put brackets round it). Here is your chance to lead, cellist, and to play yet more freely than you would in a concerto, whose conductor and orchestra couldn't follow you as flexibly as, I hope, your quartet pals can. My advice is not to accept the authentic editors' slur over the second bar's second triplet: the increasing articulation of this entire upbeat phrase is well served by the first triplet on one bow, the second *detaché*. In fact, I distinctly remember Franz Schmidt, in my experience the greatest interpreter of this variation, playing the upbeat phrase exactly as Haydn wrote it and as I am advising, utterly unaware that he actually followed Haydn's notation. The autograph he can't have seen as a growing cellist, when it was still in the possession of Brahms. And the part he played from, which I saw, had the slur our editors are suggesting. Their next suggested slur over the dotted motif in bar 3, on the other hand, is entirely plausible.

The third variation the leader should accept as a radical cure of his rubatophobia. In *tempo giusto*, the variation would be robbed of its entire sense: intense re-creative phantasy is needed throughout; one can just imagine Dittersdorf remembering his composing self when he played the variation with Haydn and Mozart – and the two, for once, joyfully adjusting to his (co-)composing intentions. Seriously though, the three lower instruments have to be wholly at the leader's disposal, enabling him to improvise with maximal spontaneity, and yet serving him with the acutest rhythmic finesse – two-dimensionally so, one ear concentrated on him, the other on each other.

By the end of the movement, it will at last become clear what I meant by dynamic economy at the outset of the present chapter: both the first and the slow movement finish stressedly *pianissimo*. And while Haydn did not mark the finale's end *pp*, the *diminuendo* of the end of the coda is so clearly composed that any dynamic marking has become superfluous – would look downright tautological. Thus it is only the gipsy minuet whose cross rhythms would render a soft ending absurd; otherwise, the quartet's introspection, its eminently private emotional weight (as opposed to that of a symphony from this period in his creative life) is well supported by these highly charged, concluding understatements, from which Mozart must have learnt a thing or two.

The gipsy minuet itself is polyrhythmic and would have been notated polymetrically by a composer of our own time. So far as the tune (Ex.30) is concerned, if you change the 'minuet' (which, admittedly, is the melody's background) into an exceedingly opposite dance form, namely, a gavotte (Ex.31), you can lose Haydn's *sforzatos* (marked '*forz* each time). This,

Ex.30

Menuet alla Zingarese
Allegretto

Ex.31

at any rate, holds true up to bar 4½ after the double-bar, when the 'one-two', which in any case hides behind every substantial gavotte rhythm's 'three-four' (quite especially, therefore, in all of Mozart's not so called gavottes), usurps it temporarily. In the cello and viola, the minuet background is more pointedly implied, yet never more than implied, for at the same time, there is again a ⁴/₄ rhythm which, mind you, doesn't coincide with that of the upper parts (start the first main beat as 'one'). In sum – and this the players have to remember, whatever else they forget – the *forz* accents invariably mark a ⁴/₄-scheme; they are never three beats apart. Before we leave the principal section, we note that Haydn's harmonic adventurousness needs more even than homotonality's unifying power. The middle movements' themes are sub-thematically – downright serially – unified: A-D-E-F♯! The notes are treated like – as – a tone-row.

The trio – whose first bar I quote (Ex.32) in order to show what are

Ex.32

Trio

Haydn's bowings *throughout*, as opposed to those of virtually all available editions – is not a piece of programme music describing a sewing machine, and

both its contrast with the principal section and the contrast between its reprise and its own middle section will best be introduced by a slight and varied hesitation in the cello. Such hesitations always have to decrease in repeats and recapitulations, because the first contradiction of expectation is the strongest: what's new has to be made clearer than the newness one knows. And whereas the contrast of the reprise is retained in the second repeat, the contrast which the opening forms to the principal section obviously vanishes in the first repeat, where the hesitation will therefore have to be reduced to vanishing point, too. If the occasional two-quaver slur helps to clarify the cellist's hesitations, the spirit of Haydn not only nods approval, but actually expresses gratitude for the imaginative, unpedantic handling of the melodic line.

For the rest, as an extreme example, this so-called minuet is a highly welcome, early warning about the nature of the Haydn minuet – immature, tediously insignificant cases apart. The mature Haydn-minuets are always composed against the background of the minuet; widely varied as are their complex meanings, these always depend on, indeed consist in, the tensions he establishes between the minuet-like expectations he creates and what, in the foreground, in the actual music, he does instead. So far as the symphonic minuet is concerned, literally all great composers followed this course of creative action, and to reduce any of his or their minuets to their minuet-like background (as, alas, frequently happens) is, simply, to divest them of their meaning.

In the whole of Haydn – in fact, in our entire literature – there is nothing remotely like the finale's upbeat phrase, which consists of the whole first bar together with its own upbeat: it only makes sense, and can only begin to define the *Presto e scherzando* (not '*Presto scherzando*'!) character, if it is played absolutely *senza misura*, emphatically *presto* (though subdued in tone, ignoring the authentic editors' proposed *forte*), and with only one aim in mind: bar 2. In other words, there is no trace of an accent before the other instruments enter. At the repeat, moreover, the wholly accentless *senza misura* extends over almost two bars: it includes three quarters of the *prima volta* bar. Nor is the most fruitful juncture for the basic tempo character to be defined as bar 2: if the impression of a rush is to be avoided, bar 2 will rhythmically balance the initial *senza misura*, will get a firm grip on the tempo, and will thus, metrically speaking, be infinitesimally slower than the eventual basic tempo; and the same rhythmic assertion will, of course, happen in bar 4. In fact, bars 7 f. (which I am quoting – Ex.33 – because Haydn's tie and final *staccato* are quite unknown: I have never heard them in any

Ex.33

performance not coached by me) would seem to me the ideal juncture for the long-postponed definition of the main tempo to take place; this highly original, crystal-clearly rhythmic, stressedly masculine phrase invites the most articulate, rhythmic characterization which, if it succeeds, won't be forgotten for the rest of the movement – and a playful, yet calm, unrushed *presto* will have been ensured.

Op.20, No.5, in F minor
(Hoboken III:35)

With the fifth work of the Op.20 set, and the composer's third minor-mode quartet, we reach a crucial point – the great Haydn at his most personal, intimate, searching and – dare we attribute this creative character trait to him? – tragic. It is the first of his two quartets in his most personal key (the other being Op.52, No.2), which was to him what G minor was to Mozart, and whose effect on Mozart is as fascinating as the fact that it didn't affect anybody else. For the virginal player, the work is the most fortunate event in the composer's entire output – a perfectly manageable playing introduction, that is to say, to the greatest Haydn.

Helped by its objective key characteristics, we have noted (pp.19–20) that Haydn's D minor inspired Mozart's – which, in its turn, had an equally stimulating influence on the old and wise Haydn. But Haydn's F minor, whose objective characteristics, such as they were, could not play an equally incisive role, was too personal to become a central attribute of another great creative personality. At the same time, I firmly suggest that Haydn's own F minor did affect Mozart decisively – though in a totally different manner from the effect of Haydn's D minor: if F minor meant tragedy to Haydn, Mozart, however unconsciously, pulled his intimate creative friend's leg by turning it into his key of mock tragedy; the scores of *Figaro* and *Così fan tutte* do not leave the faintest doubt about the consistency with which Mozart pursued this self-appointed task of irony.

Further Haydn's F minor did not reach, though F minor as such continued to play a characteristic role in great creative minds. There is, for instance, no doubt about the personality of Beethoven's F minor, for instance in one of the two quartets which make nonsense of his three periods: Op.95 is neither second nor third period, and Op.135 isn't third period either, nowise; it would have started a new phase in his output, had he lived. But deeply characteristic as Op.95's F minor is, it has nothing to do with Haydn's F minor. The case of Beethoven's Piano Sonata Op.2, No.1, in F minor is more intriguing: while its homotonality is identical with that of Haydn's two quartets in that key, its F minor could not be more different from Haydn's! So far as the F minor of Op.95 is concerned, being less privately personal than Haydn's, it proved itself capable of impressing itself upon another great creative mind, to wit, Mendelssohn's, whose own F minor Quartet, Op.80, is unthinkable without Beethoven's. But Haydn's own F minor has to be approached with the same reverence as Mozart's G minor, Beethoven's C minor – or indeed Mendelssohn's E minor, the key of the fiddle Concerto and one of our literature's greatest quartets (Op.44, No.2).

That Haydn would decide upon homotonality for both his F minor quartets was, for once, to be expected: only thus could he concentrate on his favourite key the way he did. The first F minor quartet is distinctly popular – at any rate amongst players, and not only or even chiefly because of its musical weight, but because it is not very difficult to play. It is certainly easier than the other F minor, though any failure in natural musicality would, of course, be calamitous. Perhaps the most critical point altogether, one that is not confined to this quartet nor indeed this composer, and which, in principle, we have already been in touch with in our examination of the interpretation of Op.9, No.4 (p.22), is nothing more complicated than the first movement's basic quaver accompaniment. This problem is at its most glaring at the (*allegro*) *moderato* level, where any slightly unsuccessful articulation makes itself obtrusively felt. If you play several notes of equal value and pitch with, physically speaking, equal stresses, the first will nevertheless seem the strongest, for psychological reasons. If, therefore, it does not demand a rhythmic accent, you have to de-accentuate it carefully, which means, in Schoenberg's symbolology, Ex.34:

Ex.34

and never mind the first dot: the slur counteracts it anyway. Otherwise you irreparably obstruct the flow of the melody.

That the minuet comes second is, in this instance, hardly experienced as a reversion to the old order of symphonic events, for the simple reason that the dance form is pushed so far into the background that the feeling of tragic drama which dominates the foreground invests the movement – still in F minor! – with an innovatory significance without precedent – the more so since, paradoxically, it is in the ensuing *adagio* in the tonic major that a dance form, the *siciliano*, makes itself felt nearer the surface; at least its characteristic rhythm is retained purely metrically, though violently contradicted by the tempo character of this intrinsic *adagio*.

As for the minuet's own tempo, nothing is more disastrous than the '*tempo di minuetto*' which, in the absence of any tempo indication, thoughtless ensembles readily adopt. What would they do with the countless Bach movements of contrasting tempo character which define their tempos, not verbally, but through the music? Quite obviously, the tempo character of the principal section is darkly urgent – the very opposite of a relaxed, metrical, 'galant' *allegretto*, of a rococo invitation to the dance! An outstanding example, this, of how a historically authentic style can murder the music of a great composer; it's the small composers that should be played authentically – or, better still, not at all: they represent, rather than oppose their age, which is why they die with it.

For the rest, it is the tonic major relaxation of the overlapping *Trio* which will thus come to form a maximal contrast to the principal section; its own, light-hearted, smiling agogics will not only have to heed this contrast but serve it and, at certain junctures, actually create it: the first violin's solo upbeat phrase in quavers is such a crucial spot.

The emphatic *adagio* character of the slow movement is never disturbed or interrupted by the first violin's playful behaviour, which imposes on the others, especially the second violin, a heavy re-creative obligation, for the leader's figurations, far from being able to tolerate an inhibitory, de-personalizing 'seriousness', have to be developed with what is best described as subtle, imaginative abandon – almost as if he invented them while playing, in aural view of the pre-composed tune! For this is exactly the sense in which they were composed.

The first subject of the final double fugue is, of course, a contrapuntal eighteenth-century tag which all of us have come across somewhere or other, survive as it did well beyond the baroque era, whose *Messiah* example isn't all that unknown either. Its attraction is the attraction of any good idea – the simplicity of its complication, which boils down to simplicity in a new or unusual guise. The theme's falling diminished seventh, that is to say, is, *simply*, the harmonic minor scale's augmented second inverted. Mozart took the cue, in the first quartet dedicated to Haydn: his own double fugue for string quartet, likewise, starts with a tag. What, then, attracted virtually all great composers to *clichés* – and not only in polyphonic music? In the last movement of Mozart's 'Dissonance' Quartet, for instance, we find what is, perhaps, the eighteenth century's most used homophonic *cliché* (x in Ex.35):

Ex.35

The answer is clear: the challenge of investing the meaningless with unprecedented meaning. Our fugue does indeed offer superabundant evidence. Accordingly, the second fiddler has to characterize the theme sharply from the outset; the fact that Haydn didn't compose it is no excuse for the kind of neutral, phrase-less realization (or rather, obscuration) one hears all too often. The tag is a challenge to the player too, not only to the composer! And as in the case of the C major quadruple fugue (p.45), it must be remembered that the texture can only be clearly defined if all loudness is audibly postponed until Haydn demands it – until the canon starts, 40 bars from the end.

Op.20, No.6, *in A major*
(Hoboken III:36)

With the first of Haydn's two great A major quartets (the other, and easier, being Op.55, No.1) we reach the least known, and least played work of the Op.20 set. *Pace* Mozart's A major fiddle Concerto and the Dvořák Concerto, A major (not to speak of its dominant key, in which Bach allowed himself to write a violin concerto) isn't as welcome a violinist's open-string key as is the instrument's own tonality, that of D, and its very feeling of partial discomfort seems to have stimulated, tickled Haydn into producing plenty of incidental problems. Frankly, the quartet is exceedingly tricky to play, and one readily forgives those who don't – the more so since experience shows that people who attempt it before feeling very safe in the realm of the Haydn quartet invariably come to grief.

The first movement's first subject even includes double-stoppings, admittedly not difficult to begin with, but more demanding at the end of both the exposition and the movement. And even where, in bar 4, they look easy, they equally easily produce distonation, if only because the first violin's *e'* has to be absolutely at one with the viola's! Similarly, at the end of the exposition as well as the very end, the leader has to look after not only his own octaves, but those he simultaneously produces with the cello. Add the adventurous harmony to such technical inconvenience – Haydn thinks nothing of F♯minor on the way to the second subject or of modulating within it – as well as highly exposed textural contrasts, such as the duo for two violins that marks an inventive overlap between transition and second subject, and you will happily say, 'Another year!' when you are invited to prepare the work for concert performance.

On closer inspection, however, it will be noted that the technical and textural problems hide a fairly unproblematic musical progress, though if one doesn't give oneself the chance to hear the music well in tune and well balanced, physical problems are easily mistaken for musical ones. For once, I recommend individual, preparatory practice to the first fiddler; I hope it need not be stressed that in the case of this work, sectional study is an absolute requirement for the quartet: every tricky spot must, texturally, be isolated – confined, at first, to the leading wrong-doers, while accessories should only be allowed to join once the central crime has been expiated. Conversely, if, at any given stage, the leading player has wholly and safely absorbed his own part, he will do good to lead the wrong-doers, first singly, then together, towards a clear idea of what the music should sound like.

Significantly enough, Haydn did not decide upon the subdominant for the slow movement: that would have been too easy, and would have contradicted what we might call the technical character of the work. Instead of such dis-tension, he chose dominant tension with his sublime E major *adagio*, whose key doesn't exactly facilitate the second violin's task. But in no circumstances must the movement be allowed to disclose the second-fiddle part's frictions; on the contrary, nothing is more urgently required than easily flowing semiquavers in the second violin (not *molto espressivo*, as if they were the centre of attention!). They will, in fact, be produced with greater ease if the player remembers that they are stressless: the rhythmic structure's stresses don't lie in his part. But it is the first violin's imagination that has to fire – and subdue! – the second into an infinitely flexible accompaniment whose constant tone modulation has to provide ever-changing colour.

The minuet, however '*allegretto*', should not show the remotest trace of minuet rhythm; from the point of view of sheer pace, it will be fruitful to remember that whereas the dance minuet (prototype: *Don Giovanni's*) is a slow *allegretto*, the present one must be fast enough to turn its second bar into a mere upbeat phrase in the first violin: the rhythmic counterpoint between the first on the one hand and the second's and cello's main beat on the other must be feelable without the lower two disrupting the first's upbeat through an exaggerated accent on the first beat. In fact, much of the secret of quartet-playing lies in the kind of tone production which simultaneously expresses contrapuntal opposition and homophonic agreement.

Like the *Trio* of the first Op.20 quartet (which, however, overlaps with the principal section) and that of the fourth, the present trio is in the minuet's key; nevertheless, it achieves a truly incredible contrast: where, in homotonal structures, Haydn's harmonic adventures make you forget the unchanging tonic, he turns his back on harmony altogether in the creation of this maximal contrast within the same key. How the hell does he do it?

Texturally as well as melodically. The broadly unfolding melody requires, of course, a markedly slower tempo, nor is that unfolding breadth confined to the leader: by way of that typical quartet texture which is neither homophony nor counterpoint, and through compressing such a quartet texture into a trio, Haydn enables both the viola and the cello to do the same thing as the first violin – sing on the lowest string exclusively, with the necessary *portamentos* becoming an indispensible element in the melodic build-up. For as opposed to the trio for two violins that is the three-part trio of the D minor Quartet,

Op.9, No.4 (see p.26), the present trio is a real, normal string trio – for violin, viola and cello. Ironically, by the way, none of Haydn's actual string trios reaches this trio's level of inspiration and formal perfection. In short and in sum, the contrast between trio and minuet corresponds, and not only textur-ally, to the contrast between solo and tutti, except that both the present 'solo' and the present 'tutti' are immeasurably subtler than this contrast can possibly be in either a concerto for one or more solo instruments or the juxtaposition of *concertino* and *ripieno*.

Technically, the final triple fugue belongs to the least problematic aspect of the quartet, whereas texturally, it is its most difficult part. So long as two guidelines are remembered, however, ultimate success is more than likely. First, the dynamic climax is postponed as never before: it will meaningfully begin with the *rovescio*, not to reach forte level until four bars (minus a quaver) from the end! Secondly, so long as one genuinely concentrates on the unfolding of the texture, it will always be abundantly clear that at no point in this fugue does a contrapuntal textbook situation arise: there is one leading part at every given stage, which the others have to adjust to whole-heartedly, however important their own parts. What is yet more important is the need to balance them against the temporary leader. These two guidelines should open the players' ears to what is actually happening, and a clear awareness of what is happening will be found to be more than half the battle.

Op.33, No.1, in B minor
(Hoboken III:37)

A decade or so after the Op.20 set came the fateful Op.33, again comprising
six quartets. It wasn't so much Haydn's fate of which these works proved full
as Mozart's: they prompted him to return to the string quartet and write his
own first six masterpieces in the medium – the set that bear a more affectionate
and admiring dedication to Haydn than does any great composer's work
dedicated to any other great composer, with the possible exception of
Schumann's dedication of his own three inspired, but unmasterly string
quartets to Mendelssohn, the master of the string quartet.

It is true that Haydn himself described the six quartets as having been
composed 'in quite a new, special way, for I hadn't written any for ten years',
but you can show his every single quartet masterpiece to have been composed
in quite a new, special way, and while each of five of these six is indeed
overwhelmingly new, they have no such newness in common. As a matter of
fact, it is a rather extra-musical innovation they do share: their dance movements aren't called minuets, but bear the titles 'Scherzando' and 'Scherzo'. As
before, they are, of course, all anti-minuets, but of a scherzoid character there
is as little trace as there is in the so-called minuets of Op.20, though four of
them increase their tempos to the *allegro* level. It was at a far later, indeed the
latest stage of his creative life that Haydn did introduce the scherzo into his
symphonic build-ups: hear Op.76 or Op.77. Wise after the event, we may
assume that Op.33's new titles were a bit of verbal magic and had prognostic
significance, that Haydn felt the creative desire to do something unprecedented about the symphonic dance movement – and that when he actually
came to do it, there was no more psychological need to revert to his verbal
prognosis in the shape of a realistic verbal diagnosis; far from calling his late
scherzos 'Scherzos', he simply called them minuets again, notwithstanding
the fact that one couldn't even misunderstand and play them as minuets if one
tried: try to dance a minuet to a *presto*!

If anything, and superficially, the first quartet of the set sounds fairly
early, with its distinct recollection of Boccherini metre. In a way, a numeri-
cally definable way, it is, of course: 37 great, utterly different masterpieces
were to follow. And there is another sense in which the work is early – well
over a century early, so that in this respect, it actually sounds late. The first
movement, that is to say, starts with another D major trio for two violins (see

Op.9, No.4, p. 26) – except that this time, the home key is B minor! Nine years later, at the beginning of his other B minor quartet, Op.64, No.2, Haydn was going to mislead us the same way, now opening with a violin solo in D major; in either case, it is the entry of the other instruments which, belatedly, takes us home. Haydn thus anticipated what was going to be known, more than a century and a half later, as 'progressive tonality'[1] – i.e. tonal structures which were to replace 'concentric tonality'[2] with a progress (or, for that matter, a regress) from one key to another; Mahler symphonies were the name-giver's (Dr Dika Newlin's) prime example. It is no exaggeration to say that again and again, we come to realize that from classical times until the present day, all of musical history's compositorial innovations can be traced back to Haydn. The question here arises why he adopted this novel approach in his two B minor quartets. If we may assume that for a start, he wanted to 'progress' no further than the opening key's relative minor, D major's unequalled violin sonority and brilliance must have given him the ideal deceptive platform whence to plunge into the unsuspected home key. I would go further and suggest that the interpretation might heed my interpretation of Haydn's creative intentions – to the extent of a convinced, sonorous opening *piano*, which the second violin's easy chords – the first with the open string and the second the easiest, best-sounding double-stopping altogether – will support without friction (though in the sound-conscious excitement, care must be taken to avoid the misaccentuation analysed on p. 59, apropos of the basic quaver accompaniment of the first F minor Quartet's first movement: double notes increase the risk of an unintentional accent on the first quaver.

There is another link with Op.9, No.4: this B minor quartet is another sonata festival (cf. p.20), in that three of its movements are in fully worked-out sonata form. However, at the present, mature stage, Haydn's beloved monothematic, or near-monothematic contradiction of polythematic sonata form makes itself richly felt, in that he thus exploits the sensational tonal ambiguity of his first subject to the full, for at the second-subject level, that of the relative (D) major key, there is no more need to contradict and overcome the theme's D major implication with which, at the very beginning, he had misled us by way of a joke so serious that it must needs improve on closer acquaintance – with foreknowledge, that is, of its point. Again, the shaping of the second subject will do good audibly to delight in its confirmation of D major, as opposed to the original reinterpretative contradiction of the key. The selfsame delight has, of course, been composed into the theme in the first place: we are now able to indulge in a 4-part *forte* sonority of the violin's own key. It need hardly be pointed out that in the development section, too, the blunt major-mode edge of the two-edged melody is explored and indeed sharpened: so long as one makes the movement's clear thought (stressedly

[1] Dika Newlin, *Bruckner, Mahler, Schoenberg*, New York, 1947.
[2] Ibid.

clear, in the unprecedented circumstances) one's own, it really seems to play itself and happily absorbs one's own phrasing delight at Haydn's structural delight.

With the not so called minuet, we are back at the earlyish impression the quartet superficially makes, at least so far as the movement's position is concerned: once again, it comes second. But within a few bars, we encounter another innovation which, believe it or not, anticipates the end of Schoenberg's book on *Harmony*[3] (as well as one of his Five Orchestral Pieces of 1908):

> Tone-colour melodies! How refined are the senses which thus differentiate, how highly developed is any mind enjoying such subtleties!
> Who dares demand theory here?[4]

Certainly not Haydn who, like Schoenberg, convinced through the logic of his creative thought which, in bars 6–7, and again towards the end of the principal section, produces precisely the new 'tone-colour melody' Schoenberg is talking about, i.e. a thematic phrase which replaces the melody's differences of pitch with differences of colour, the pitch remaining identical: the leader surprises us with slurred quavers between the $f\sharp''$ on the A-string and the $f\sharp''$ on the E-string; in the finale of the 'Frog' Quartet (Op.50, No.6) four years later, he was going to promote such a tone-colour melody from a thematic thought to the actual theme of the movement.

The double-stop-like stretch involved, between the fourth and first fingers, is technically unprecedented too: nothing like it can be found in any previous string quartet that has survived. The phrase's difficulty depends, of course, on the size of your hand – but in any case, the closest possible identity of pitch must be achieved, so that the respective colours of the two strings are thrown into relief as the only element of differentiation. Many decades ago, when people still played gut A's, life was made too easy here for the first violinist, who tended to forget that Haydn himself played a gut E as well!

In any case, one quite often hears carelessly different pitches here – which ought to be avoided at all costs. Arnold Rosé used to say, demi-semi-jocularly, that 'octaves have to be a bit out of tune, for otherwise you don't notice that they're octaves' – a saying which many a leader seems to be taking to heart in the present situation, notwithstanding the fact that the very opposite of octaves is involved: a differentiation between, as opposed to a combination of sounds which aims at a blend.

It is not, perhaps, unnecessary to draw attention to the circumstance that in the *Trio*, one should not *technically* be aware of its B major key and its modulation to F$\sharp$ major at the end of its first part – of a key signature Mozart would never have allowed himself. There are two types of difficulties, those

---

[3] *Op.cit.*, p.471 of the third edition, p.422 of the translation.
[4] My translation.

which are an expressive part of the composition (Beethoven, Brahms!) and must therefore remain audible, and those which aren't – and in the present instance, they aren't. The trio's dynamic level is low, its texture sparse – and its contrast with the principal section, therefore, complete; the performance has to emphasize both contrasting aspects, rather than employ the usual, chronic utility *mp* or even *mf*.

Where the opening movement was 91 bars long, the (not so) slow movement, in the liberatingly brilliant relative major, amounts to 93 bars – nor is the comparison altogether artificial: the different proportions of the two sonata structures are illuminating and have to be realized (in both senses of the word) in performance:

	1st movement	3rd movement
	Allegro moderato	*Andante*
Exposition	37 bars	40 bars
Development	*21 bars*	*14 bars*
Recapitulation	33 bars	38 bars

But compressed as the slower movement's development is, there is no question of a mere transition back to the recapitulation: the modulatory activity is too intense, producing one of the movement's culminations. The leadback itself is sharply articulated by a pause on its last, solo note on the cello – and no wonder: listen to where I'm leading you back to, Haydn seems to say, if 'back' is indeed the word; from the note 'go', the recapitulation is lavishly modified.

As for the *Andante*'s *sforzatos*, the best approach to the meaning of dynamic and rhythmic marks is to imagine how one would tend to play the passage in question if they weren't there. If there were no *sforzato* on the second bar's principal beat, for instance, we might well thoughtlessly follow the metrical upbeat to bar 1 by an accent on *its* first beat. In musical reality, however, this is still an upbeat phrase, and all the *sforzato* at the beginning of bar 2 means is – no accent at the beginning of bar 1! Any exaggerated pushing on the *sforzato* is therefore quite out of structural place; if Haydn had known the de-accentuation sign used in our examples, he would have put it over the first beat of bar 1 instead.[5]

The finale's subtle and natural assimilation of the gipsy idiom (which Haydn himself verbally noted in the case of the *Menuet alla Zingarese* that is the gavotte-like anti-minuet of Op.20, No.4: see pp. 55–6) reminds us of the Austro-German tradition's unhappy love affair with gipsy-like improvis-

---

[5] Incidentally, many of Haydn's mere accents appear as *sforzatos* in print – not to speak of the *sforzatos* habitually added by copyists under syncopations.

ations – or rather, only three of its composers were able to turn it into a happy affair: Haydn, Johann Strauss, and Franz Schmidt. The unhappy affair, on the other hand, reached its critical climax in Brahms, where, admittedly, we do find a single happy moment – the slow movement of the Clarinet Quintet.

By way of completion of the sonata festival, the finale does not evince any trace of rondo anywhere, unless you want to regard the 12-bar theme itself as a rondo theme that is prevented from fulfilling itself, or what you consider its self – for the fact that the movement is not turning into a rondo is indeed its first major event, none the less creative and substantial for being negative. Now, if sonata expectations were thus disappointed, that would be a different matter!

It wasn't Mozart whom this enriching structural disillusionment inspired in the first place, but the late Beethoven – in fact the latest: compare the second finale of Op.130, still quite wrongly described as a rondo all over the place. Haydn's second subject injects an astonishing degree of contrasting lyricism into tiny motivic entities that fly past at *presto* speed – which must not inhibit or obstruct their interpretative expressiveness. The development section avails itself of the material of the transition, which is really development itself: the development section proper ought therefore to be called a second-degree development. There are, needless to add, overwhelming reshapings in the recapitulation; the interpretation will show its awareness of them. The coda renounces any temptation to aim at a Picardy third, a tonic major resolution; after, or rather, before all, we've started it all in the relative major! Hence, a stern, firm, emphatic B minor concludes the last movement with two *fortissimo* chords – as it had concluded the first. A sensitive performance will succeed in making us alive to this relation.

Op.33, No.2, in E flat major
(Hoboken III:38)

When I first came to this country as a pretty grown-up chamber musician at the age of 16, I was horrified to hear this E$^\flat$ quartet referred to as 'The Joke'; no such nickname attaches to it in the languages Haydn spoke. It need not be thought that I played the end of the work without employing my sense of humour, that I was unaware of its witty (rather than jocular) aspect; but to reduce what I thought was a doubly revolutionary compositorial device to the level of a joke which, by its very nature, makes its strongest effect when it is first heard, seemed to be equivalent to a childish misunderstanding, and the intervening decades have done nothing to improve my impression; on the contrary, they have substantiated and thus deepened my admiration for Haydn's far-reaching innovation. But, chronologically speaking, first things first – except that so far as the opening theme's continuation and quaver accompaniment is concerned, enough has already been said – in respect of Op.9, No.4 (see p. 22) and Op.20, No.5 (see p. 59) – to make a renewed warning of misaccentuations unnecessary; only, since the accompaniment's three quavers don't aim at a crotchet on a strong beat, it is the second quaver that takes what there unavoidably is of an accent.

As in all but the last two quartets of the set, the wishfully scherzoid movement comes again second; the only element that removes it yet further from the minuet background than were the Op.20's minuets, i.e. the *allegro* tempo, is very often ignored in performance because of the opening's outspoken triple rhythm. In deplorable fact, amongst Haydn's 45 great anti-minuets, this is one of those which are most frequently reduced to the minuet level, *allegretto* and all, and thus robbed of their essential meaning. As for the *Trio*, one can hear how Haydn actually needed the key of the principal section in order to throw the extreme contrast between the thematic characters of the respective melodies into relief: an additional key contrast would have obscured the elemental differences between the two, which demand, needless to add, a more relaxed tempo character for the *Trio*.

The *Trio* structure's relaxation has to express itself multi-dimensionally; so far as its melodic realization is concerned, single-finger *portamentos* in bars 1–2 and 5–6 will be found to be part and parcel of the actual melody. Each of them has to produce, or be produced by, a graceful *diminuendo*, disproving the twentieth-century convention according to which any so-miscalled *glissando* is the expression of uninhibited, 'romantic', cheap emotion or sentimentality. The 'normal' contemporary fiddler, incapable as he is of the rich variety of *portamentos* which the music of the great masters demands, is unaware that the truth is exactly the opposite: the chin-rest was introduced by Spohr (probably because he had a very long neck), prior to whom changes of position could not be managed inaudibly, whence the *portamento* was as much a composing consideration as, or even more than, the breath in vocal parts: one can specifically demonstrate that the great pre-classics and classics, Bach included, used it as a positive means of articulation, and not only in slow movements. Haydn even notated fingerings in order to make sure that we would understand his sliding intentions.

The *Largo sostenuto*, a combination of sonata and rondo form, is the viola's finest hour: had the time come when Haydn foresaw that he'd be playing quartets with Mozart at the viola desk? Mind you, he himself was an enthusiastic viola player too: when he travelled to England, he took his viola along, not his violin. The present E♭ Quartet is his first, anyhow, using the viola – which, *qua* solo instrument, had been omitted from the variations of Op.20, No.4 – in this leading role.

The theme is, in fact, exposed by the viola, in a duo with the cello, while the violins look after the restatement, with the help of the cello's two-bar punctuation. Is what one might describe as an extended textural climax in the offing? For once, Haydn meets one's expectations – but only because they are hope- rather than fearful: at the first return of the theme, the duo is between second violin and viola, but it has turned into a trio, in that the leader extends what was the cello's punctuation into a continuous figuration which almost assumes the significance of a counter-subject, though it is careful to remain a subordinate part. It remains for the second return and the coda to widen the texture into a full quartet.

The movement's basic interpretative problem, then, or rather, its basic solution, is the shaping of its repetitions: the second violin repeats the viola's theme, and the first the second's as well as the viola's. In good music, it must at the same time be remembered, there simply is no repetition: contextually and/or essentially, intrinsically, every seeming repetition is a variation. It follows that if one player repeats another's theme, he cannot possibly rest content with imitating the model's phrasings. He has to introduce a variation, which is to say that he must retain his predecessor's fundamental structure, on whose basis his imagination will introduce new elements that don't contradict it, but, on the contrary, substantiate it. In the present instance, moreover, the textural and, hence, structural climax has to be taken into account, so that the viola's will have to be the simplest statement, while the first violin's restatement will set the unfolding variations in motion. The second violin's variation will be helped by the first's superimposed subordinate part, which will, itself, contribute variational imagination; it is important for the second not to go one better, but to realize that its own theme now forms a basis for what is to be the leader's variation. And all three of them will have to save something up for the leader's eventual, victorious return and a half: the subordinate part, now in the viola and, in the coda, in the second violin, is no longer superimposed, but properly subordinated; the concluding triumph is the coda's half-statement, in view of which the first violin's preceding full statement must be a highly expressive *piano*, not again a utility *mp*, rising, via a three-quaver crescendo, to the coda's decided, confirming *mf* – but not beyond! For within the cello's semiquavers, an equally decided *piano* level has again to be reached – the necessary fundament for the concluding bar's *pianissimo* with its accent displaced on to the shorter second beat.

And so to the 'joke', behind whose entertainment hide two compositorial innovations that were to prove of decisive consequence for Mozart, Beethoven, and indeed beyond. Its understanding interpretation will lead us to its nature, for it has to be understood that the 'joke' is on the first sentence of the movement, as distinct from the returns of the rondo theme. Rests apart, the antecedent remains identical, whereas the consequent is modified towards greater conclusiveness, so that the first expectation is that the movement will finish with the completion of the oft-interrupted sentence. By then repeating its opening phrase, however, Haydn makes us expect the repeat we heard at the beginning, and it is at this very point of the intensest, utterly specific expectation that the strongest possible contradiction of expectation arises, for it isn't music that contradicts our expectation, but the fact that it's all over; with shocked gratification, we realize that this end, identical though it is with the beginning, makes perfect sense. The interpretation of the last phrase has to express the conflict between the beginning *qua* beginning and the uncontinued end *qua* end by way of a wittily half-hearted hesitation which does make clear that now, it is not a first phrase; countless senseless *ritardandos* are being played at the end of movements, regardless of the structure in question, but in this instance, a subtle combination of a *ritardando* and a *ritenuto* makes perfect sense: it does define the end and, at the same time, points to the fact that this needn't have been the end – that the most unexpected end has been chosen as the most logical.

The end that is absolutely identical with the beginning: outside downright circular structures, it hadn't happened before, and must have left a particularly deep impression on Mozart who, far less of a developmental composer than Haydn, must have liked this idea even better than its own inventor did – a fact for which there is profoundly meaningful evidence at the maturest stage of the younger composer's development. Significantly, it is evidence of two kinds, which I would describe as structural and autobiographical respectively.

As a hefty piece of structural evidence I would remind the reader of Mozart's D major Quintet which, it will be remembered, Haydn and Mozart played together, changing to and fro between the violas from movement to movement. The 8-bar sentence with which the body of the first movement starts is, note for note, identical with its concluding sentence – though at the beginning, it sounds as if it could only be a beginning, and at the end, as if it could only be a confirmation of finality.

From the point of view of Mozart's personal creative interests, my autobiographical piece of evidence is yet more fascinating, just because it is without structural signficance: it must have meant a lot to him, and can't have meant anything to anybody else – except, possibly, Haydn, who is bound to have discovered it. What I am talking about is the highly charged A major duet from the second act of *Così fan tutte*, whose opening is, again, wholly identical with the end of the first movement of the Piano Concerto K.414 in the same key, the 'little A major'. In neither structure, moreover, does this phrase play a leading thematic role – yet once again, it seems the perfect beginning or the perfect end, according to which piece one hears: the two are, of course, eight years apart.

The other compositorial innovation which the coda of this finale introduces is yet more elemental and does, in fact, start the history of a fundamentally new way of composing – a history that has remained alive until the present day, when it is proving even more alive than ever before. For to my knowledge, at any rate, we here have the very first structuralization of the very opposite of structure – of a process of formal disintegration. Haydn thus enters an entirely new field of expression whose attraction even a Mozart, the integrator *par excellence*, who felt that music must never cease to be music, found himself unable to resist: at least on a single occasion, he tore his own music creatively to bits – in the opening of the development section from the finale of the great G minor Symphony, where the disintegration of the theme assumes such proportions that in order to structuralize it, Mozart has to anticipate a century and a half of composing history: as I have shown else-where,[1] the passage is re-integrated by way of strict serial technique, with the result that the expressive value of its formal disintegration is nowise reduced. (Of Haydn's own serial technique we have already encountered an example: see p.56.)

It was, however, Beethoven in whom Haydn's new expressive conquest awakened highly characteristic creative needs; in fact, he continued the exploration at precisely the formal juncture at which Haydn had started it – though hardly by way of imitation: his first great advance into this field, the end of the *Eroica*'s funeral march, is no joke.

Op.33, No.3, in C major
(Hoboken III:39)

'The Bird' is both the most popular and the most 'celebrated' quartet so far encountered. Its opening innovation had such a wide and long influence on the history of composition that it almost became one of many opening conventions; as a result, it has become difficult for us to experience it as an innovation. I am, of course, referring to the beginning before the beginning, the initial accompaniment to nothing – a procedure which led through such works as Mozart's second G minor Symphony, Beethoven's Ninth, Schubert's A minor Quartet, Mendelssohn's Violin Concerto and several of his string quartets, to the symphonies of Bruckner and beyond (Schoenberg's Third Quartet, for instance). The structural purpose is to increase the range of a movement's, indeed a work's tension (Haydn's later introductions serve the selfsame purpose), historically an ever more urgent purpose in proportion as themes themselves came to unfold on higher levels of tension, owing chiefly to the development of harmony and the rising norms of consonance and dissonance. Apart from the present writer, nobody seems to have observed

[1] 'Strict Serial Technique in Classical Music', *Tempo*, No.37, London, 1955. For an early example of Mozart's strict serial technique, see also my 'The Chamber Music', in H.C. Robbins Landon and Donald Mitchell (eds.), *op cit.*, pp.95f.

this phenomenon: decades ago, he pointed out that it was awaiting detailed examination, but apart again from his own work, nothing seems to have happened in the meantime.

This opening is hellishly difficult, and few are the public performances which allow the melody-less accompaniment to come from nowhere, as it obviously should. For since the second fiddle – or, at any rate, one of the middle parts – has to lead, public tension almost invariably produces an accent on the first quaver. Ironically enough, the work's popularity has been promoted by this misinterpretation, which gives the asymmetrical antecedent a slightly more symmetrical feel. For the rest, the middle parts' problems are not confined to the beginning of the accompaniment to nothing and its reiterations: there is another, almost universally played wrong accent whose avoidance is not easy – the first, *forte* beat of bar 4, reached by way of a *cresc.* that has to adjust itself with great finesse to the first violin's entirely different *cresc.*, unfolding as this does during the rhythmic acceleration of the extended upbeat phrase. It isn't easy to land in a *forte* bar and postpone the phrase's main accent until the next beat, but this is precisely what Haydn wants with his implied cross-accents between the leader and the middle parts: the leader's first main accent is, of course, bar 4's first beat. In the middle parts, what one usually hears is a musical absurdity, to wit, two main accents per phrase – one on the first beat, and one on the ensuing *sforzato*. It is shattering to observe how few players clearly realize that in good music and good music-making alike, a phrase cannot contain more than one main accent; where it does, something has gone wrong with either the composition or the performance or indeed both of them – for one can improve a composer's faulty split-up of a phrase by reshaping it by means of one's own phrasing. There is one consolation for the middle parts at that tricky moment: the difficulty of reaching *forte* level without an accent is even greater, far greater, on a keyboard instrument, where the classics – Haydn, Mozart, Beethoven – none the less require that course of (in)action on an awe-inspiring variety of occasions.

Haydn would not be Haydn if he did not immediately exploit his innovatory beginning before the beginning by complicating his beginning – the theme, which develops on an unexpectedly high level of tension: 'develops' is indeed the word, for the theme modulates, thus anticipating the manifestly developmental themes of the romantic era; we have observed that Haydn is the source of everything.

The second subject can hardly be introduced without rubato on the upbeat phrase; the contrast does not otherwise make sense. The free upbeat should incorporate a *diminuendo* rather than a *crescendo*, in order to prepare for both the dynamic level of the entire second subject and the lightened 'bird' texture, i.e. the two violins which are to resume and expand their two-part sound in the downright duo that is the *Trio*. The climactic phrase of the theme, where the crushed notes appear in the rhythmic diminution produced by the quavers, ought to be given its full, witty value so far as the *acciaccaturas* themselves are concerned, with more of a fuss over the first than the second;

the second violin has to support this deliberate execution by a miniature *tenuto* on the *b'* and – less so, of course – on the *a'*.

The *Scherzando*'s position as second movement and its *allegretto* tempo are, come to think of it, its only traditional aspects; in all other respects, it overflows with originality – even texturally, for the contrast between the principal section's tutti and the *Trio*'s duo casting is transmuted into two sharply contrasting sound pictures the like of which one had never heard before. In the principal section, Haydn contrives dark brightness by subjecting C major, in an utterly unrelieved, *sotto voce* quartet texture (there's not a moment where you don't hear all four instruments!),[1] to the darkening influence of the four instruments' lowest string. The opposite precedent is to be found in the previous set's A major Quartet (pp.62f.), where it is the (largely literal) trio that is thus coloured. The low dynamic level should be strictly retained.

The *Trio*, on the other hand, whose uncontrasting tonicality once again throws its extreme contrast in all other respects into relief, switches, not to the trio for two violins we have encountered twice before (cf. Op.9, No.4, p.26, and Op.33, No.1, pp.64–5), but to an actual duo for those instruments: if Haydn had felt in a verbally realistic mood, he could have called his *Scherzando*, anti-minuet and all, '*Menuetto. Allegretto*', and his *Trio*, '*Duo*'. During the phrasing of the *Trio*'s tune, now confined to the upper strings (as well as in the phrasing of the first movement's second subject), the leader had better forget the work's nickname: extra-musical considerations won't contribute to a characteristic shape, and without its wit, the trio loses much of its significance; I am not an ornithologist, but to my knowledge, birds are not particularly witty. In a well-improvised performance of the duo, the second fiddle must be at the audible (and, as it were, appreciative) disposal of the leader's wit.

The *Adagio*'s symmetrical theme is *its* only traditional aspect, which has made it one of Haydn's most popular slow movements altogether, though its comprehensive structural originality has remained quite unnoticed – even by normally insightful analysts. Haydn's enthusiasm for combining forms now widens into a *ménage à trois* – between sonata, rondo, and variation. I feel tempted to widen the metaphor in my turn, and to speak of a little harem consisting of variation and rondo, with sonata emerging as the dominating principle binding the two together and to itself. The movement's – indeed all four movements' – *sforzatos* need no longer be discussed: what we said about those in the B minor Quartet's *Andante* applies to them throughout, if *mutatis mutandis*. Yet how many performances can the reader remember whose 1st, 5th, and 9½th bars were clear, unambiguous upbeat phrases, recognizable as such before the respective phrase's main stress ensued – rather than retrospectively, after the accenting event? Which would be too late, of

---

[1] Cf. the slow movement of Op.20, No.1 and, later, that of Op.42 – pp.30 and 84f. respectively.

course: retrospective intellectual recognition is no substitute for a musical experience that hasn't happened, and legitimate retrospective experiences are confined to those which the composer intends and, through his definitions, causes.

The final rondo must be as fast as rhythmically calm – which means very fast. There is no objection to *ricochet* (i.e. a thrown down-bow *staccato*) in the semiquavers right at the end if imagination dictates it: in this very fast tempo, the respective two instruments can't help being together, and the virtuoso touch is not as such unmusical in chamber music. What is more unmusical is its unsubstantiated suppression, with nothing except an empty good-boy attitude to replace it.

For the rest, it pains me to assault as musical an observer as D.F. Tovey, but when he says that 'the first movement is at once the quietest and the greatest Haydn had so far achieved',[2] all he demonstrates is his surprisingly superficial knowledge of nine other opening movements. But then, notwithstanding his shafts of esoteric insight, he remained a lifelong outsider, whose perusal of the present book I'd have deeply welcomed. Maybe there are one or two Toveys around.

Op.33, No.5, in G major
(Hoboken III:41)

With the G major quartet from this set we have arrived at the first of its two homotonal works (whereas no fewer than four out of Op.20's six had been homotonal), and at the second of its two works that start before the beginning; only this time it isn't with an accompaniment to nothing that Haydn extends the range of structural tension, but with a two-bar introduction excluded from the exposition's repeat but reappearing unchanged as what, therefore, we can regard as either the last stage of the leadback or the first stage of the recapitulation – or, most understandingly, as both: we shall come to see that in the further course of his quartet development, and most systematically at its maturest stages, Haydn was to explore every possible introductory function. Meanwhile, the present introduction and its structural consequences offer us an opportunity to discuss an interpretative question I have been suppressing for many thousands of words, since I wished to postpone

---

[2] In *Cobbett's Cyclopaedic Survey of Chamber Music*.

the answer until there was an occasion on which one could discuss it simply, unambiguously, and incontrovertibly. Why all this fuss? Because it is my submission that the answer which virtually our entire playing civilization, Western and beyond, gives to what I consider a burning question is wrong, demonstrably, stupidly, inexcusably wrong – and our most distinguished artists give it as readily as any old fool; they don't even bother to think about the alternative answer.

The question? Let me first pose it negatively – or rather, in a way which will elicit a negative answer. Confine your recollections to your most admired performers, and tell me whether you've ever heard them play a second repeat in any Haydn, Mozart, or even Beethoven work wherein the composer asks for it. No, will be your most likely answer; even the possibility of one or two exceptions is so remote that I for one can't see it without a telescope.

I have, from this point of view, analysed every single second repeat in important works and it is now my definite, demonstrable and provable submission that so far as the great composers' mature works are concerned, every second repeat they have notated in a sonata movement must be played, because it involves, indeed contains, what are among the most essential inventions of the movement in question, so that its omission is equivalent to something none of the omitters would ever as much as consider – a straightforward cut in a masterpiece.

The loss of the composer's thought is, moreover, twofold – and the two types of inventions that are withheld from the recipient tend to be intimately interconnected. On the one hand, that is to say, what we lose is the composer's carefully created transition from the end of either the recapitulation or the entire movement to the opening of the development, a transition in view of which the transition to either the coda or the very end had been contrastingly composed; neither of them can be fully understood without knowledge, without experience of its contrasting basis.

On the other hand, I put it to every performer of our time that in every single mature sonata movement by a great composer who has requested a second repeat, and with the sole and obvious exception of the last movement of Beethoven's last string quartet, the development section is not only, sometimes not even chiefly, concerned with the exposition, but also, sometimes even chiefly, with the recapitulation. It follows ineluctably that the recapitulation has to be heard, not only after the development, but also before it. Ironically, therefore, the never-played second repeat emerges as yet more important than the oft-played first; as against the considerations of sheer meaning, of fundamental sense, I have here adduced, considerations of formal balance clearly take second place.

Now, why have I chosen this particular G major quartet for my passionate lecture to our entire music-making world, more urgently necessary than which no observation, analytical, educational, or both, will be found in the present volume? (The lecture is, of course, both.) Because either type of Haydn's inventions, and above all the *unity* between the development and that on which it is based in the recapitulation, largely manifests itself in the *continuity* from the end of the recapitulation into the development. As a result, the absolute need for the second repeat is glaringly obvious to the naked ear whose attention has been drawn to it, specifically and in all its concreteness.

Despite its nature, the cadential introduction, which proves both dispensable and indispensable (the mark of genius is the capacity for having it both ways), gradually turns out to be the main protagonist of the first movement's action, both in itself and thematically; it will, as I shall try to show concretely at the end of this analysis, have to be played with full – if concealed – consciousness of its role. Both the first repeat and the progress from exposition to development rub in its dispensability; the very fact that the development starts with a tonic minor version of the theme shows us that even though the introduction as such has now been absent from the movement for a long time, such a structural point is made of its absence that we may expect much of the rest of the movement to be about its structural function. And indeed, the leadback combines, successively, its replacement (which precedes both the first repeat and the development) and its original version; in fact, the two bars' GP between the two makes it at least as much part of the recapitulation proper as of the leadback: only the experience of the first repeat prevents us from simply accepting its reappearance as the start of the recapitulation.

And now we come to its six crucial final versions, arrived at sequentially on its very own basis, without three of which – i.e. in the case of an unheeded second repeat – the movement simply does not make sense. In the coda's sequences, its thematic role gradually and naturally develops into, or is naturally enveloped by, its original shape, that is succeeded by its final octave-unison simplification, for which the preceding octave in the second violin has been a subtle preparation, utterly unnoticed by any quartet I've heard that hasn't been coached by me. The one-bar GP preceding the second repeat is thematically determined – yes, rests can be thematic, too! – by the GP preceding the recapitulation: a warning of a violent contradiction of expectation. At the recapitulatory stage, the *introduction* was least expected; after the coda, its *continuation* is. With the resumption of the theme after the coda, the introduction's indispensability is rubbed in whith a vengeance: even the theme's tonic-minor version needs it! In fact, the variation on the introduction produces a variation on the theme, whose minor-mode version the unison version of the introduction neither anticipates nor contradicts. In other words, without the second repeat, neither the beginning of the development nor the end would have been composed as they were: the end would have been the normal introduction, and the beginning of the development would have been like every other such structure in great Haydn, to wit, not tonical. In yet other words, the eventual end of the movement only makes sense in the light of the beginning of the development that had succeeded it: now the warning GP tells us that nothing is to follow. Just as the theme proved capable, in the first repeat and only there, of emerging without the introduction, so the introduction proves capable, at the very end and only there, of emerging without the theme. The final, relatively inconclusive octave unison loses any residual anxiety that may attach to it as soon as we realize that, though it is not now followed by the G *minor* of the opening of the development, it *is* followed by another G minor – that of the *Largo*'s opening! We hear now that *the work's homotonality has become an unalterable fact as from the opening of the first movement's development section.*

It will, I hope, be obvious from the foregoing analysis that the absolute need for the second repeat has to be specifically demonstrated in each individual case: the concrete reasons are, of course, never the same in any two great works. But once alerted, the musical reader will, I am confident, be able to find them for himself in any given case; my teaching experience tells me that this is the normal course of musico-intellectual events. It only remains to be added that so far as such mature sonata structures are concerned, the presence or absence of a *seconda volta* does not make any difference to the need for the second repeat, whose own absence produces a visible cut in the case of second-time bars, and an invisible, but none the less devastating cut in the case of their absence: that is all.

And now for the interpretation of this two-bar perfect cadence – which has to be smilingly knowing, both stressing and winkingly denying its pseudo-banality. For once, in fact, the interpreter is invited to confuse the recipient – to puzzle him. There are countless ways in which this aim can be achieved, but they all share one condition: the introduction must precede the definition of tempo character; as a matter of fact, it will be characterless, aside from its ironical cadential gesture, and hence marginally slower than the basic tempo – hesitating, in fact.

We remember that the structural large-scale purpose of any beginning before the beginning is an extension of the range of tension – and as in the case of the opening movement of 'The Bird', Haydn immediately exploits his beginning before the beginning by his theme's modulatory complication: he lets his first subject modulate to the dominant, thus again anticipating the modulatory themes of a much later stage in the development of symphonic thought.

At the end of the first subject's recapitulation, in what one might realistically describe as the transition to the transition, the playing reader will not fail to be reminded of our remarks on the first movement of Op.9, No.4 with reference to Ex.2 (pp.21f.).

In the aria (not, as Tovey says in his grossly misleading note[1] on the work, the 'arioso') that is the ensuing *Largo*, the second violin has to shun both over-distinctness and the contemporary accompanimental malaise – a *sempre espressivo*. The necessary flexibility will manifest itself automatically as soon as, in his mind, the second fiddler plays the first-violin part too – an absolute

[1] *Op.cit.*

condition, this, and not only for the realization of the present accompaniment!

The amazing rhythmic structure of the *Scherzo* is clearly stressed by Haydn's dynamics: *the entire antecedent is an upbeat to its last note*; only if the *allegro* character is immediately defined will the first three bars be meaningfully and utterly accentless. They should, moreover, be thoroughly extra-metrical, turning time-beating into an insoluble problem, and whole-heartedly expressing the single-minded urge up to bar 4. The tonical trio is a powerful, or rather, and extremely relaxed contrast in almost every other respect; its own *allegro* character will, of course, be very different, and distinctly slower for a start.

The final variations are, again, on a *siciliano* theme (cf. p.59), this time closer to the tempo character of the actual dance form. Both theme and variations will inevitably remind players of Mozart's final variations in his second Haydn Quartet, which is putting the cart before the horse that is the present movement and, of course, the inspiration of Mozart's; that at this stage, Mozart's dedication has become a little ambivalent, in that he wanted palpably to go one better, cannot, perhaps, easily be denied. In any case, in either movement, the definition of the *allegretto* has to take the eventual speed-up into account.

Op.33, No.6, in D major
(Hoboken III:42)

The opus' second homotonal work concludes it in the key in which the whole set had started, however deceptively.[1] From the interpretative standpoint as distinct from that of execution, it is one of the least problematic – so long as everything we have so far said about misaccentuation and the precise meaning of Haydn's *sforzatos* is clearly remembered: see, particularly, p.67 with reference to Op.33, No.1, as well as p.59 with reference to quaver

---

[1] I am, of course, using the adverb ironically – for in great music, there is no deception, as which the contradiction of expectation cannot be described, unless he who expects narcissistically confuses expectation with reality. The term 'deceptive cadence' is, therefore, aesthetically inadmissible; 'interrupted cadence' is its realistic alternative – which, unfortunately, German terminology does not provide for *Trugschluss* (deceptive cadence).

accompaniments (*cf.* Ex.34). The first two movements, that is to say, will not take kindly to accents on the half-bar, which, in the *Andante*, are heard as often as Haydn's *sforzatos* try to forestall them – in bars 2, 4, 6, etc. The *Andante*'s entire first bar, in other words, is a single upbeat to the second; once again, the fact that the middle parts go together intensifies the danger of misaccentuation, because audibly wrong accents readily slip in unobserved, each of the players feeling that he is not to blame, whatever the composite picture may sound like. Each of them, then, has to be alive to his inescapable responsibility for the composite picture.

Its *Allegro* character once again removes the *Scherzo* one step further from its minuet background; at the same time, the antecedent's and consequent's opposing accentuations have to be clearly heeded: the antecedent goes with the first and third bar's accents, whereas the consequent goes against its own first, second, and third bar's accents, and unless these are as decisively de-accented as the respective upbeats are accented, Haydn's displacements will turn into phrase-destroying tautologies – into two disruptive main stresses per phrase.

The trio (this time not so called) once again uses its tonicality as a common background against which the thematic and textural contrasts between it and the principal section are thrown into relief; in fact, five eighths of its first part are as literal a trio as the first quarter of its second part is a duo, the second quarter a trio, and the second half a full quartet: another textural climax, different from anything we've had before. The character definition is, of course, down to the cello, which will naturally have to relax the *allegro*: the time when one had to put in a separate tempo mark for unmusical players had not yet arrived.

Just as the dance movement was an *allegro* instead of the expected *allegretto*, the finale is an *allegretto* instead of an *allegro*; with its strictly alternating D major and D minor, it represents an apotheosis of the work's homotonality, and uses this alternation towards a combination of no fewer than three forms. But whereas in the case of the *Adagio* of 'The Bird', we had sonata, rondo, and variation combined, the present movement combines not only variation and rondo, but also Haydn's own new double variation form. Nevertheless, it outlines its structure with such abundant clarity that a verbal outline would make me guilty of a sterile, sheer pleonasm; suffice it to say that double variation form, i.e. variations on two themes, is one of those forms which Haydn, as distinct from any other composer of the Western World, introduced single-handed into the evolution of composition, where it cele-brated many a climax within his own output, though most people chiefly, or even only, know it from a more often played climax – the slow movement of Beethoven's Ninth.

The interpretation of the finale will have to heed two elemental require-ments above and below all – the sharp contrast of character between the major-mode and the minor-mode sections, and the demand for variation not only, and self-evidently, in the variations themselves, but also in the repetitions of the theme, whose repetitive repetitions have given rise to many an embarrassing performance.

Op.42, in D minor
(Hoboken III:43)

The 53-year-old Haydn created a miracle within the miracle that is his output of great string quartets: to put it briefly, its closest relative is Mozart's 'easy' C major Piano Sonata, K.545. The Quartet could indeed bear the sub-title 'a little string quartet for beginners', except that apart from its actual duration (it is Haydn's shortest quartet of stature), it isn't all that little; but together with its sublime perfection, its careful avoidance of any technical demands makes it not just the ideal but, upon comprehensive reflection, the sole uncomplicated introduction to the playing of great string quartets, as which it is urgently and unreservedly recommended. It is the only great quartet that is easy to play – so far as anything great is easy to play. The deplorable level of our literature on the string quartet can be estimated in view of the circumstance that this amazing fact has never yet been pointed out.

The tragedy is that almost certainly, there were at least three of them, the other two having gone 'down the Spanish drain', as H.C. Robbins Landon puts it: 'Typical, I fear, of everything Haydnish in Spain; all the known, unknown works are lost . . .'[1]

Haydn never wrote an isolated quartet, and Landon has indeed considerable evidence to suggest that three had been commissioned for an unknown Spanish purpose; Haydn himself mentions, in a letter, three 'very short quartets' intended for Spain. The type of purpose for which they were written is abundantly clear from the nature, the technical limitations of the extant work; what is downright incredible is the stature, in respect of both substance and originality, it nevertheless achieves with the most carefree, uninhibited mastery, and with its winkingly 'simple' style – though Jens Peter Larsen,[2] aware maybe of the absence of playing difficulties but utterly unalive, evidently, to its musical weight, does not even grant it a mention. In view of the fact that no substantial commentary on the work is in existence (even Tovey misleads more often than he illuminates, especially with his remarks on the slow movement), we shall have to examine it in some considerable detail; it will perhaps be agreed that its original substance definitely outweighs that of

[1] From private correspondence.
[2] Op.cit.

the aforementioned, comparable Mozartian masterpiece.

The originality of the quartet's invention and its textural contrasts are, in fact, as incisive as ever, and strikingly in evidence as from the opening thought, whose phrasing is not at all obvious: the easy is not always simple. The first note of the model and its quasi-sequence is the main note; the rest of the phrase, which radically changes its shape from the model to its offspring, is after-beat, epilogue. Once again, the single purpose of the *sforzato* is de-accentuation – of the middle of the bar (cf. Op.33, No.1, p.67), though now it is a downbeat phrase, not an upbeat one, which the *sforzato* clarifies. At the same time, what was an echoing motif at the end of the model turns into its very opposite at the phrase's recurrence, namely, an upbeat motif to the consequent: can a subtler maximal differentiation and contrast be found in any theme by any composer?

This metamorphosis is, of course, the opening sentence's crucial event, more profoundly thrilling than a detective novel's climactic surprise, in proportion as it isn't a surprise at all, but an essentially different type of contradicted expectation whose effect, far from being reduced by one's foreknowledge, actually deepens with one's familiarity with its nature: one's precise intellectual foresight prepares one's emotions for a full experience of the event – and this is true of all so-miscalled musical 'surprises' which convey meaning, as opposed to real surprises produced, say, by sound effects, which do indeed wear off with familiarity.

It would be foolish, therefore, to destroy the event, as frequently and quite inanely happens, by making the upbeat drive immediately manifest; there simply is no upbeating energy in the model, whose three last notes cannot, therefore, be standardized according to what happens to them in the quasi-sequence. In short, one cannot contradict the model to the point of inconsistency; it is quite enough to know inwardly that the structural function of the three quavers is undergoing a total change, and, for the rest, to keep the phrasing of the model characteristically alive – true to its own character, that is, as opposed to the violently contrasting character of its offspring.

The compression of the opening movement's recapitulation is unprecedented in Haydn's own quartet output: observe how, in the reprise, he cuts straight across from the exposition's fourth bar (as early as that!) to its nineteenth, i.e. right into the beginning of the second subject, availing himself of both his monothematic design and, of course, the tonical residence of the subsidiary subject in the recapitulation.

The minuet – which, in this easy and, perhaps, allegedly, officially simple quartet had to come second, I suppose – is no less subtle, no less complex, in fact. What does the *sforzato* in bar 5 mean? The first bar is an upbeat to the second, the third seems a corresponding upbeat to the fourth – but the *sforzato* turns the fourth bar into a continuation of the second upbeat phrase, so that the phrase's main accent is now delayed by one bar, whereupon the two foreshortened sequential phrases defined by the two *sforzatos* establish the consequent's counterbalance *vis-à-vis* the antecedent's extension of the basic idea. So long as the players are clearly conscious of these structural conditions, they can't go wrong – not with their tempo, either, which the opening upbeat bar will have to turn into a light and lively *allegretto* – the opposite, needless to add, of a minuet's *allegretto*.

Where the lively tempo will show its utter indispensability, however, is at the climax of the rhythmic structure's contradicted expectations – before and at the return of the ternary principal section's outer part: a forward-urging, two-bar *crescendo* makes one expect the strongest downbeat bar of the piece – which, unbelievably, proves a downbeat bar and an upbeat bar rolled into one, in that the downbeat is confined to the first beat of a bar in which the section's strongest downbeat and its strongest (opening) upbeat overlap; rhythmically, though not melodically, the upbeat phrase has thus been robbed of a crotchet, of whose rescue the leader might make a witty show. After all, his part in the overlap is merely dynamic – his *forte* on the first beat which, with refined, knowing bowing, he might yet invest with upbeat significance, so that the second fiddle's and cello's downbeat and the first violin's upbeat are actually heard to overlap.

At the end, incidentally, *pace* Haydn's concern for the technical limitations of his Spanish players, he does let the first violin ascend to top D – but only in order to help the virginal leader lay claim to being a virtuoso: if he happens to be reading these lines, he will agree, upon his first reading of the passage, that the brilliant concluding run in the violin's most characteristic and most comfortable key is dead easy.

The *Trio*'s more rhythmic version of the monothematic movement's thematic material invites a slightly slower, more 'held' tempo, of which the opening crotchets – as distinct from the minuet's opening quavers – are immediately expressive: one has to think in terms of a maximal contrast between these two, thematically related, superficially 'similar' opening bars. The repeated dominants have proved basic ever since the work's second bar. For the rest, the turn to the relative (F) major within the eight bars of the *Trio*'s first part is almost abrupt, an emphatic change in emotional atmosphere which still sounds 'modern' to an unjaded ear. The same is true of the parallel switch-back to the work's tonic in the second part of the *Trio* – a mere eight bars again.

The culmination of textural as well as structural originality, however, is reserved for the profoundly characteristic Haydn *adagio*, the miraculously continuous four-part writing of whose twelve-bar theme doesn't let the slightest whiff of air into the texture, which is, in fact, unrelieved by the tiniest rest, and would thus have sounded thick, un-quartet-like, in the hands of any other composer: two previous textures, the *Affetuoso e sostenuto* of Op.20, No.1 (see p.37) and the *Scherzando* of Op.33, No.3 (see p.74) had given us an inkling of Haydn's unrivalled mastery of a full, unrelieved quartet texture – which can, of course, be endangered by an insensitive performance; in the case of the present theme, the three lower instruments have to listen two-dimensionally all the way – to their balance on the one hand, and their blend on the other. And I hope I shan't be accused of mysticism if I add that in a really masterly realization of a quartet texture of this type, the first violin has to hear, and has to be heard to hear, the lower instruments' two-dimensional listening.

As soon as we turn from the texture to the structure, we suddenly realize that Haydn's last and first D minor quartet's slow movement, likewise a B♭[3] *adagio* (see pp.26–7), had introduced a structural innovation of far-reaching importance, one which he here resumes, immeasurably more subtly, complexly – in fact, still more innovatorily, for the monothematic structure itself is a combination of ternary form, variation form, and sonata without a thematic or even harmonic, i.e. dominant, second-subject stage, nor does Haydn simply vary the repeat of the exposition; what he varies is, of all things, the implied repeat of the continuation of the theme. Why, for heaven's sake? Because it is this continuation which becomes the subject of the development: the varied repeat serves the very purpose the repeat of the exposition used to serve.

The fact remains that Haydn hits upon this novel idea of a varied repeat in his two B♭ *adagios* of his first two D minor quartets. In the case of his two B minor quartets, we could at least divine a reason why he chose this particular key for the purpose of 'progressive tonality' (*cf.* p.65), but his concentration on D minor works and the B♭ movements is as inexplicable as his concentration on C major works for a purpose we mentioned apropos of Op.20, No.2 (see p.39), or Mozart's concentration on B♭ works for the purpose of postponing his second subject until it is least expected, i.e. after the double-bar: hear the first movements of the 'Hunt' Quartet and his second B♭ Piano Trio. I have to reiterate that it is important to own up to the fact that one has no answer to a question, for only thus does one ensure the survival of a question which most investigators hide because they don't know the answer.

There is another intriguing and unanswered question here. Unanswered? To my knowledge, it hasn't even yet been asked – though myself, for one, it fascinates. The quartet was written in the year of Mozart's dedication to Haydn of his own first set of great quartets. We have observed that Haydn's only previous D minor Quartet – his first great work in the medium – must have influenced Mozart's second Haydn Quartet, itself in D minor. Is it conceivable that with Op.42, the reciprocal inspiration had started, that Mozart's D minor Quartet stimulated not only Haydn's 'Fifths' (Op.76, No.2) but, long before and far more immediately in a temporal sense, our present work, Haydn's only other quartet in this key apart from the Introduction to the *Seven Words* and what would have been his last quartet (whose slow movement is, again, in B♭, which is why it was illiterately described as a B♭ quartet: see footnote 5 on p.7)? My own answer is a definite yes: the

---

[3] This quite usual, submediant slow-movement key must, of course, be understood as the relative major's subdominant – the reposeful region *par excellence*.

respective themes are of one family, with their birth certificates being analytically available. I well remember, moreover, that when as a boy I first played Mozart's first Haydn Quartet and, as second fiddler, tremblingly started the fugal finale, I immediately recalled my strictly parallel trembles at the beginning of the present quartet's finale – nor is this relation confined to my autobiography: Haydn had not previously started any movement in this manner which, although not fugal, does enlist fugue-like counterpoint quite unlike his own finale fugues. In short, Mozart's second-fiddle opening may well have prompted Haydn's.

In any case, the latter makes little ado about much. In its miniature sonata form, again monothematic, it accommodates fugato as well as playful homophony, asymmetry as well as dance-like recreation. Exceptionally announced by the second violin in a four-bar duo with the viola, whose subordinate part (rather than accompaniment) beautifully explores the contrasting colours of the two instruments, the *marcato* theme at first shows its uncomplicated face and must in fact be played as 'innocently' as Haydn wants the other outer movement to materialize; in the coda we shall even play its first phrase in octave unison. Immediately after the opening announcement, however, the theme displays its contrapuntal features, *stretto* included.

In all the circumstances, and in view of both the intensive development and, once again, the violently modified, drastically compressed recapitulation (28 bars as against 40 of the exposition!), which steals in, on the cello, under polyphonic cover, it is amazing in playing to note how Haydn remembers all along, whatever his commission was which produced the self-commandment, to keep his instrumental technique 'unassuming' – if I may use the expression which Carl Ferdinand Pohl, Haydn's one-time standard biographer, misapplied to the style of the slow movement, as if there was nothing behind it. Of course, the entire work is stressedly unpretentious, but then, stressedly or not, so is all mature Haydn. However, the claims and demands it makes on our musicality are nowise modest; it must finally be re-emphasized that only the demands it makes on our playing ability are.

Op.50, No.1, in B flat major
(Hoboken III:44)

Published and possibly composed in 1787, in Haydn's mid-fifties, Op.50 shows Mozart's reciprocal influence – though paradoxically, the extreme characterological differences between the two composers thus emerge all the more strongly and clearly: the present quartet's third, E♭ minor variation in the slow movement, for instance, Mozart wouldn't have been seen dead with; in fact, Mozart never went beyond four flats or four sharps for any of his home- or temporary home-keys – and even four of them he used but rarely. Nevertheless, a *circulus virtutis* unique in musical history here completed its first round.

The very beginning of the quartet, the two bars of solitary B♭ crotchets in the bass (which can't have imposed too heavy a strain on what must have been the impressive technique of the set's dedicatee, the cello-playing Friedrich Wilhelm II, for whom Mozart wrote his last three quartets), represents and presents a double innovation overflowing with self-contradictory meaning as only music logically can. On the one, representative hand, that is to say, like 'The Bird', the quartet starts before the beginning with an accompaniment to nothing, which this time is a tonic pedal without anything on top; however, it comes to assume basic thematic significance. On the other, newly presenting hand, our impression of having started before the beginning is rudely interrupted by the discord with which the music proper opens, the 'theme' in the conventional sense, and which now gives the impression that on the contrary, we are starting *after* the beginning, after something that's been left out: we hear a sequence without a model. The cellist will best foreshadow this paradoxicality by way of total, yet slightly play-acted innocence: 'I know of nothing, believe me or not'. Well, if he knew nothing, he wouldn't have thought of his rider, which his imaginative tone production as well as a marginally irrational distance between the first two crotchets will easily insinuate – between ourselves, as it were. As for the leader's contribution, he will have to act as if the introductory pedal had suppressed a model for the ensuing sequences: he will have to start as if he continued something he hasn't in fact been playing.

Another of Haydn's multifarious introductions, then. If 'The Bird' is one of its sources, the other fully describes our *circulus virtutis*: which other great quartet starts with a tonic pedal of repeated equal values with nothing on top –

which proves unexpectedly thematic? None other than Mozart's only mature quartet which starts with a Haydnesque, slow introduction that almost shows off a downright un-Mozartian, stressedly Haydnian harmonic adventurousness and dissonant demeanour – 'The Dissonance', in fact, the last quartet Mozart dedicated to his closest musical friend! It was at a private quartet evening where 'The Dissonance' was first performed that Haydn described Mozart as the greatest musician he knew or knew of.

This time, the repeat of Haydn's exposition includes, of course, the introduction, but not the wildest imagination – unless there is a Haydn amongst my readers – can forehear what is going to happen at the lead-back and recapitulatory stages. First, we get the beginning before the beginning in G minor, hence introducing, not the reprise, but the lead-back, and by the time we hear the actual pre-beginning again, foreshortened but in its proper tonicality, we have, as it were, missed the beginning of the recapitulation; for, as if the theme's initial start after the beginning hadn't been enough, its recapitulation starts in what was bar 5 of the exposition, with the result that its antecedent now is no longer than a bar and a bit!

The interpretation of this, the most thrilling moment in the fate of Haydn's introduction will have to be proportionately subtle. The viola's pseudo-introduction, or its real introduction of the lead-back, will have to allude to the cello's opening without slavishly imitating it, but when the cello itself enters with its proper introduction reduced to less than half its original structure, it will have to anticipate the ensuing, stunning compression by contradicting its original opening (which will meanwhile have been varied in the repeat of the exposition), to the extent of unexpectedly urging forward – without the slightest suspicion of a rush, of course, which would destroy the entire rhythmic structure; but a feelable *tempo giusto* will, at this point, be experienced as freer than the most daring rubato.

There are no more than three variations on the rich, reposeful theme of the none too slow *Adagio*, whose relatively lively tempo must not be allowed to rob it of its *adagio* character, for the movement is emphatically reposeful, not only because of the easily graspable personality of both the theme and its variations, but also because of the traditional withdrawal into the subdominant. True to his own creative personality, his passion for thematic (as opposed to Mozart's harmonic) economy, Haydn was fond of turning his variation-movements themselves into structural *cum* textural variations on the *passacaglia* principle; to put it simply, the theme as such is rarely ever absent, however lavish and contrasting the variations. In the first variation, the second violin plays it, while the first is engaged upon variation. The second variation we have already referred to: it is the E♭ minor one, whose superabundance of flats does not prevent the leader from playing the modified theme in a relaxed *dolce* style – much of it: there now are basic departures from the original, both harmonically and, therefore, melodically. In the last variation, the first violin does what the second did in the first variation, to wit, play the theme, and the cello does what the first violin did in the first variation, only more so: at last, the King of Prussia is coning into his own, supplying downright virtuosity in spite of the *adagio* tempo – with demisemi-quavers more brilliant even than the leader's *staccato* scales in the first variation. Follows a weighty coda of fourteen bars – two bars longer, that is, than the theme or any of its variations, in which circumstances, as so often elsewhere, the term 'coda' seems a metaphorical misnomer: after all, the tail is but rarely longer than the dog.

The movement's first *sforzato* has more positive significance than the next two, which only re-establish the bar-accent, add the half-bar accent, and thus define the respective upbeats: if these are played as such, they fulfil the *sforzatos'* entire function (cf. Op.33, No.1, p.67). The cross-accent of the first *sforzato*, on the other hand, has to be played in view of its as yet hidden meaning in the first variation where, on the second violin, it becomes a model or, to be precise, an anti-model, for the first violin's imitation.

Even at first hearing, not to speak of first playing, the theme of the minuet can be felt to be closely related to the theme of the slow movement, which has been heard over and over again – not the only example, this, of thematic interrelations between movements in classical works, which makes the usual musicological practice of confining the concept of so-puzzlingly-called 'cyclic form' to nineteenth-century music a little unrealistic. From the playing point of view, musical meaning will be enriched, or rather, done full justice, if the phrasing of the four-semiquaver upbeat audibly remembers the phrasing of the previous movement's four-demisemiquaver upbeat.

Although in the unifying tonic and, again, thematically related to the principal section, the *Trio* couldn't be more of a contrast. For one thing, the texture of the principal section, pretty full and partly contrapuntal, is succeeded by a 'trio' with a vengeance: eight of the *Trio*'s twenty-eight bars are not a trio but a duo and indeed – if I may switch to Greek – a 'mono', which covers the most important phrase too, i.e. the leader's opening basic motif and its continuation. For another thing, an element of wit enters the structure in the modified return of the *Trio*'s own principal section: each note of the basic motif, now enunciated by the second violin an octave lower, is aped, at the original pitch level and at a quaver's distance, by the first, as if the leader couldn't keep proper time and, by way of revenge on the metrically accurate second fiddle, were correcting its pitch level all the way; the second is right in time and in the wrong octave, while the first is in the right octave but consistently behind in time. The interpretation of the *Trio*'s opening will naturally be freer than that of the return, wherein, however, the second fiddle has to be heard to be as proud of its metre as the first will be heard to be of its pitch corrections – which will discreetly retain, perhaps even emphasize, the *piano* level. A straight-faced, humourless performance of the *Trio*, in the style of a quartet composed of German academy professors, would destroy the music altogether.

Nor are the smiles over yet. The *Finale*, one of Haydn's beloved mono-thematic sonata shapes, pulls our own legs with *two* false recapitulations, abandoned quickly enough, the first of which is not only in the tonic, but preceded by pauses, a little first-violin cadenza, and the impression of an ineluctable lead-back: Haydn's masterly escape route represents the very height of purely musical comedy, so that we must beware lest we laugh out aloud; who needs an opera in aural view of such dramatic events? To advise on their interpretation would surely mean to spoil the fun; I'd go so far as to suggest that whoever feels in need of interpretative advice at this stage – whoever wants suggestions as to how to phrase the cadenza, for instance – shouldn't venture anywhere near this particular masterpiece, and consult a psychoanalyst instead.

But the subtlest piece of comedy is reserved for the end. Just as Haydn had started the work before the beginning, he pretends to finish it after the end. However, listening players and eavesdroppers sensitive to structural balance and the relative finality of different cadential formations will not be taken in altogether by his false conclusion, succeeded though it is by a GP of 2½ bars, after which we start all over again, with a complete statement of the 8-bar theme, now preceded by an upbeat phrase introducing it in a leisurely manner, as if nothing had happened. A metrical approach to the upbeat would be murder; it has to be played hesitantly, assuming, at the same time, a relaxed and winning shape: please, if you don't mind, go on listening!

Together with at least one of the false recapitulations, then, the coda lends the total structure a distinct rondo tinge, which the structure of the theme itself has led one to expect in any case. And the complete restatement of the theme forces the coda to produce its own coda – which, again, is longer than the (8-bar) theme, namely, 12 bars: they continue the comedy right to the end, containing as they do no fewer than three further false conclusions. To be sure, we are invited to take them less and less seriously, and gradually to resign ourselves to the unprecedented circumstance that the *Finale* will never end – for if it hasn't ended yet, how can it ever?

The interpretation must not ignore the serious side of all true, substantial comedy: the penultimate end's *pianissimo* is not jocular deceit, but takes its expressive structural place between the implied *piano* of the pen-penultimate end and the *forte* of the real end which, by now, sounds – in fact, has to be made to sound – like an intervention, a rash, precipitate interruption of a never-ending shape. A *ritardando* would be inane, the remotest suspicion of a 1½-bar *stretta* both comically and seriously meaningful.

Op.50, No.2, in C major
(Hoboken III:45)

Without symmetrical or, on the other hand, taste-inspired prejudices and with, very much with, equally uninhibited imagination, the set's second quartet ought to prove downright easy to play so far as its interpretation is concerned: notwithstanding its wealth of original invention, it poses no interpretative problems, for Haydn's masterly definition of his complex build-ups does not at any stage leave any doubt about how the music goes; any interpreter who encounters a musical problem in these pages has created it in the first place. For my part, I can, of course, only deal with such problems, all created by players (outstanding players admittedly amongst them), as I have come across in the course of my teaching and coaching.

Right at the beginning, symmetrical prejudices tend to make themselves felt, whereas Haydn's actual nine-bar structure, outrageously asymmetrical as this opening sentence is, is so clearly, indeed helpfully articulated that an instinctively natural interpretation ought to be inevitable. The first three bars immediately contradict the basic metre which, at Haydn's time, invariably defined the background, whereas in our own time, it is the rhythmical foreground that tends to be metrically notated – whence a modern composer would write the opening either in ⁷/₄-time, or else let a ⁴/₄-bar follow the opening ³/₄-bar. In any case, the contradicted expectation is an accent on the first beat of the third bar, which Haydn turns into the least accented note of a three-crotchet upbeat phrase: without total de-accentuation of the note preceding it, his first *sforzato* loses its entire significance; his second contradicts his first and, at the same time, belatedly meets the expectation which the first had contradicted. Clearly conscious of these facts, the first fiddler will find nothing easier than to shape the antecedent into a natural phrase. Mozart, it must be admitted, wouldn't have dreamt of imposing such asymmetry on us; the furthest he went in this direction were the 7- and 5-bar phrases in his last quartet's minuet and trio respectively.

In the *Adagio* – the '*Cantabile*' is not Haydn's – the second violin must resign itself to the deeply imaginative fact that its solo prepares for the first's. There is no musical point, therefore, in forcing the beginning and trying to play it in the grand style. The attempt would be doomed to failure anyway, because the first fiddle plays in the upper octave, where the theme lies better and sounds better and, most important of all, the harmonization of the restatement's first bar beats any previous attempt at a grand opening state-ment out of existence. The second subject, too, must be stressedly *piano*, in view of, and until, the one-bar *crescendo* leading up to the movement's first *forte* at the end of the exposition; meanwhile, players can rest assured that the contrasting theme cannot fail to make itself heard under the inverted pedal.

In view ot the development's contraction into a virtual transition and the recapitulation's intense compression, an improvised or, if absolutely neces-sary, pre-composed first-violin cadenza before the recapitulation would be more than welcome; on those rare occasions when we actually hear one it tends to happen after the second pause – though I would recommend its body between the two pauses, with a final, imaginative figuration of the dominant chord after the second pause. In the minuet, the leaps can, as occasion arises, be taken *glissando* in order to support the *sforzato* on the first beat and stress the composed strain of the leap – if, that is, the players are sufficiently uninhibited in this respect: compare the need for the equally free, but struc-turally and dynamically opposite, *glissando* in the second subject of the first movement from Op.20's G minor quartet, pp.49f. The lack of inhibition will mean an absence of nervousness on the one hand, or of over-compensating vulgarity on the other. Of course, any *glissando* approach must be established at the very beginning by way of directive exposition, in which case an imperceptible *tenuto* on the upbeat will help to define the basic idea behind the interpretation. Now, almost all the leaps are between two strings, and a sensitive 'gipsy *glissando*' (with the finger of the new note) will occasionally be to the point. Should the orthodox, 'tasteful' player-reader recoil in horror, I may remind him that the newer (Flesch-Rostal) orthodoxy proved more perceptive than the old. In the first volume[1] of his *Art of Violin Playing*, Flesch writes about the 'gipsy *glissando*', which he calls the 'L-*portamento*', as opposed to the well-educated, conventional, 'tasteful' one, which he calls the 'B-*portamento*':

> When we consult the best-known violin methods with regard to this point, we are obliged to admit that all their authors, without exception, recognize the B-*portamento* as the only road to salvation, while the L-*portamento*, on the other hand, is excommunicated as a devilish invention of bad taste. This ostracism reminds us of a similar occur-rence, when, nearly two centuries ago, Leopold Mozart stigmatized the *spiccato* as an 'indecent bowing'!
>
> In this field, however, there exists an intimate inter-communication between individual taste and technical execution; since the latter, in a way, is the logical sequence of the former and is absolutely dependent upon it.

If the viola wants to participate in the sliding orgy, it will find itself

[1] *Technique in General: Applied Technique*, trans. Federick H. Martens, New York, 1930.

involved in a *glissando* from g to g'. In this particular instance, I would not recommend an artificial manoeuvre necessitating a change of string, which is almost bound to sound self-conscious, 'good technique' and nothing else; the natural thing to do is to employ a sham *glissando* from the open string, sliding, that is to say, with the first finger which comes in from nowhere just below a♭ and thus pretends to have played the g.

The leader's and, later, everybody else's, intervening interplay in the *Finale* stands or falls by its wit; how often one hears it fall with a heavy thud! A condition is, of course, a *vivace* that doesn't drag; the '*assai*' is Haydn's. It must, in fact, be a very different *vivace* from the other outer movement's – immeasurably lighter, self-evidently, right up to the last bar: a broad, weighty, *meno mosso* conclusion on the part of the cello, officially announcing that 'This is the end!' would destroy the final understatement, whose all-important, unaccented last note must really be heard alone: on top, the upper three instruments' crotchet-long quintet, which accompanies the cello's semiquavers, has to be safely out of the way by the time the cello repeats its open-string quaver; four bars earlier, the middle parts had extended their (trio) accompaniment over that quaver, the lonely sound of whose final repeat is, therefore, the last, drastic contradiction of expectation.

Op.50, No.3, in E flat major
(Hoboken III:46)

The third of Haydn's six great E flat quartets evinces a distinct family relation to the second, Op.33, No.2 (pp. 68ff.), and not only because they both start with a dominant upbeat and a tonic main beat: that particular opening formation is, after all, nothing to write home about. More relevant are the first movements' respective short, sharply articulated opening phrases – in which respect the present movement goes one better: its first phrase is a one-bar utterance where Op.33, No.2 needs two bars for the definition of the opening idea.

The respective tempo characters, however, might be thought not to show any family traits – *Allegro moderato* as against *Allegro con brio*. But the family relation between the thematic structures inevitably produces a closer character resemblance than meets the verbally preoccupied eye: the '*brio*' applies much more to later events than to the opening – and conversely, the '*moderato*' of the first movement from Op.33, No.2, is more of an invitation to articulate the short phrases as distinctly as Haydn composed them than a demand for relative slowness.

In fact, articulation is all in either case, and if a verbal combination of 'con brio' and 'moderato' didn't sound too ridiculous, Haydn might well have decided upon it in the present case, where shortest-term articulation is an absolute requirement: the opening motif (x in Ex.36) functions as mini-antecedent, the following, yet shorter motif (y in Ex.36) as mini-consequent – which latter, however, is not an answer but, on the contrary, a question provoked by the opening assertion (x):

Ex.36

The harmony of the ensuing sequence exchanges the roles of antecedent and consequent, while the following sequence of the mini-consequent alone resumes its original, questioning role, which is sustained until bar 4, where-after the 'official', four-bar maxi-consequent, itself divided into questions and answers, provides the reply to the four-bar maxi-antecedent. For these constantly changing articulations which, in the opening four bars, happen within the shortest possible space, phrasing space is an urgent necessity, and the merest suspicion of haste would de-characterize the theme beyond recognition: I recommend, for a start, progress in slow motion, so that the changing character of the theme will have clearly established itself before the 'con brio' is taken into account – necessary as it will prove for the purpose of sustaining continuity in spite of everything.

The question may well be asked why I am making such an unprecedented meal of the interpretation of the opening, the immediate definition of the movement's tempo character. The answer is practical – solely experiential, in fact: apart from Oskar Adler's approach half a century ago, I have never come across any interpretation which, as yet unenlightened about the ambiguous, but none the less clearly defined nature of the theme's character, has not either raced ahead in a process of continual de-characterization, or else lost both itself and *brio* as well as line in the relaxed characterization of successive motifs. One simple fact above all others must never be forgotten – that the sequences articulate the half-bar of this ⁶/₈-time very strongly.

A single little phrase in her *BBC Music Guide* to the Haydn quartets[1] proves Rosemary Hughes an outsider – her descriptions of the cello-viola duo and the following duo of the two violins that are the first twelve bars of the slow movement's theme as one of Haydn's 'most finely drawn pieces of two-part harmony'; to be precise, harmony is never finely drawn: it is a *contradictio in adjecto*. Drawing produces line, and the viola part is indeed far

[1] London, 1966.

too linear to be describable in vertical terms; on the other hand, it is far too accompanimental to be read as counterpoint: the theme, the tune, is first the cello's, and then the leader's. Although confined, for the moment, to two parts, the texture is exclusive quartet-writing whose style has remained name-less, since it is neither polyphony nor homophony; 'subordinate part' remains the closest possible description for a line that prevents the texture from being either. The usual interpretative fallacy is to tackle it contrapuntally – although it remains true to say that it's despite its subordinate station, which the player has to heed well, that the part has to be played, phrased as a line.

The E♭ minor variation introduces a fundamental innovation into the very technique of composition, one which Beethoven – as opposed to Mozart – availed himself of and which has left its mark on variation technique ever since, even in extra-tonal circumstances, such as those of Schoenberg's Orchestral Variations. What is happening in this movement is that the universally accepted, fundamental criterion of variation form is meaningfully and expressively abandoned – the retention of the theme's harmonic structure throughout all variations. Instead, the model's harmonic structure is itself subjected to variation – an almost 'shocking' event of which the interpreter has to be clearly conscious if the shock is to be conveyed to the recipient without the harmonic aspect of the varying process being glossed over; in proportion as a variation unsettles the theme harmonically, it moves, of course, a little closer to what normally is variation's diametrical opposite, to wit, development. The E♭ minor variation, for instance, replaces what was the perfect tonical cadence with a perfect cadence in the dominant minor, which has been preceded by the necessary, unsettling modulation, whose interpretation will have to be fully and clearly conscious of this injection of destabilizing development into what used to be the stablest of all methods of musical continuation, sheer repetition apart, i.e. variation.

Again and again, we realize that the Haydn quartets are more pregnant with future developments, in the twentieth as well as in the nineteenth century, than any other group of works, perhaps even Beethoven's included. In point of fact, Beethoven's apparent innovation in the first part of the trio of his Op.130 Quartet's *Alla danza tedesca*, whose variation includes variation of the theme's harmonic structure, leads us straight back to the present movement, whose harmonic shocks are, in fact, more incisive than Beethoven allowed his shocks to be in this playful dance movement. (On the other hand, Haydn never out-Beethovened its contrast with the *Cavatina* that follows it!)

From the interpretative standpoint, the minuet's central textural com-plexity is indeed its centre – the *Trio*. The middle parts are quite right, that is to say, if they think they are important, but they're wrong if they follow the all too usual procedure of dominating the first violin, which remains leader; the second, as subleader, has to look after an easy and flexible quaver motion.

If the first movement leaned towards monothematicism, the other outer movement, though likewise sonata, outspokenly challenges the sonata need for polythematicism. In view of the close relationship between the two first subjects, moreover, one might go so far as to suggest that the outer movements of this work are not only internally, but mutually monothematic! At the same time, the character differences between the themes are extreme: there certainly is no ambiguity in the *Finale*'s, which can therefore afford a wholehearted *Presto*; in order to realize this singleminded *presto* character, the merest trace must be avoided of any bar accent which is not a structural stress: the opening bar must be recognized as leading up to the second bar before the second's accent is heard.

The most intriguing point in the entire *Finale* is no doubt the opening of the development. We have heard the theme at both the first- and second-subject levels, and we've heard it repeated after the unexpected dominant seventh arpeggio *cum* flat sixth (not perceived as turn to the minor, but as the dominant's Neapolitan sixth) with which the first violin has returned us to the tonic at the end of the exposition; how can we now not expect the tonical theme again at the beginning of the development? After all, the dominant seventh creates one instinctive, spontaneous expectation, and one expectation only.

And sure enough, the upper three parts play precisely what they played at the beginning – but the cello, by slipping down a tone, contradicts our expectation most violently at the same time as the upper three are meeting it exactly, for the D♭ turns the expected tonic chord into the dominant seventh of the subdominant. Never has expectation been simultaneously so minutely met and so totally contradicted! But playingly, the upper three have to behave as if they were in the know; after all, or rather, after the first play-through, they are. In other words, in no circumstances can the opening phrasing be thoughtlessly repeated or imitated; it is the drive towards A♭ that now has to be expressed: now it's the first two bars which must be heard to lead up to the third – even before you have heard the third.

An unanswered and unanswerable question remains: precisely why did Haydn write as many great quartets in E♭ (6) as in the readily explicable D major? When he does write in E♭, it does not emerge as a personal key the way F minor does; even D minor (3 quartets) has greater personal significance for him. It isn't a particularly comfortable key from the players' point of view, nor do its objective characteristics arouse enthusiasm comparable to the joy with which he and other great composers write in brilliant D major. For Mozart it was, in fact, unattractive enough (see pp.13–14) to let the viola play, in effect, in D major while the violin overcomes its difficulties in E♭. And while it must be admitted that whenever Haydn writes in E♭, he perfectly adjusts the character of his music to the characteristics of the key, one does not notice a greater involvement with his E♭ characters than with the character of keys in which he wrote fewer quartets. Rare are the questions which, at least to one investigator, seem so wholly unanswerable; he would be delighted if he found a reviewer who could tell him where to get off – if only by way of finding a tiny fragment of an answer.

Op.50, No.4, in F sharp minor
(Hoboken III:47)

The present chapter is the only one in this book whose writing I am approaching with a considerable degree of uncertainty and an equal amount of trepidation. For it is my experience that whenever I talk or write with analytic enthusiasm about a work, there are plenty of performers amongst my listeners or readers who feel both stimulated and indeed artistically obliged to try their hand (or throat, or stick) at it – and it is indeed jolly difficult to suppress one's analytic enthusiasm about the F♯ minor Quartet, what with its exceptional position in more than one dimension and the fact that not only structurally, but even formally, it contains innovation: Haydn is indeed the only composer, great or small, who invented forms.

At the same time, it is not only my conviction, but, more convincingly, my lifelong experience that this work cannot be played by any – repeat: any – quartet which has not been playing Haydn quartets together for many years – and the majority of ensembles which have been playing Haydn for decades can't play it either. So whom am I writing for? Should one not rather be writing against? Against any attempt, that is to say, to make sense of this towering masterpiece, if the players are not absolutely – i.e. well-foundedly – sure that they are ready for it. For otherwise, the result will be definite deterioration: as soon as a quartet renounces its normal aims and ideals, as in this case it is often bound to, its development as an ensemble is not only arrested, but easily subjected to painful regression, none the less harmful for usually remaining unnoticed.

If, as a writing musician, then, one is determined to face the facts and figures of musical life, one has to admit that so far as the present chapter is concerned, one's receptive and, subsequently, productive readers will be about four or, at the outside, eight; aware that, simultaneously, too much analytic fervour might well result in people having a go at the work who shouldn't, the writer will have to remember constantly that in the first place, the present book is about interpretation – not about the countless innovatory thoughts of that which is to be interpreted.

Great masterpieces for string quartets in F♯ minor there are, altogether, two which we find at either end of our symphonic tradition – the present work and Schoenberg's last tonal quartet, which is his Second (or his third, if we count the very first, which was published posthumously). The distance between the two works is far more chronological than musical: both can easily be described as sonata festivals, which is to say that either composer's variation technique evinces developmental incursions. And both works are packed with innovations which, as we have pointed out, even include formal innovations in Haydn's case: the slow movement is in his very own double-variation form, whose harmonic implications have not even yet been fully recognized. As for Schoenberg's harmonic innovations in his F♯ minor Quartet, they were recognized, from the interrupted first performance, with an audible vengeance.

In addition to these gigantic masterpieces, there are two further F♯ minor quartets by outsiders, Reger's Fifth, Op.121, and Tippett's Second – substantial, lasting works both of them. As are, in fact, two other F♯ minor masterpieces by Haydn himself – the 'Farewell' Symphony, and the Piano Trio, Hoboken XV:26; Haydn evidently liked, upon occasion, to make life difficult for his string players, the King of Prussia included (the dedicatee of the present set); as a matter of fact, the only previous great quartet in which he showed the same tendency bears the same key signature: it is the A major work from Op.20. Both it and the present work are the diametrical opposite of both Op.42 and the next work of the present set; Op.42, in particular, shows his genius for making life easy without sacrificing an ounce of originality, without even inhibiting his innovatory fervour. For the rest, the only other key which he confined to a single great quartet is E major; the difficulties of Op.54, No.3 we shall inspect in the work's proper place (p.125).

In one respect, however, the present work is altogether exceptional from the point of view of approaching its execution: for once, I would strongly recommend individual practice – and not only, as in the case of the aforesaid A major work from Op.20, to the first violin; if the interpretation is to succeed at all, every single awkward bit – and there are plenty of them, in all instruments – has to feel as if it lay well, as if one were playing a D major quartet (well, almost). Only thus prepared will one be able to adjust to current circumstances, intonation included. It is fascinating to observe how quartets which are capable of exquisite, downright creative intonation regress, in the present work, to mere in-tune playing, if that: quite often, they rest content with a 'well-tempered' performance (if that!).

Is there a single reader who can honestly say that he has ever heard a fearless opening gesture, an octave-unison that formed a triumphant tutti basis for the leader's ensuing solo contrast, which turns the meaning of the opening three-quaver upbeat on the same note into its virtual opposite? So far as my limited experience of gramophone records goes, we don't even encounter the required sound in commercial recordings – the total blend, that is to say, which this short antecedent demands. And such seems to be the case despite the equally total absence of any real difficulties at this initial stage: it's all in the mind, which immediately insists on expressing its all-pervasive fear, a well-founded fear in all conscience, of F♯ minor.

What some far-hearing, or far-divining readers may have suspected in the case of the finale of Op.33, No.6 (see pp.80f.) is becoming quite obvious in the case of the fully developed double-variation form that is the slow movement of the present work – but however obvious it may be becoming, it has not yet, to my knowledge, aroused critical comment: Haydn's new form offers him the possibility of a bi-dimensional 'double', in that he can base his structures not only on two themes, but also on two keys within a single tonality, thus anticipating the major-minor structures that were to emerge at later stages of symphonic thought. There are countless instances, amongst which Mendelssohn's Op.13 Quartet (really his first, although listed second) occupies a special position, owing to its mis-titling in many learned books and even scores: it isn't, as they say, in A minor, but in A; how indeed can you describe a work as being in A minor that starts and finishes with an A major theme?

Likewise, the present slow movement is in A, and the A minor theme also forms a similar textural contrast to the A major theme as its D minor forerunner in Op.33, No.6 does to the theme of that movement: it stresses the contrapuntal end of our nameless, intrinsic quartet texture, whose homophonic end the A major theme had emphasized. The parallels between these two movements do indeed deserve close inspection, and interpretative mastery of the D major work's finale will very concretely help towards mastering the present *Andante* – which, in any case, is the work's only movement whose mastery can be attained without years of Haydn-playing: it is, marginally, at times more than marginally, easier than the rest of the work.

But let us not shout for joy too loudly as we see the accidental-less key signature of the *Andante*'s second theme, for the next new key signature will be the six sharps of the minuet, whose relaxed character demands the subtlest and clearest intonation: it has to sound palpably unstrained, as if the comfort of D major, rather than the headaches of F♯ major, were at the back of the player's minds.

The *Trio* does not only return to F♯ minor but consistently pursues the minor mode's preference for the contrapuntal side of quartet texture, in which respect it presents a strict inversion of the normal relation between it and the principal section. Normally, that is, the minuet surrounds the trio's relaxation, whereas it is the minuet's relaxation which here surrounds the intensive *Trio*. From the playing point of view, the simple observation that both of them are equally and fiendishly difficult comes closest to the musical reality's discomfort.

The climax of its contrapuntal preference, however, the minor mode celebrates in Haydn's only great fugal quartet *Finale* on a single subject. Not that intrinsic quartet texture is forgotten over this contrapuntal orgy, which compensates for the absence of more than one subject by incorporating enough homophony for the movement to be clearly audible against the background of sonata form. Mozart's sonata fugue in the first of his Haydn Quartets may have something to do with it, even though it is a combination of sonata and fugue, whereas Haydn's fugue relegates its sonata elements to the background, where they patiently waited for later geniuses to explore and exploit their possibilities – above all Beethoven: his Grand (and nowise monothematic) Fugue, Op.133, shows beyond a shadow of doubt that he must have occupied himself just as deeply with this particular Haydn fugue as with the polythematic fugal finales of Op.20 (see pp.45, 52, 60 and 63).

At the Summer School of Music at Dartington, I once gave a lecture of more than two hours' duration on this Beethoven fugue, its sonata background and its unplayability by a string quartet. Little did the audience know that for the duration of the lecture, I felt honoured to share a teacher with Beethoven – Haydn. As I have pointed out before (p.34, n.3), Haydn's essential influence on Beethoven seems to be confined to the younger genius' later years; when Haydn actually was his teacher, Beethoven must have been too youthfully ambivalent to be able to bring himself to profit from Haydn's discoveries. And even at this late stage, a certain amount of sublimated aggression towards Haydn, ennobled admittedly, seems to me to permeate the Beethoven fugue – a desire to out-Haydn Haydn. For one thing, he refuses to accept Haydn's monothematic reason for the sonata background, preferring to marry the polythematic fugue to its implied, polythematic sonata expectations; for another, and for once, he just as decidedly refuses to accept Haydn's unconditional framework – the retention of an intrinsic quartet texture with its equally unconditional playability. Where Haydn's F♯ minor fugue strains the player and the quartet sound to their respective extremes, but meticulously keeps within the bounds of playability, Beethoven's B♭ fugue goes beyond these extremes and envisages a quartet texture which is physically unattainable; I have no doubt that when he returned from inspiration to the hard facts of acoustic life, he came to realize the unrealism of his adventure: one reason, this, for the withdrawal of the movement as finale for Op.130, and the only reason for its transcription.

As in the Op.20 fugues, Haydn's special dynamic situation has to be immediately established – though one should not, perhaps, merely describe it as dynamic: the *mezza voce* is a question of colour too, of tone production and tone modulation; in order for the texture to realize itself, the tone, in addition to lacking volume, had to be contained, almost tangibly repressed, rather than straightforward and open – and unlike the Op.20 fugues, this one turns the tonal aim into a problem. This is to say, as soon as the player is confronted with technical difficulties, however superable, his audible strain will interfere with any type of tone production that doesn't aim at expressing such tension – and the desirable, contained tone should confine its tension to the expression of the repressive element, of emotional rather than physical strain. Tone quality is a musical dimension not readily accessible to words – but fortunately there is a reason why I am not likely to be misunderstood: if the players understand this fugue at all, they will be dissatisfied with any dynamic level and colour that do not meet the conditions I am trying to define, and happy only when, at last, their *mezza voce* produces the required sound – for whose achievement the inaudibility of the movement's technical difficulties, including its precarious intonational junctures (quite a few of them!) is an absolute condition.

As in the Op.20 fugues again, the tonal containment must be heard to harbour a contrastingly open, dynamic climax which, for the greater part of the fugue, cannot be released. Only, this time, the dynamic climax, when it eventually arrives at the end of the movement's first, 1½-bar *crescendo* and, significantly enough, by way of a homophonic explosion 22 bars from the end, has not only its own culmination, to wit, the *fortissimo* five bars further on, but actually consists of two distinct waves with an intervening *piano* and, therefore, a renewed, 1-bar *crescendo*; the coda, moreover, once again withdraws to the *piano* level before it discharges its own *fortissimo* for the duration of less than a bar – by which time not much of the fugue is left, its opening phrase apart, conclusively announced by the second violin and now embedded in a four-part, typical quartet texture which, as we have seen (pp.4ff.), is neither homo- nor polyphonic.

Have I, then, written well over 2,000 words for four readers or, at the outside, eight? My hope is that the present chapter will stimulate all its illegitimate readers into trying their hand – not at the F♯ minor Quartet, but at a sufficient number of other great Haydn quartets, for a sufficiently protracted period, to turn their eventual, delicate, by then deeply quartet-sound-conscious assault on the present work into a realistic proposition. However, so long as they don't know what I'm talking about when I speak of a delicate assault, they'd better not move anywhere near this music.

Once they feel they are in a position to tackle it, they might, as the final stage of their preparation, first study by playing the more difficult of Haydn's two A major quartets, i.e. Op.20, No.6, and then the equally inconsiderate E major Quartet, Op.54, No.3, which, surprisingly enough, behaves more ruthlessly towards its players than does the only masterly violin concerto in that key towards its soloist. This comparison between two works which have little to do with each other is not altogether fanciful, since both of them were written with a high degree of technique-consciousness, their composers being excellent violinists and viola players. Even structurally, the concerto I am leaving unnamed lies far nearer to Haydn's forms than any music history will tell you: not only is the last movement in clear rondo form, but the other outer movement approaches sonata form far more closely than any critical observer has realized – and with this supremely easy quiz I conclude my chapter on Haydn's only supremely difficult quartet.

Op.50, No.5, in F major
(Hoboken III:48)

From the point of view of playability and therefore also from that of under-lying character, the whole of Haydn's quartet output, not forgetting Op.42, does not show a stronger successive contrast than that between the present quartet and its predecessor: was it perhaps the dedicatee of the set, the cello-playing King of Prussia, who provoked Haydn into an almost leg-pulling succession of supreme difficulty and surprising ease? We are aware that he must have been a highly capable cellist, in any case, as well as an interesting musical personality: what with Mozart's last three quartets and the two cello sonatas of Beethoven's Op.5, he should probably rank as musical history's most richly endowed dedicatee, whose name and musical fame has been kept alive by three great composers. Speaking as a well-endowed dedicatee myself, for instance, I must confess that among the dozen com-posers who have dedicated works to me, I can only find a single one on whose greatness the world will come to agree.

As a cellist, moreover, and notwithstanding our glib theories about the advance of instrumental technique, especially ours, the King must have been superior to many a leading quartet-cellist of our own time, for there are passages in the Mozart and Beethoven works as well as, of course, Haydn's F♯ minor Quartet which simply wouldn't have been written if these three giants had not felt concretely inspired by the King's playing style and his sheer virtuosity. Mozart's B♭ 'Solo' Quartet is almost as acute a shocker for the cellist as Haydn's F♯ minor – but personally, I can't hear the *Trio* of Mozart's D major 'Solo' without thinking of the King: my reaction is, almost invariably, 'Why don't you play it the way the King played it in Mozart's mind – and, therefore also, in all likelihood, in reality?' And like these two Haydn quartets, Mozart's three indulge in contrasts between extreme difficulty and almost equally extreme ease, except that whereas Haydn does it between works, Mozart does it within them.

This F major Quartet, then – the very first of Haydn's surprisingly few (three) quartet masterpieces in that key – can be tackled at a relatively early stage of an ensemble's development – after about three months' regular study, I'd suggest (and by 'regular' I mean at least one weekly session). In fact, with equal care and attention devoted to meaningful phrasing (only one main accent per phrase, please!) and the colorific side of intonation, there simply should be no difficulty if the lower parts consistently listen two-dimensionally – to the leader and to each other. What I mean by the colorific side of intonation becomes obvious as early as bars 5 and 6, where it isn't good enough for the viola and cello to be 'in tune' – or rather, where they won't be in tune if they are content with playing in tune: the C♯, especially, which must be played as the subdominant's mediant's leading-note (rather a mouthful, this, but the feeling thus verbalized is straightforward, simple and elemental), has to be, partly for this very reason, so perfect a blend that it sounds as if it came, as an octave, from a single player and a single instrument. On this particular occasion, we have to disregard Arnold Rosé's (oral) advice, according to which 'octaves have to be a bit out of tune so that one notices that they're octaves', for the perception of octaves is, in any case, guaranteed by the different instruments, not to speak of the different players.

The perception of the two parts is, at the same time, all-important, for the two are questioningly answering the upper two. The opening period, then, develops as a subtle climax of quartet textures, thus initiating yet another innovation for which, manifestly, the twentieth century has been responsible – the structuralization of texture as practised by György Ligéti and, perhaps more structure-consciously, by the Israeli composer Josef Tal.

First, that is to say, we get the two violins' exposition of the antecedent – a continuous duo which, with the start of the consequent, expands into a dialogue between the upper and the lower duo that, in its turn, expands into a full quartet texture from the moment, i.e. the quaver upbeat, which announces the cadential, confirmatory consequent within the consequent. The ensuing, varied restatement structuralizes the texture further and yet more varyingly: duo, cello-less string trio, and quartet are all involved, with the textural basis being the full quartet sound, in view of which the second violin will have literally to change its tone to the extent of a very different *piano* from the first's (and its own) opening *piano*; more generally, too, the ideal restatement will evince as much difference from the start as it will show an underlying sameness – like the offspring and his identifiable parents.

The movement's sextuplets never occur in what would be tonally unsatisfactory combinations of three instruments, but invariably either as solo lines, or in alternation, or in combinations of two instruments or, quasi tutti, in all four parts, and in view of their extremely variable textural contexts, they ought to make us think twice – quite especially about our ready smiles when, but a few pages ago, we learnt what Leopold Mozart had to say about *spiccato* bowing. How often have we heard these sextuplets produced by a wrist-conscious *spiccato* which gravely, 'indecently', interrupted any phrasing that may have surrounded them? A well-phrased *détaché* will, in fact, prove immeasurably preferable. And in more general support of old Mozart it cannot be too firmly emphasized that the undeniable satisfaction which a good *spiccato* causes the player to feel tends to overshadow structural requirements of the passage he is playing.

Which purely factual and widely experienced observation should not, on the other hand, encourage any abandonment of *spiccato* in classical quartets as a matter of principle: the deeply phrase-conscious *spiccato* (which Leopold Mozart may never have heard!) has powerfully enriched our technique and both refined and multiplied our methods of musically motivated differentiation. I shall never forget helping to give birth to the Lindsay Quartet who, just before I came in, had been coached by our century's most overrated quartet player – Rudolf Kolisch, the leader of the Kolisch Quartet, which was responsible for the premieres of Schoenberg's twelve-tonal quartets; as his brother-in-law, he was able to present interpretations that had been directed by the composer.

But his performances of Mozart or Beethoven hadn't been, and you could hear it. The Lindsays he forced to play all classical quartets on the string, including their most natural *spiccato* passages, with the paradoxical result that in the case of that prenatal quartet, it was artificial *détaché* runs and other quick passages that interrupted their natural phrasing before and after the unnatural event. Kolisch also compelled them, incidentally, to play from the score – a habit which, likewise, I immediately abolished: by staring at the score, you inevitably delay its musical assimilation through the ear, and, in fact, weaken your powers of unaided aural perception. Will the playing reader therefore kindly note, please, that apart from those easily recognizable problems which a twentieth-century work may present, the only possible way of 'learning' a quartet, any classical or romantic work, of becoming aware of how it goes both structurally and texturally, is through playingly listening, visually unaided listening (except for the help the four separate parts provide) – that the circumstances necessitating recourse to a score simply do not exist? This absolutely factual statement is based on over half a century's experience of countless groups on every conceivable level of achievement and failure.

Why the *Poco Adagio* (and hence the whole quartet) is known as 'The Dream' I don't either know or care; what I do care about is what I've noticed to be two alternative obstacles in the way of its theme's characterization – though even at this late stage in my own musical development, I wholly fail to understand how one or the other obstacle can arise in a truly musical mind, as I have heard it arise on many an occasion, and even on the level of alleged quartet mastery.

One basic point to be remembered is that however '*poco*', the movement bears distinct *adagio* character; as soon as, at the beginning, the middle parts start running under the pathetically helpless first violin, it's all over, and any performance of the movement will prove far worse than none.

Maybe it was in view of the alternative, opposite danger, however, that Haydn inserted his qualifying '*poco*' – certain middle parts' tendency, that is, especially certain second fiddlers', to spell out the first two bars' quavers instead of submitting them to the *adagio* flow (yes, there is such a thing) of a phrase-conscious definition of rhythmic character. In any case, the second fiddler has to be aware, from the note f', that the establishment of the movement's tempo is altogether up or down to him, and has to lead accordingly.

The leader's own phantasy, clear-eared rather than dreamlike, has to emerge later, and will celebrate its maximal freedom in his solo triplets: like the opening movement's sextuplets, the triplets appear in textural variations, the quartet tutti included – with which, this time, the movement ends, whereas it is the first violin's solo sextuplets that bring the first movement to a close, over the thematic middle parts. And it is this solo which lands, by way of a *crescendo*, in a *forte*, whereas the slow movement's tutti achieves a *piano* conclusion, notwithstanding its own *crescendo*: supreme mastery of quartet-writing was needed for this paradoxical contrast of textures!

If one word had to describe the underlying mood of the *Poco Adagio*, it would be 'repose', which has to be felt throughout, though the degree of its primacy or dominance does, of course, vary – but one cannot think of a single slow movement by any of the great masters whose reposeful subdominant is contradicted by any of its otherwise contrasting events.

There is all the difference in the structural world between the upbeat that is the upbeat to bar 5 of the minuet (*y* in Ex.37), and the upbeat that isn't the upbeat to bar 1 (*x* in Ex.37):

Ex.37

The first violin's entire opening solo line (down to bar 3) is, of course, an upbeat phrase, which mustn't be disturbed by the slightest accent: the very first accent occurs with the arrival of the first violin's *forte*. One would not even object to the tempo definition taking place as from the *forte*: a marginally faster, forward-urging upbeat phrase would sound quite natural and actually contribute to the definition of tempo character, which will not be contradicted by the upbeat to bar 7 not being played as an upbeat either: now it is up to the string trio to shun any accent on the first beat of bar 7, in order to aim the upbeat phrase at bar 8.

In the stressedly developmental *Trio* in the tonic minor, which the minuet has foreshadowed (is it an accident that Haydn goes characteristically developmental immediately he reaches his most personal key?), the upbeat phrase has to be realized by a texture whose reinforcement is without precedent: the four of them are now playing in octave unison, and at *forte* level too! Only, the aim of the phrase, however intensely suppressed dynamically, is not now bar 3, as at the beginning (see Ex.37), but bar 5. It is for this reason that the minuet's *forte* is now replaced with a *sforzato*, whose sudden, unsustained accent will enable the players to aim at a main accent that never comes, but is replaced, in its turn, by a *piano* that has been prepared by a *diminuendo*, and whose purpose is the definition of the overlapping function of bar 5's first beat, which is the aim of the *Trio*'s opening phrase on the one hand, and its diametrical opposite, i.e. the first note of the ensuing upbeat phrase, on the other. With the help of Haydn's meticulous dynamics, these opposing functions of the selfsame note can be clearly expressed.

The developmental nature of the *Trio* is emphasized not merely by its thematic material, which is the principal section's, but above all by the fact that the modulatory instability which is the essential element of any development section manifests itself before the *Trio* has a chance to establish or even as much as outline its own home key. No sooner do we expect to land in F minor than the opening phrase cadences perfectly in A♭: not a modulation in the strict, technical sense (since no implied new key signature is reached), but the musical fact remains that relative keys are further removed from each other than are the keys of the minuet and trio, whose different key signatures cannot hide the fact that they share their tonic as well as their dominant, and hence their tonality.

Nor is the modulatory drive thus exhausted: B♭ minor is to come in the ultra-developmental middle of the developmental *Trio*. Once again, then, Haydn allows himself a strict inversion of the normal relation between minuet and trio (cf.p.99): far from relaxing the structure, the *Trio* represents the climax of instability, of tension, which the relative stability of the principal section relaxes upon its return – a structural situation to which the players have to be deeply alive if they are to realize the contrast between *Trio* and minuet in terms of structural tension and discharge; thematic contrast there is, of course, none.

No, the *Finale* does not prompt me to withdraw anything I have said about the relative ease with which the present work can be mastered: its difficulties, if any, are purely psychological, not musico-technical. Once again, that is, Haydn invites, in fact demands, single-string *portamentos* (cf.pp.49 and 69) whose technical execution does not present any problems, despite the over-stretched fifth positions in which they involve the leader; if, nevertheless, he feels inhibited about them, he might actually welcome this opportunity to rid himself of inhibitions created by the pseudo-taste of our time. If, in each of these climbs, he aims at a delicate *diminuendo* rather than a crudely climaxing *crescendo*, he will find, to his own surprise, that the very *grazioso* character he has in mind, and which he irrationally fears the *portamentos* might upset, will, in musical reality, be far more readily definable with their help. Only, he has to imagine, to hear these *diminuendos* distinctly and concretely before and as he plays them; as his self-confidence gradually increases, he will enable himself to introduce subtle variations into the successive climbs, rather than producing a string of boring replicas. A different *kind* of variation will fruitfully and imaginatively introduce the recapitulation: there is, after all, an essential structural difference between successive repetitions and repetitions which occur after something contrasting has happened in between, which is why we talk about restatements and repeats on the one hand and recapitulations or reprises on the other.

For the rest, despite its intermittently full texture which, in effect, produces, in places, a quintet sound, the quartet-writing never abandons its finesse and makes balance as well as blend so easy for the understanding ear that all one has to remind players of is something that should go without saying – the need for continuous, comprehensive listening, for constant awareness of the ever-changing and subtly contrasting textural situations.

Another requirement which goes without saying is the need for the clearest possible definition of character, which only leaves something to be desired when some of the *grazioso* element is sacrificed to the *vivace*, or when some of the *vivace* character is sacrificed to the attempt to produce a delicate sound picture: any imaginary polarity will have to be replaced with the reality of mutual reinforcement.

Op.50, No.6, in D major
(Hoboken III:49)

Of the 'Frog' Quartet it can be said that it is as great as it is famous, and that in addition to the finale's 'Frog' theme, its fame rests on its relatively symmetrical rhythmic structures, its four-bar and eight-bar phrases, as well as its exceptionally brilliant sound, with the outer movements written in an easy-sounding virtuoso style. Like the earlier of the six great D major quartets from Op.20 and Op.33, but unlike the later ones (Op.64, No.5, Op.71, No.2, and Op.76, No.5), the work is homotonal – and more than usual Haydn achieves greater variety within the same tonality than many a composer who dives into $G^{\flat\flat}$ for his *adagio* at the slightest provocation, since he doesn't know what else to do.

The principal section of the minuet apart, this is another quartet in which the phrasing cannot easily go haywire, which is not to say that anything in it plays itself: great music never does. In the first movement it is particularly important to make the dynamics part and parcel of the phrasing rather than superimposing them on it – which immediately means, of course, that one can't confine oneself to the printed dynamics: in order to achieve the truly dramatic *crescendo* of bar 8, for instance, the first violin cannot start it on the *mezzo forte* level defined in bar 4, but has to start it on a lower dynamic level, which he will have to have reached with his four-semiquaver upbeat in bar 7, where the other three's four-part texture will have to follow his dynamic withdrawal with perfect blend in the middle parts and the cello quavers' equally perfect balance.

As the culmination of the *crescendo* is reached with bar 9's *forte*, there will have to be all the difference in the structural world between the first violin's four-semiquaver motif and its imitation in the second violin, where its introductory quaver and its repetition produce an onward-going flow notwithstanding the two *legatos*: accents on the first semiquaver of each would tear the phrase asunder; it is a pretty selfless upbeat anyway, in that it leads more to the first violin's than to the second's main beat in bar 10, where its resumption leads more to the cello's leading part, intended no doubt for Friedrich Wilhelm II, than to the second fiddle's subordinate (rather than merely accompanimental) syncopations.

As on a previous occasion – in the finale of Op.50, No.3 (see pp.96f.) – the development seems to resume the opening and its repeat, but once again the semitonal change of a single note (the cello's A♯ instead of what was the viola's A♮) revolutionizes the harmonic situation: far from the development starting in the tonic its first bar pressages, the resulting diminished-seventh chord produces the relative minor as opening key. We remember that Haydn's two B minor quartets start in D major (see p.91), and now note that the opening B minor of this development is preceded by an apparent D major too! The cello's A♯ must, of course, be fully conscious of this state of harmonic affairs.

By inverting the *siciliano* rhythm's elements and subjecting one of them to diminution, the monothematic sonata structure of the *Poco Adagio* in the tonic minor creates a new thematic type whose parentage renders it all the more meaningful: the dotted motif is transferred to the second half of the ⁶/₈-bar and, in addition, gives rise to an upbeat diminution which, in the listening (as opposed to the compositional) event, is experienced the other way round, as giving rise to the *siciliano* motif – whereafter it reappears cadentially at the end of the phrase, a *sforzato* throwing its central importance into relief. While the further evolution of the melody bears this displaced accent in mind, the leader (and later the middle parts) mustn't, so that he establishes a clear rhythmic contrast between the accented diminution and the later, upbeating demisemiquaver motifs which lead to the stressed quavers: the build-up of the melody stands or falls by these contrasting accents, to which first the second violin's and then the cello's demisemiquavers add further contrasting variations, in that the phrase's aim and accent is now deferred until the next bar. A modern composer would have written bar 6 as two ³/₈ bars, but in Haydn's time one could still rely on the players immediately realizing such metrical variations without their having to be spelt out: quite generally, our increased notational differentiations and sheer *addenda* are a measure of the unmusicality the contemporary composer has to fear on the part of his interpreters; we have noted that Bach even trusted his performers to the point of letting them define his tempo characters on the basis of his thematic structures, often without verbal help.

With his extended D major peroration – much more than a mere coda, since it starts with the recapitulation of the second subject – Haydn limits the only remaining key contrast of his homotonal structure: all four movements – or, if you like to include the tonical trio, all five main structures – develop towards, reach, broaden out and fulfil themselves in a D major destination; yet these tail-pieces are so contrasting that one has to remind onself of what, in less inspired circumstances, would be an over-obvious fact. The reminder is not unimportant from the interpretative point of view, for it will prompt the players to tackle the recapitulated second subject in a different spirit from their approach to its exposition, despite the latter's major mode: now we're turning the *tonic* into the major, and the underlying relaxation (that of a gigantic Picardy third, as it were) is an unprecedented, profound structural event which has nothing to do with the exposition's turn to the relative major; the home-coming is unexpectedly complete – completer,[1] that is to say, than was the home from which we started out.

The interpretation has to express this climax of dis-tension as from the first violin's dotted upbeat, whose demisemiquaver heralds the unexpected extent of emotional discharge: the upbeat will already have to be different from the exposition's, a requirement which Haydn even expresses dynamically; where, in the exposition, the preceding *forte*, which had been reached by way of a *crescendo*, is countermanded by the upbeat's 'm.v.', this moderation and restraint is confined, in the recapitulation, to the lower parts. But the dynamic dimension should not remain the only one in which the new mood expresses itself; the definition of tempo character has to help, too, by sounding slower than it is and was at the corresponding juncture in the exposition. Haydn's new *sforzatos* on the half-bar (whose absence from the exposition does not, of course, imply a different centre of gravity) are evidently designed to support the characterization of this broader tempo character, which can thus be achieved without any, or with only the very slightest, change of actual pace.

In the principal section of the minuet, we encounter the quartet's, or rather its interpretations', sole example of wellnigh invariable misphrasing; instead of a detailed description of the horrors one tends to have to face at this stage, let us tackle the problem which countless leaders have here created by clearly concentrating on the shapes in question: during the downward drive of the little conjunct two-note motif, and despite the chordal punctuation in the lower parts, there is – has one actually got to say it? – not the remotest trace of any bar-accents. The single immediate aim of the passage is the tiny turn to the subdominant which is indeed stressed by the *sforzato*. Now, if the player is unambiguously conscious of the structure, he can certainly afford to play this rush down *senza misura*, with what one might realistically describe as well-measured haste, *viz.* just a little too fast; the chords will have to follow

---

[1] For once, the comparative makes sense: what had been experienced, and is still recalled, as complete proves capable of comparison with something completer.

suit unobtrusively, and not lose their blend in the excitement. In order to restore the rhythmic equilibrium, generous value will have to be given to the dotted minim and to the quaver-plus-crotchet rest before the cadential phrase, and a minute *ritardando* will have to be felt if not played in bars 6–7, where the two-note motif moves up again, so that the *total* time for the first repeat will be the same as that of a *tempo giusto* would have been.

The tonical *Trio*'s *sforzatos* de-accent the first beats not only of their respective bars, but of the preceding bars: they turn the entire structure leading up to them into an upbeat phrase consisting of six non-beats.

Why the second part of the *Trio* is an ideal study for string quartets at any level, for their textural behaviour, including their blends and balances, need hardly be mentioned – and I do mean 'hardly', for there is one reason, as crucial as any, which will easily be overlooked. The jocular entries and re-entries of the *Trio* theme's opening phrase, at both *piano* and *mezzo forte* level, need continual, precise leadership from the first violin and the viola respectively. Unfortunately, it happens very often in such circumstances of led upbeats, and in the most distinguished circles too, that both the leading player and also the anxiously led invest their first notes with an accent that has no place at the utterly unaccented beginning of an upbeat phrase; on the one hand, this unintentional stress is caused by the leading player's leading as such: this is the ideal place for him to learn that a different, utterly accent-less type of leading is required, more often than not, in the context of a string quartet. On the other hand, it is the led player's triumphant (yet anxiety-ridden) precision, his all too obtrusive 'following' which reinforces the accent, with the frequent result that the upbeat motif turns into its opposite, and two main stresses split the entire phrase asunder and thus make it meaningless. For study purposes, the '*mf*' should be replaced with a '*p*', the '*p*' with a '*pp*': so far as the respective first notes are concerned, at any rate, not much will have to be changed dynamically on the way back to *mf* and *p*!

With the theme of the *Finale*, the so-called croaking of whose upbeat phrases is responsible for the work's nickname ('The Frog', which derives from the German 'Froschquartett' – not, as various English sources have it, 'Der Frosch', which in German would be meaningless), we reach Haydn's revolutionary melodic innovation: he introduces Schoenberg's 'tone-colour melody', which we have heard foreshadowed as early as the *Scherzando* from Op.33, No.1, bars 6–7 (see p.66). It will be remembered that what Schoenberg means by a 'tone-colour melody' is a melody in which successive pitches are replaced with successive colours.

In Paul Griffiths's history of *The String Quartet*,[2] the present masterpiece is thus dismissed: '. . . and Haydn remains occasionally capable of pure silliness, as in the finale of the D major quartet from Op.50, whose bouncing on one note has given the work its nickname of the "Frog".' The fallacy of this

[2] London, 1983, p.53.

observation cannot be overemphasised; it behoves me, therefore, to have a close look at the finale.

More likely than not, the reader will in playing have convinced himself of the theme's substance. But we are invited to assume that for the purpose of pure silliness, Haydn went to quite extraordinary structural as well as textural lengths. Structurally, he not only explored all open-string possibilities, but introduced two types of variations on the initial 'tone-colour melody' – (a) changes of fingered colour without the participation of open strings, and (b) combinations of changes of colour and pitch (such as Ex.38):

Ex.38

Texturally, he not only introduced dialogues between tone-colour melodies (such as Ex.39), but placed his colour melodies in a fascinating contrasting variety of textural contexts (such as Exs.40 and 41).

Ex.39

Ex.40

Ex.41

At the end, moreover, we get the texturally climactic effect of contrasting tutti textures, each of which evinces three simultaneous colour melodies, fingered throughout in the case of the first violin and viola, and with the open string in the second violin – while the cello furnishes the contrast with its equally thematic, chromatic bass (see *x* in Ex.42), which resolves, in the very last phrase, into an interplay between the tonic and the leading-note (see *y* in Ex.42):

Ex.42

These two cadential phases produce an unprecedented sound, an unheard-of harmonic texture whose wit, first *piano* and concludingly *pianissimo* is in fact deeply moving; the cello's chromatic bass (*x* in Ex.42), is, moreover, the retrograde version of a previous combination of the colour melody with the cello's variation. Needless to add, this entirely new type of quartet texture, 'old' only in the sense of being typically quartet-like, *viz.* neither homophonic nor polyphonic, has been well prepared in the course of the *Finale*, both structurally and texturally.

It also has to be noted that Haydn takes the greatest care to write the purest possible form of colour melody, which is to say that the changes from note to note are only perceptible through the change of colour, that no other element assists our perception. For this purpose, his colour melody consists of equal note values throughout, so that the melody has to make do without rhythmic articulation or characterization. Likewise, he even insists that we should not recognize the different notes because one of them stops before the next one starts: the colour changes are produced by legatos from one colour to the other – which, since they involve a single bow for successive changes, excludes the remotest possibility of identifying the duration of the two notes in question by anything but the end of one colour and the beginning of the next. Had Haydn employed *staccato* or even *détaché* notes of equal value, one could still have said that he hadn't written pure colour melodies, because the infinitesimal silences between the notes, or the changes of bow, would have enabled one to distinguish between the notes without colour being the sole means of distinction.

It will now readily be understood that what I find most unacceptable in Griffiths's reference to the movement is the irresponsibility of such a playfully critical remark, made quite thoughtlessly, evidently without concrete knowledge of the score, not to speak of the unconditional need to extend a credit account of trust to a genius of Haydn's calibre, and to follow up, conscientiously, the (clearly audible) reasons why he did something, anything, before describing it as pure silliness. Incidentally, there is no 'bouncing on one note': a bouncing bow, which can be heard in *spiccato* or *ricochet*, would indeed have produced the aforementioned notes, one of which would have stopped before the next one started, whereas what Haydn here requests is the diametrically opposite bowing, i.e. a smooth legato across the strings – the most unbouncing bowing there is.

The colour melody and its structural and textural variations are, in fact, so characterful that Haydn has to forego his usual monothematic urge in order to find the strongest and most unexpected second-subject contrast possible. Now, thematically, it isn't easy to search for unexpectedness: there are no contrasting thematic structures which a composer can expect us to expect, and then duly contradict. But whereas we are without thematic expectations, our sonata expectations of tonal and harmonic contrasts are, in the classical creative world, firmly ingrained: anybody who plays or hears the 'Frog's' finale for the first time will, as soon as he becomes aware of the sonata build-up, expect a modulatory drive to the dominant and a second subject intimately related to the first or strikingly different from it, but in any case firmly embedded in that contrasting key, which he has instinctively come to accept as the second corner-stone of any classical sonata movement, whatever its contradictions of his other expectations.

And this is where Haydn goes all out to throw the colour theme, his 'pure silliness', into relief against that which it and its variations surround: the sonata world itself is shaking in the player's and listener's experience, for the dominant theme does not ensue! Instead, upon establishing the dominant via the dominant's dominant as of old, Haydn embarks on his second subject in the dominant's relative minor, and while both it and its restatement move back to the dominant, its centre of melodic gravity remains F♯ minor – a nostalgic backward glance, perhaps, on top or at the bottom of it all, to the sensational events of two quartets ago?

In any case, Haydn curbs his monothematic passions to the extent of having this single theme as a decided thematic contrast to his 'pure silliness', which dominates everything else in the movement; the second subject is, literally, the movement's only thought which is unaffected, directly or indirectly, by it – unaffected, that is, by the colour melody, though not – let us hasten to realize – by the first subject as a whole. For though Haydn abandons any thought of monothematicism, he remains aware, of course, of the need for what we might call mono-subthematicism – the simple need for unity between the subjects. As on a previous occasion (cf. p.56), he adopts a serial approach, except that in both instances his series is not a note-row, but a degree-row. When the colour melody changes into a normal melody, that is, it moves down conjunctly from the dominant: dominant – subdominant – mediant – supertonic – tonic (x^1 in Ex.43), and this first motion of pitches in the first subject becomes the first motion of pitches in the second (x^2 in Ex.44):

Ex.43

Ex.44

If you like, there's even a trace of thematicism left, inasmuch as the colour melody's enormous initial stress on the dominant is recalled at the beginning of the second subject, which features its only repeated note as introductory upbeat and main beat – the dominant again.

Otherwise, Haydn has gone out of his and the classical sonata's way to make the second subject an extreme, three-dimensional contrast – an unparalleled contrast of keys, a total thematic (melodic) contrast and, encompassing both these contrasts, a contrast of fundamental types of melody, a new type having been invented. The only remaining element of unity is experienced through the second subject's consistent conjunct motion: its every phrase consists of neighbouring notes – which, let us not forget, are his principal means of varying the colour melody itself in the rest of the movement, above all chromatically!

From the viewpoint of essential symphonic contrast, which we have recognized to depend more incisively on the contrast between statement and development than on thematic contrast or key contrast, this *Finale* is, in fact, the world's only sonata structure which, under the influence of its colour melody, depends as heavily on its thematic contrast and its unprecedented key contrast as on that between statement and development. So much, then, for Haydn's pure silliness.

The reason why this book on interpretation had to go into such analytic detail on this occasion is that it will now easily be seen that without fully appreciating the elemental contrast between the subjects which involves, of course, an extreme contrast of moods, one cannot hope to do justice to this unique structure and the astounding continuity which its unity gives rise to despite its exposition of different melodic worlds.

Amusingly enough, penultimately, it so happens that in the viola part, the very last two variations, both structural and textural, on the colour melody (Ex.42, x and y) present a problem whose solution (if any) belongs more properly to the present book's central terms of reference. If the viola player has small hands, that is to say, and/or if an outsized modern instrument maltreats him, he will find the necessary stretch between the first finger on the G-string and the fourth on the C-string distinctly unpleasant, if not imposs-ible. Artistically speaking, there is no harm in hearing a bit of difficulty here, a little strain which would accompany the change of colour, but rather than practise himself into a muscular inflammation, the player might be well advised to cheat and produce the *a*s on one string. If he has the necessary imagination, he will be able, within the total texture, to simulate the required sound – on the C-, not the G-string.

Finally, there is another unanswered question – which is, perhaps, answerable. How was it possible for Schoenberg to invent, and then climac-tically[3] to write about, his colour melodies without drawing attention to their inventor? For decades, I played in a quartet led by the man who led Schoen-berg's quartet for many, many years, and in view of his countless reports on their quartet sessions, I don't have the slightest doubt that Schoenberg must have played, if not Op.33, No.1, then certainly 'The Frog' on numerous occasions. My all too human answer is that Schoenberg repressed the model that had inspired him, in order to be the inventor himself. There was plenty left for him to invent in his new melodic world, anyhow.

---

[3] The paragraphs in question appear right at the end of his book on harmony (*op.cit.*).

Op.54, No.1, in G major
(Hoboken III:58)

Perhaps, before we inspect the interpretative problems (if any) of the next masterpiece, a further word is needed on the omission, from this book, of *The Seven Words of our Saviour on the Cross* (Op.51, 1–7), quite especially in view of the regrettable fact that many a pseudo-masterly string quartet has accorded the work a prominent place in its repertory; it goes without saying that it is, above all, the Haydn specialists who have turned *The Seven Words* into veritable stars amongst Haydn's master quartets.

The musical fact is, however, that these pieces cannot possibly be called string quartets: no reason has yet been advanced from any competent source why they should be. And apart from everything else, no natural musician will readily play seven successive slow instrumental movements (until the thunderstorm eventually ensues) if no extra-musical purpose is involved – and is there an instrumental combination which, at its greatest, is freer of extra-musical purposes than the string quartet? It cannot be too decidedly maintained that the passion certain ensembles show for the work is an indisputable sign that they have not even begun to understand the true nature of the string quartet and its texture.

And now for the present work's interpretative problems, if any: strictly speaking, there are none. It is the first of the twelve so-called 'Tost' quartets – and it was, incidentally, with Johann Tost that Haydn and Mozart played the Mozart quintets (see p.3, n.3). Since Tost seems to have been an outstanding fiddler, virtuosity has duly been read into the first-violin parts of the Tost quartets, but the musico-technical fact is that many another Haydn quartet makes greater demands on the leader's virtuosity than any Tost quartet. The present one does not, in fact, contain any outstanding difficulties; it is altogether amongst the most popular Haydn quartets – which, as we have seen (*cf.*, for instance, p.107), owe much of their popularity to their symmetrical rhythmic structures. In the minuet, however, Haydn cheats the listener into believing that he is hearing symmetrical phrases, whereas in rhythmic reality he isn't.

First movement first. The opening antecedent's third-bar aim must, of course, be pursued not merely by the first violin's theme, but also by the accompanying quartet, whose quartet-producing second fiddle can, at this early stage – i.e. just after the players have tuned – safely use the open D-string for its double part, which accompanies the entire antecedent: there is no need to create problems where there aren't any. Of the creation of such problems I have, in point of fact, some entertaining practical experience. I've heard the second fiddlers of no fewer than three well-known quartets, one of them in a coaching session with me, play the first three bars in the third position – with the result that in respect of both intonation and blend, the part stuck out, throughout the 4¼ bars, like a gravely injured thumb: there wasn't even any attempt at gradual adjustment in any of these instances. An example, this, of a very typical, wellnigh neurotic, anti-musical removal from reality: in order to solve a non-existent problem, a course of action is taken which produces the very problem it was intended to solve.

For it must be realized that in any case, the D- and A-string give rise to a far better blend with the first violin's E- and A-strings than the G- and D-string; besides, the first violin's opening double *acciacatura* will just have sounded the second violin's very notes on the D- and A-string, in which respect the second is actually committed musically to follow suit! The recapitulation, coming as it does from somewhere rather than from nowhere, omits the *acciacatura*, half of which the opening of the development does retain in order to issue the earliest possible warning of the theme's tonic minor version. We are indeed led to expect – and the leader has to lead us further into that expectation of – a complete tonic minor version of at least the antecedent, before the development embarks on its first modulation. Instead, the tonic minor proves a mere upbeat, as it were, to its relative major's subdominant, in which key this metamorphosis – not a mere variation – of the antecedent ends: the quartet has to effect the modulation with full emotional anticipation of the contradiction of expectation, even if it decides to behave as if nothing had happened: one distinct possibility, this, of doing full justice to the drama of $E^\flat$.

The sonata structure of the slow movement avails itself of the *siciliano*'s characteristic dotted motif, which both Haydn and Mozart explored and exploited, (cf.pp.59 and 79) without turning itself or even its background into this dance form: by delaying the first appearance of the motif until the third bar, Haydn makes sure that we don't experience it as the most essential element of the basic thought. Its performance, likewise, even though it must remain eminently rhythmical, cannot suddenly throw what now assumes the significance of a cadential phrase into dramatic relief: the phrase is, and must be unambiguously heard to be, on the way out.

But the tempo character of the suppressed dance form is retained, whereas many a distinguished ensemble turns it virtually into an *adagio*, even though one of the work's subtlest, yet most clear-cut contrasts is the very difference between the respective *allegretto* characters of the middle movements, each of whose *allegretto* should, nevertheless, be audible, palpable, virtually tangible to any musician who has never seen a score of the work. Like *adagio*, *allegretto* is a tempo whose character retains identical features in its most dissimilar manifestations.

With its first part's two pseudo-symmetrical 5-bar phrases, the minuet flowers into one of the most refined rhythmic structures in the entire literature. How does Haydn persuade the simple-minded recipient of the opening sentence's non-existent symmetry? In the first place, by actually retaining one element of symmetry, to wit, the equal length of the two halves – but in the second place, or rather, in the shared first place, by moving his symmetrical background (Ex.45) sufficiently close to the foreground (Ex.46) to make it clearly audible, or at least concretely divinable:

Ex.45

Ex.46

It will be noted that the first-beat significance of bar 2's and bar 7's second beats is retained in the foreground; in fact, in the foreground's structural event, bar 2's second beat will have to be played as the phrase's main accent altogether, a circumstance which will be clear enough to the leader, but which the cello's crotchets and especially the middle parts' dotted minims will have to respect as convincedly and convincingly as if their players were themselves responsible for the principal part.

The overpowering contrast of the *Trio* is, once again, achieved without change of key, even though there is the relative minor and its subdominant in the middle; the *Trio*'s first part is indeed a normal string trio, though the cello is the leader, without however robbing the violin of its own intervening leading role: a wonderful test piece, this, for the two's complementary, imaginative liberties and the viola's equally imaginative adjustment to both – or rather, each! Although only three people are playing, one couldn't easily find a more characteristic quartet texture; the string trio is, after all, but a variation on the theme of the string quartet – as is, on the other (fifth) hand, the string quintet, with which the present work has started.

The *Finale*, an ultra-characteristic Haydn paradox in that it is that sheer impossibility, a rondo with thematic episodes and, needless to add, with developmental and hence sonata incursions, has to be strikingly delicate on the *piano* level, despite the semiquaver motion in the middle parts, the 4-part writing, and the *presto* character, whose definition and characterization must, of course, take place immediately, despite the opening *piano* and its delicacy which, ideally, should emerge as an essential element of the *presto* character, not as its opponent. Even in the more masculine and assertive *fortes*, the delicate nature of the opening will have to be remembered; the occasionally-heard alternative is an intolerable quasi-orchestral texture. And above all, *no two 2-quaver upbeats can possibly be alike*, nor can any repeat be like its model. The freest upbeat, the playing reader may agree, will probably be the very first, as it cautiously and smilingly leads us into the piece; its repeat is a vastly different matter.

Op.54, No.2, in C major
(Hoboken III:57)

It can safely be suggested that there is no more original Haydn quartet, nor any that contains more prophetic innovations, than the second 'Tost' Quartet, whose first-violin part does suggest, if not yet that Tost was an exceptional virtuoso, then that he was an exceptional musician with an intense and rich imagination; it would indeed have seemed unlikely in any case that Haydn would write a dozen quartets for any old fiddler, that, whatever the practical and financial circumstances, the man for whom he wrote them was without such musical character traits as would stimulate his invention.

The third of Haydn's seven great C major quartets – not even in the violin's own key, D major, did he write as many – has one striking structural characteristic in common with his first, Op.20, No.2: the slow movement, an *adagio* C minor fantasy – the two works are homotonal – which both stimulates and invites improvisation, leads without a break into the *allegretto* minuet with its tonic minor trio (cf.pp.44ff.), thus anticipating a continuity between movements which later ages were to explore with enthusiasm. We have noted personal associations between structural peculiarities and keys (see for instance pp.64f.). From the player's point of view, this unifying continuity between the middle movements involves a double attitude towards the slow movement, far more so in the present case than in that of the Op.20 work: he has to treat the *adagio* not only as the highly characteristic tempo any mature

Haydn *adagio* inevitably is, but also, notwithstanding its own weight, as an introduction to the minuet.

From the opening, asymmetrical five-bar phrase (3 + 2), whose sixth bar is a G.P. which the recapitulation will fill in with an echoing motif that turns the relative symmetry of the two-bar consequent into a three-bar asymmetry, we know that we are in for invention without concession. And sure enough, before we know where we are but as soon as the player knows where he is, this first subject switches to A♭ major, thus immediately reminding us of the need for a unifying, homophonic framework. The initial exposition of the first subject has to be played, therefore, with a C major conviction that is given the lie as early as that sudden A♭ dislocation in bar 12, compared to which Prokofiev's comparable manoeuvres in, say, his Fifth Symphony are child's play from both the conductor's and the listener's standpoint, nor indeed is this the last abrupt shift that has necessitated the homophonic structure. Harmonic consciousness is therefore of overriding importance in the interpretation of the movement; such audible awareness has to prepare for every new contradiction of harmonic expectation by knowingly asserting that which will be promptly contradicted. I should think, then, that to give a logical account of the *Vivace* without ever having seen it before is, even for a very mature quartet which otherwise knows its Haydn, a virtual impossibility – though technically, it could be read without difficulty. And in the second subject, one cannot exaggerate its *piano dolce* contrast to the assertive masculinity of the first, even though both of them make great play of the shortest possible – i.e. two-crotchet – motifs; in fact, it is in the very character of these miniature entities that much of the contrast lies, a circumstance whose clear recognition will help the leader to achieve what amounts to a polarity of characters.

As for the tonic minor *Adagio*, every single reader will agree that it is one of the most astounding slow movements ever written – a very profound assimilation of gipsy style, probably the profoundest ever (the second place might be granted to the slow movement of Brahms's Clarinet Quintet, his only total success in this direction, though indeed a sovereign one). Although in principle, all the rubatos, if not indeed the agogics, are written out in the first-violin part, a quartet which really knows the movement will be able to afford countless complex additional agogic shadings, but of course the lower instruments, and above all the second violin, have to be dead sure of every note the first is playing. That is not, alas, difficult if the leader indulges in pseudo-improvisations which, in unmusical reality, are well-tried 'liberties' which he repeats unchanged year in, year out: more than one world-leading ensemble has been guilty of this act of utter musical unrealism, this phantasy-less approach which can even be studied (as distinct from musically experienced) on their gramophone records together with their live performances, or on successive recordings of the same work. No, these shadings depend for their life on their uniqueness, their once-only appearance, whether at home, in the concert hall, or in the recording studio: they can certainly not be rehearsed. In general, what a string quartet's rehearsals ought to promote is what Mahler said he rehearsed for – 'in order for the orchestra, the individual players, to get to know me', not in order to fix and thus calcify phrasings, robbing them altogether of their spontaneity. In the quartet, and quite especially in the present movement, it is, of course, the leader whom the other three have to 'get to know' in rehearsal: in proportion as they know him, he will be able to invent spontaneously, to keep the movement intensely alive, Tost-like, through genuine improvisation.

He must, in a word, be free to rhapsodize to his heart's and mind's content (in that order), inhibited only by the consideration that his own freedom can already be found in clear rhythmic outline in the note values he has to bring to life. Experientially speaking, the movement has proved quite a job, even for very experienced, first-rate players – or perhaps especially for them: a 'normal', 'professional' approach to it condemns it to death. The artist, the whole artist and, above all, nothing but the artist has to re-create this rhapsody. For the sake of the experiment, I have taught it to amateur players who came to render it better than some professionals or advanced students. For it is no empty statement to claim that when you really know it, there simply is no difficulty at all: metrically speaking, you can then play it in your sleep.

Structurally speaking, I trust the reader won't need the present writer's reminder that Haydn here combines passacaglia, monothematic ternary (another characteristic Haydn paradox: cf. Op.54, No.1) and, of course, sonata, inasmuch as the middle is developmental.

Is it too much to hope that we have reached a stage in this book where the reader can foresee that the *sforzato* in the minuet's third bar will be described as not only the main, but in fact the only accent of the opening phrase? For the duration of the entire principal section, we have indeed to remember that the most important questions about any *sforzato* in any great composer's music are (1) what would happen if the *sforzato* weren't there, and (2) which accent(s) the *sforzato* removes. With this reminder, I can safely leave the minuet in the player-reader's hands and mind (in reverse order), for the fact that Haydn's dynamics are an essential structural element is, I hope, too glaringly obvious to be in need of emphasis.

A textural warning about both minuet and trio might not, however, be out of place: both of them contain not only an unusual amount of four-part writing, but also quadruple octave-unisons whose blend is not a foregone conclusion. Nor, for that matter, is the balance of the four-part writing, especially on the *piano* level: a thorough knowledge of (not about) what each of the others is doing, and by 'knowledge' I mean concrete forehearing, is an unconditional requirement if the necessary textural clarity is to be achieved.

The minuet's unison will have to explode as a stark contrast to its model, which is the first violin's preceding solo line, whose *piano* must not be negative (i.e. 'not loud'), but delicately positive – indispensable, that is to say, to the phrase's *grazioso* character. It is a very difficult unison – in view of its *crescendo*, to which Arnold Rosé's habitual *crescendo* advice cannot, for once, be applied: '*Crescendo* means *piano*' – by which he in his turn meant that one ought to start a *crescendo* on or near the *piano* level. It was a helpful reminder, if one remembered too well the almost invariable *mf*, if not indeed *f*, of most mechanical approaches to *crescendo*s. Exceptionally and explicitly, however, the present *crescendo* is a climax from *forte* to *fortissimo*; quite clearly, it wouldn't otherwise make sense.

Now, my advice is to employ the kind of tone production which makes a mere *mezzoforte* sound like a *forte*, in order to create the desirable maximal range for what will have to be a powerful climax to the *fortissimo* at the other end. Much will depend, of course, on the blend the unison is going to achieve, and much can thus be achieved by adjusting fingerings to each other with a view to the closest possible monochrome of the greatest possible number of adjoining notes. It is indeed staggering to find that even in emphatically professional circles, players will often in this type of situation either slip into any old fingering, or else plunge for a fingering they personally prefer, regardless of what is happening around them.

The fingering aspect assumes immeasurably greater significance even in the *forte* octave unison that opens the *Trio* – greater significance not merely in degree but also in kind. Owing to the fact, that is to say, that the fiddles here play in actual unison while the viola's octave below enables the player to finger like the fiddles and, moreover, to avoid their single inevitable open string, a monochromatic minimum is attainable on the basis of near-identical fingerings of the upper three, and the monochrome of the one note that need not be fingered identically, i.e. bar 1's G, is actually improvable by way of the viola's fingering! In my experience, the closest monochrome is obtained if the upper three play the four-bar phrase in the third position. Whether the viola should contribute to the likely distonation of the open G by playing its own open G, or play the note on the C-string, is an ideal question for the purpose of illustrating the precise meaning of the concept of a dilemma, a position that only leaves a choice between equal evils – except that some evils are more equal than others: the decision will altogether depend on the viola-player's instrument, whose C-string may be one of those which seem to belong to another instrument or to none, in which case the distonating open G-string will still be preferable, for the C-string will sound out of tune anyway. The cello is, of course, in the viola's situation, except that its C-string is not likely to be a foreign body, so that the fingered G will be advisable.

The work's most shattering and, if I may so put it, untimely innovation is, of course, the *adagio* finale, which turns the typical symphonic structure with two *allegro*s upside down, throwing up two *adagio*s instead. History books credit the nineteenth century with the symphony's slow final movement, whether it came about by accident (Bruckner's unfinished Ninth) or design (Tchaikovsky, Mahler). To my inadequate knowledge, not a single historian has noticed that Haydn was responsible for introducing this new symphonic form. His combination of forms challenged the course of musical history, which had made the Italian Overture the mother of symphonic structure; in its turn, he now married symphonic structure to the French Overture.

Mind you, the finale's opening *adagio* raises expectations of a following quick movement, to which it would then be found to have formed an introduction, and when Haydn actually meets these expectations with his *Presto*, the feeling arises that the body of the finale has arrived – a feeling which he contradicts as radically as possible: the *Presto* turns out to be a mere middle section; the body of the movement is, on the contrary, the *adagio*, which duly returns.

The players have to go with both the expectations he meets and the expectations which what seems his accommodating creative behaviour appears to confirm beyond any remaining doubt, only to contradict them finally with an unprecedented structural step into wholly uncharted symphonic territory.

The forms he combines in this finale are, once again, his own, paradoxical monothematic ternary variation, and sonata – monothematic, too, needless to add. By characteristically drawing his variation technique into developmental unrest, moreover, he introduces a new way of musical development in the wider sense, of musical evolution, which enables him to turn the *presto* middle section itself into a variation on his initial theme and thus to unfold a structure which, while strictly monothematic on the one hand, usurps as it were all the contrasts that are the normal property of polythematic structures – on top of which the *Presto* doesn't change key, though its major mode follows the *adagio*'s C minor variation: his homotonal framework does not allow movements within movements – the *Trio* and the finale's *Presto* – to escape it. The intererepretation will have to be proportionately tonality-conscious, for only thus will the playing imagination be inspired by the work's extreme harmonic variety and extreme harmonic contrasts as well as the contrasts between statements and developments and the ultimate combination of the two. There is, in fact, no other Haydn quartet which offers the interpreters a richer chance to take part in its composition – so long as they keep as conscientiously within his frameworks as he does in the first place.

In the *adagio* finale, however, it is the flexibility of the middle parts' accompanimental framework – a string trio for most of the time which even flowers into a quartet! – that is the *conditio sine qua non* for the free and natural growth of not only the first violin's profusely ornate melodies but also the cello's contrastingly simple, deep-breathing subordinate part, less subordinate than which no subordinate part will be found in our entire literature; at the same time, it is not a counterpoint nor indeed a counter-melody, but, on the contrary, serves to provide the theme with homophonic support by way of, once again, a paradigmatic quartet texture.

What about the middle parts' all-important flexibility, then? How is it going to be attained? Ideally as well as realistically, by means of what I have described as 'Carmirelli bowing' in the case of the present quartet's sister work, Op.20, No.2 (see p.42): thus, and only thus, have I heard the middle duo, trio, and quartet supply, paradoxically, a perfect framework for their top and bottom leaders, who remain, of course, ultimately responsible for the shape and sound of the framework. Its sound is indeed a crucial consideration: not only do we have to cope with a consistently full quartet texture, but this description amounts to an understatement, in that in effect, it usually is a quintet and sometimes even a sextet we have to blend and balance. Throughout the work, in fact, the players will have to be conscious of its innovations not simply being structural, but involving entirely new types of quartet sound at virtually every corner. At the same time, the desired sound is, again throughout the work, self-evident, so long as we have a proper look at what Haydn wants both structurally and texturally, and translate our understanding of his intentions into a clearly audible, mental, aural picture of the required sound. With silent, mental practice, this inner picture will arise spontaneously, as a result of the aforementioned proper look.

Op.54, No.3, in E major
(Hoboken III:59)

That Haydn should write his only mature E major Quartet (the two immature ones are, with respect to one of mankind's greatest geniuses, not of the slightest interest) for Tost makes this fiddler ever more fascinating: by now we must be sure of his rich improvisatory spirit, of which the slow movement of the present work offers further, confirmatory evidence. But on the technical side, the two preceding Tost quartets don't evince any difficulties which are remotely comparable to the technical pain in the neck that is this E major Quartet, which thus seems to show Haydn's confidence in Tost's sheer fiddling ability: 'If I want to write an E major quartet,' the mature Haydn must have said to himself, 'this is my chance!' The work is, in fact, as difficult as Mozart's E major Piano Trio, and indeed as outstanding – which means more outstanding, because it's a quartet.

Musical problems there are, at the same time, very few, though the most glaring one is to be found right at the outset: the second violin's opening of the antecedent and the first violin's response to it (in no way yet a consequent) overlap without the second becoming less important with the first's entry; what, two simultaneous principal parts? Yes and no. Yes, in that the first violin's entry does not relegate the second's end of its phrase to a subordinate role; no, in that acoustically speaking, and hence also in the composer's mind, there simply can't be any such thing as two simultaneous leading moments. Haydn took indeed great care to let the second fiddle start as low as at all possible in the tonal circumstances, so that when the first comes in over the second's lowest fingered notes, it assumes natural, indeed acoustic leadership despite the second's continued melodic significance; Haydn goes out of his way structurally to confirm this textural event with his *sforzato* in bar 4: the preceding motif ends where the first violin came in at the beginning, i.e. after the three crotchets which are introduced by an upbeat.

And now to the solution of the problem: in terms of balance, our observations mean that the second violin need not retire with the first's entry, which will push it into the background anyway, but that the viola will, as it were, notice the entry, in view of which it no longer contributes to the sounding together of two notes, but has become the lowest of three. The solution applies to bar 5 too, of course, whereas in bar 9, Haydn has actually composed it – with his first-violin *sforzato* as against the upbeating middle parts.

This is not a book on the art, or rather the craft, of string playing, and I propose not to waste the reader's time with an investigation into the work's E major difficulties (not to speak of the second subject's B major triplets), beyond reminding him of the work's once again exceptional need for individual practice – not just of the leading part as in the case of the A major Quartet from Op.20 (see pp.61–2), nor again of all four parts as in the case of the F♯ minor Quartet (see p.98), but, this time, of the two violin parts. And here again, there is little point in trying to cope with the work early on in an ensemble's Haydn development: the later, I should say, the better, and not only for musico-technical reasons; the finale's unparalleled developmental flood needs a lot of experience of Haydn developments and their controlled resistance to harmonic control – to predictability.

In the middle section of the *Largo cantabile*, my advice, more musical than technical, is 'Carmirelli bowing' in the lower parts (see p.42), with the most concentrated attention to the indispensable flights of the first violin's imagination: if there aren't any, the movement had better not be attempted; what the first fiddler has firmly to decide is to out-Tost Tost at what is easily recognizable as every characteristic corner. It may indeed be conceded at this stage that Haydn's characterization of Tost's imaginative personality has been completed.

The minuet doesn't do us the favour of changing key for the *Trio* – but then, no hair-raising difficulties await us there, so long as the intonation and blend of the opening octave unison is conscientiously (rather than orchestrally) tackled. The *diminuendo* and the ensuing *piano* have to be a major event as they prepare for the first violin's consequent.

In the excitement of also starting the other outer movement, this time with a protracted solo, second violins sometimes accent the second halves of the first, third, and fifth bars. This must not, of course, happen: aim at the second and fourth bars. The sixth is itself only half an aim, if that, because the structure drives on after the sequences.

Now, in the case of the finale, the second violin's opening theme doesn't have to face the first's overlapping intervention; when the leader does intervene in bars 10 and 12, it is up to him to do it with discreet playfulness: to err on the loud side would be disastrous; to err on the soft side, with a firm phrasing intention behind it, might prove the happy assumption or impression of a mistaken error. For the rest, the finale's compression of development and recapitulation produces a developmental intensification of the total structure which is altogether unprecedented – even in Haydn's output. From the interpretative standpoint, it is not only the excitement of instability which is intensified, but also, proportionately, the emotional discharge of the movement's stability eventually regained – and 'eventually' is indeed the word: even the dominant seventh under its hopeful pause a mere 25 bars from the end does not yet introduce the expected relaxation!

Op.55, No.1, in A major
(Hoboken III:60)

The second of Haydn's two great A major quartets (*cf*.pp.61ff.), whose
probable date of composition is 1788, is definitely easier than the first – not, in
fact, a problematic technical proposition at all. And its originality certainly
exceeds its parent's or elder brother's; the special type of asymmetry which
opens the work is, of course, prophetic of things to come: the only properly
symmetrical bit is the first four bars – which, however, are a complete melodic
statement,

Ex.47

as the first four bars virtually never are, and notwithstanding what is going to
prove their antecedent significance. And consequents there are, equally extra-
ordinarily, two, the first of which turns itself into a renewed antecedent – a
course of events which the interpretation has to reflect.

The second subject out-Haydns Haydn's monothematicism: it actually
starts exactly like the first; for once, it mightn't do any harm explicitly to ape
the original, initial phrasing, to the point of creatively implied structural
irony.

The slow movement, a Haydn *adagio par excellence*, opens as if it were a
string trio – as which, again ironically, it might be played, without any
suspicion, that is, of a restatement. When the leader then enters, liberatingly,
with the selfsame tune, we realize all the more clearly what quartet texture is
about.

In the tonical *Trio* of the minuet, it is again this string trio which plays a
leading role, both at the beginning and in the middle, but when the first violin
does participate, it climbs unusual heights, both on the E-string and, exceptionally at the end, on the G-string, where it reaches the *c*♯″ the soloist does just
before the coda of the Mendelssohn Concerto's finale, and for the same
purpose: in either case, the climb produces a composed hesitation; in the film
Melody of Youth decades ago, Heifetz played the passage too well – without

any hesitation, as if he had played it in the first position. The leader, then, ought to think of Tost rather than of Heifetz: one can hear Haydn's fiddler use his rich imagination towards a discreet *portamento* at the actual change of bow, from *c♯"* to *a*! It is indeed a composed *portamento*, as part of the composed hesitation. In Haydn's day, without a chin-rest, an inaudible change of position from the fifth to the first would have been a physical impossibility.

The theme of the last movement, finally, starts with a sentence that is nine bars long instead of eight – and with an upbeat that extends over more than a whole bar, which, provided that it is played calmly, can't be played fast enough, i.e. sufficiently extra-metrically: a well-exaggerated speed will remove the merest suspicion of accents on the first of each couple of slurred quavers, and they will thus emerge in accentless quintuple articulation, whereas the tempo definition will start in bar 2.

The foregoing race through the quartet is designed to make players keen on getting down to it: very much as opposed to its parent or sibling, it is indeed emphatically recommended for playing study – for which purpose I shall now add a concentric inner circle of advice to the outer circle that was the just-mentioned race, a second round, as it were, which mixture of metaphors does not cause them to contradict each other. To some extent, our remarks about the accompaniment to the theme in the first movement of Op.33, No.2 (see p.69) apply to the middle parts of the present first movement's theme; only, this time it is crotchets instead of quavers, and their pitch is not identical: it is, in fact, a subordinate phrase. Consequently, the third beat takes a real accent, except in bar 3, where the three crotchets form a pure upbeat phrase to bar 4, whose own, more manifest (*legato*) upbeat phrase they thus foreshadow. But let not the turn produce any accent whatever!

Mutatis mutandis, the second-violin solo that opens the *adagio cantabile* might heed our remarks about the *Adagio* of Op.50, No.2 (see pp.91f.): yes, it is possible to combine the requirements of our two concentric circles, to avoid the suspicion of a restatement without a grand statement, to keep within the limits of the string-trio theme without pressaging its metamorphosis into a quartet; in short, restraint is possible without the promise of its abandonment.

The first bar-line of the finale, it will now be realized, has no rhythmic significance whatsoever, and the second less than the third. The same holds true, of course, of the restatement as well as the returns of the theme, despite the lower instruments' entry into what was their empty bar at the recapitulatory stage: it doesn't change the first violin's phrase structure. As for the first and last appearance of the theme, a modern composer, unsure of his players' understanding, would have written its upbeat as a ⁵/₄ bar.

In general, but still specifically, it can finally be said that so long as you approach the work without any phrasing prejudices of any kind, letting Haydn's notation not only of the notes, but also of dynamics and expression marks be your sole directive, there shouldn't be any problem at all; at the outset, I mentioned the absence of technical problems, but every single musical point I have made in my discussion of this work could, should have struck the player forcibly and unambiguously in view of the music alone. There is no Haydn quartet whose interpretative structure and texture is better defined; ideally, the present discussion could have consisted of a single sentence: Haydn tells you precisely not only what to do, but where there are alternative ways of conveying what he means. All of them, needless to add, need your imaginatively completing the creative job; if my remarks result in your always playing the finale's opening upbeat the same way, I have failed: there are dozens of ways of, say, deleting the first bar-line.

Op.55, No.2, in F minor
(Hoboken III:61)

Considering that, as we must realize by now, Tost's musical personality as well as his individuality as a fiddler ('as a gipsy', I almost wrote) must have proved a major inspiration for Haydn, we could, I think, have foreheard that the composer would write – probably in 1788 again – the second of his two quartets in his very own key as one of the works he specially produced for a man who makes one regret, as few players of the past do, that the gramophone didn't yet exist in his time. I am convinced, in other words, that the reader who is unfamiliar with Haydn's quartets, but who has read this book consecutively until the present stage, will have exclaimed 'Of course!' in view of the present chapter's title, so long as he remembered that this was one of the Tost quartets. Nor are our expectations disappointed at any point in this F minor Quartet, even though they must have reached what might seem an unrealistic culmination; on the contrary, if anything, the present work proves our expectations pitiable, so little do we realize, even now, the possible flights of Haydn's unremittingly original imagination.

In the C major Tost Quartet, homotonal like Haydn's first great quartet in that key (see pp.120 and 39 respectively), we come up against an unprecedented slow finale; in the F minor Tost Quartet, homotonal like Haydn's other great quartet in that very personal key (see p.59), we are surprised by the other end of the French Overture, as it were, by a precedented slow opening movement – precedented in that his Symphony No.49, known as *La Passione* and likewise in his own key, had adopted a comparable ground-plan.

This slow opening movement adopts a particularly subtle structure within Haydn's self-invented double variations form (*cf.* p.80), in that the second theme, in the tonic major, itself varies the first or principal theme; there is yet another F minor work which Haydn cast in a comparable structure – his profound piano Variations. Whereas the first theme modulates to the relative major in the middle, the second modulates to the dominant, but the first theme's turn, before the end, to G♭ major, to the Neapolitan sixth, cannot hope for a counterpart in the major-mode theme: the Neapolitan sixth has been closely bound up with the minor mode's harmonic structure. It is scarcely necessary to add that these modulatory drives, which immediately justify the homotonal framework, carry considerable expressive power, which the interpretation has to reflect – most of all, of course, in the least expected, Neapolitan sixth's departure, whose pre-cadential function emerges quite naturally, owing to the flat supertonic's bafflingly close relation to the tonic, which even a Schoenberg's harmonic investigations failed to illuminate or explain; I well remember its mystifying me even as a child, when I used to enjoy, in fact indulge in, continuous alternations on the violin's G- and D-strings, between the arpeggios of G minor or major and A♭ major, delighted at A♭'s 'leading' tendency back to my tonic G.

In its *alternativo* major-mode sections, i.e. during the second theme and its own variations, the movement must not be allowed to go to sleep over the inner parts' semiquaver movement, as it can often be heard to do, even in public performance. Flow and blend, please; don't play 'beautifully', for heaven's sake, and thus destroy the beauty of the melody – which, needful to add, has to be played with Tost-like phantasy, with true individualism. The way in which Haydn injects rondo form into this variation movement need not be described in detail: any player who is incapable of distinguishing between a recapitulatory thematic return and its opposite in the circumstances, i.e. a variational move away from home, can hardly hope to cope with the work's most elementary interpretative demands.

The *Allegro* is evidently intended to follow without a break – as if the enormously expansive *andante* had been a mere expanded slow introduction! The curious, breath-taking fact is that despite the respective proportions, in a well-feelable way it actually is. A two bars' G.P. introduces the theme's switch to the afore-heard Neapolitan sixth: we remember the last C major Quartet's (Op.54, No.2's: see p.121), likewise a homotonal structure's corresponding switch of the first movement's first subject to A♭ major – which, after (or rather, before) all, is the dominant's Neapolitan sixth. Nor is this the last correspondence between the two works: once again, Haydn out-Haydns his monothematicism in that the second subject starts like the first, here availing itself of the relative major mode's mood-changing contrast; a mere aping of the opening phrasing would therefore be musically absurd: the changing mood has to be phrased.

The fugal development, on the other hand, is without precedent – unless we want to invest the other, equally homotonal F minor Quartet's (Op.20, No.5's: see pp.60f.) fugal finale with precedent significance! In any case, the interpretation must take the greatest care to be clearly and audibly conscious of the overlapping recapitulation – an entirely new type of recapitulatory climax, it will even be instinctively admitted. For the rest, so far as both theme and fugue subject are concerned, the gravest danger is, simply, bar accents, which both the semibreve and the dotted minim tend to push people into. The only legitimate bar accent, on the other hand, is the third, up to which both the semibreve and the dotted minim with the subsequent, *acciacatura*-like upbeat turn have to lead; if it be objected that there has to be sharp rhythmic definition, my reply is that it can be made all the sharper without metrical stresses, though bar 3's crotchet value has to be unambiguously heard for the purpose, towards which end I recommend the fastest possible turn before the beat: from the phrase structure's standpoint, the upbeat's main note, the crotchet itself, has to be heard, understood, as half the ensuing legato motif, half its duration.

As we reach the tonic-major minuet, we realize that the polyphonic festival isn't over yet: if the other F minor Quartet concentrated it at the end, this one centres rather than concentrates it. The principal section's two opening parts at once prove themselves invertible (no harm in varied phrasings here!). They gradually grow into a four-part texture (expanding, at the end, into five and even seven parts), whose contrapuntal nature should not induce everybody to play equally softly or loudly: even in the strictest counterpoint, there is, at any given point, one single leading part, while the respective importance of the others varies, likewise, from stage to stage – nor is only balance involved in a natural realization of this texture: as the players get to know it better and better, they will notice ever more clearly that there are crucial points (though not counterpoints) of desirable perfect blend too.

When phrasing the first part of the tonic-minor *Trio*, it may prove fruitful to remind oneself that it is in F minor so long as there is no harmony, and turns to the relative major as soon as there is.

Rosemary Hughes thinks this quartet is neglected because 'its pungency places it outside the range of expression regarded as representative of Haydn by our "type-casting" habits of mind' – which, since these lines were written, have undergone drastic changes so far as our views of what is representative of Haydn are concerned, whereas this highly personal work's relative unpopularity and neglect haven't changed a bit: Rosemary Hughes' cause has gone, but its alleged effect remains; the quartet continues to be played far more rarely than any of the 'celebrated' ones, though on the few occasions when the public does get a chance to hear it, its success is strikingly immediate, incisive, and indeed indistinguishable from the success of the famous quartets. About its 'pungency' we do not, of course, have any quarrel with Rosemary Hughes; it is, in fact, the work's very pungency that makes it a spontaneous success, nowadays, with every music lover who is allowed to hear it.

But the reason for the work's continued neglect has to be sought elsewhere, nor is it all that difficult to find: I would indeed suggest that it is the playing difficulty of the quick movements – the second and the fourth – which frightens people off whose knowledge of Haydn is not so intimate that they feel the irrepressible and utterly natural urge to get right inside every mature F minor work of his that comes their way. At the same time, it must be unequivocally stressed that the textures of these movements are not, as such, problematic. I have myself frightened players off one or two quartets in the preceding pages, but I should never dream of including the present work in our temporary black list. The one thing which has to be avoided throughout the work is any hint of rough playing. I am, threateningly, raising the subject before we inspect the *Finale*: it is in the last movement that roughness is most frequently heard on the one hand, and that it has the most devastating consequences on the other; ironically enough, players will find that without the slightest suspicion or roughness, the *Finale* is in fact far easier to play.

Haydn was the first composer to make us expect a form, not in view of his successive structural events, but in view of the sheer character of his themes. The opening theme of the *Finale* seems such a typical rondo theme that the last thing we expect is a movement without the remotest rondo implications – yet this is precisely what the ensuing, essentially monothematic sonata structure discloses. This idea of creating expectations (which are as definite as they prove definitely mistaken) by means of thematic character was taken up by both Mozart and Beethoven with enthusiasm, though both of them did also use the rondo expectations for their sonatas' later rondo implications, for the purpose of combining sonata and rondo form – Mozart in the finale of his D major 'Solo' Quartet composed a year later, and Beethoven in the last music he wrote before he died, i.e. the second finale for Op.130 – where, however, the rondo or sonata-rondo implications are extremely subtle and deliberately far-fetched, such as the inescapable experience of a central episode which, later, turns out not to have been one. But Haydn, strong as was his influence as a creator of pseudo-prophetic thematic character, remains the only one to have gone all the way – to have made us definitely expect one thing in order just as definitely to confront us with another, in fact, *the* other. Trust Haydn to go the whole hog; we would have expected the uncompromising Beethoven to do likewise, and in his last composition he virtually did – except that his rondo theme, its character, is not the only indication of a rondo that never was, is, or will be.

Such reflections don't turn their back on questions of interpretation: as a player, too, not only as a composer, one can characterize a theme as a rondo theme – a matter not only of cadential emphasis but also of playing a theme in a way which will create the expectation of more than one return. In fact, the first part of the *Finale*'s theme is composed, all the way, as a repeat: it would sound incomplete, unbalanced, without one. Needless to add, that absolutely necessary repeat never happens; Haydn replaces it with a variation, as he has done on other occasions, in the slow movements of Op.9, No.4, and Op.42 (see pp.27 and 85). But whereas previously and indeed in all 'normal' classical variations, notes have been and are added to the theme by way of variation, the present variation consists, *inter alia*, of the very opposite – the omission or deletion of harmonically inessential notes: compare the 'theme' (Ex.48) with its variation (Ex.49)!

Ex.48

Ex.49

Unobtrusively, Haydn thus introduces an entirely new principle, a new method of variation; this time it will indeed be Beethoven who will go the whole hog – at the beginning of the *Eroica*'s finale. What's more, Beethoven will have it both ways: as theme, the opening will have normal consequences in the variations, i.e. more notes; *but as initial variation of a theme which will emerge later*, the opening is reduced to its bare harmonic essentials.

Though viola and cello fill in, syncopatingly, the open spaces created by the loss of melodic notes in bars 7 and 9, the first violin will have to be active too in re-characterizing the melody, now closely followed by the second: one ought almost to be able to hear those two swallow the notes in question – an effect which can *not* be achieved by shortening the preceding notes, but, on the contrary, by turning these into imperceptible, truly microscopic *tenutos*. A basic condition is, of course, a delicate style (no roughness!), which the *piano* framework obviously demands: even the first *crescendo* leads back to a *piano*.

The second fiddle really plays a double role in the varied repeat: where, in the aforementioned bars, it supports the leader's suppression of the original melody's repeated notes, it switches, in bars 8, 10 and 11, to *supporting from above* (!), the two lower instruments' varying accompanimental rhythm, which is a pure, ultra-quartetlike example (trust Haydn again!) of an immaculate, finest-grained borderline case between accompaniment and subordinate part – or rather, a prototype of what is accompaniment in one elementary and elemental respect, and subordinate part in another. Harmonically, that is to say, we have to play these three parts as accompaniment, but rhythmically, we have to lend them the character, articulation and definition of joint subordinate parts, and contrasting subordinate parts into the bargain, for the contrast with the accompanimental rhythm of the 'theme' requires a sharply contrasting phrasing, which will aim at a distinct but discreet accent on the third of the four quavers of which the motif consists – discreet enough not to disturb the first violin's phrasing, whose main stress happened three quavers ago.

Let nobody think that Haydn's eagerness to expose the character of a rondo theme made him behave more simply or stably harmonically than he would otherwise have acted! On the contrary, it was his continued harmonic adventurousness in such circumstances which, in my submission, stimulated and encouraged the latest Beethoven's own harmonic adventure in the afore-mentioned (non-) rondo theme – the last basic idea of his creative life.

In the present context, Haydn has not forgotten his beloved homotonality and its – invariably demonstrable – purpose, to wit, daring harmonic enter-prise within the unifying tonal framework thus established: it was because the mature Mozart, as opposed to the mature Haydn and Beethoven, was infatuated with daring melodic rather than harmonic enterprise that notwith-standing his relative key economy, he showed no interest in homotonality, whereas Beethoven again followed Haydn in this respect.

Not only, then, does the alleged rondo theme modulate to the dominant (the key of the unforehearable second subject) at the end of its first part and its varied repeat, but the further course of melodic events almost assumes developmental character at a crucial, i.e. again cadential juncture: we extend ourselves as far as a perfect cadence in G minor! And don't molest Haydn with a textbook rejoinder, to the effect that G minor is but the relative minor of the home key's subdominant: if you play this emphatically – i.e. plannedly – unpredictable modulation into unsuspected harmonic territory as a matter of straightforward melodic course, you haven't begun to divine the experience Haydn is driving home – away from home. The *subito piano* at the initial swerve to G minor must be carefully heeded: its melodic significance, as a varyingly echoing afterthought, must not be allowed to hide its central harmonic function, which can only be realized if the ensuing *crescendo* starts late enough, so that the cello's overlapping, newly-found dominant pedal still enters and, in fact, unfolds for a half-bar's duration on a clear and positive *piano* level; the *crescendo*, short and, proportionately, dramatic, must not start before the second quaver of the bar and will have to have reached its *forte* aim well before the G minor cadence which, together with the phrase whose end it defines, has to unfold on the *forte* level itself. The phrase's upbeat, then, while having reached unmistakable *forte* level, must not be disfigured by an accent – which doesn't follow on the main beat either, but has to be saved up for the G minor chord's fifth-less sonority before the quaver's G.P.; Haydn is careful to help us avoid the merest suspicion of an accent on the upbeating quaver, in that he does not allow the cello to participate in the motion. As a result, the cello's own *forte* will be reached a quaver later. The ensuing *piano subito*, needless to add, is but one instance of one of the movement's structural cornerstones: a paradigmatic example, this, of how dynamics have to be understood, invariably in the mature Haydn (at and after 40), as an essential aspect of his structures. Now, if they always are structurally essential anyway, what's paradigmatic about this particular example? Its unmistak-ability, which makes it serve as a prototype for instances where one or the other player might feel that the dynamics are incidental rather than essential. A quick reminder of their role in this movement will force such a player into second thoughts about the seemingly incidental dynamics he is examining.

For an exhaustive understanding of this particular instance of Haydn's homotonality, finally, it isn't enough to feel oneself fully into the harmonic adventures which happen within this framework and depend on it for their unification and cohesion – for their large-scale, their total togetherness. There is a motive as well as a reason why Haydn cast his two F minor masterpieces in a homotonal frame, and an understanding of that motive is needed for one's comprehensive comprehension not only of the present work but, in fact, of both F minor quartets; the reason why I raise the point upon the occasion of the second rather than the first F minor Quartet is that the first seems so readily accessible that the reader might have grown impatient with me had I warned him that he might not yet completely understand it.

Haydn's motive for homotonal F minor quartets must, of course, have been his particular, personal feelings about and for that key: once he had decided to write in his most personal, most characteristic key, he would undoubtedly try to make the most of it – and an F minor composition which is homotonal offers more chances for F minor thoughts than an F minor work that isn't.

What I am suggesting may seem, at best, a vague truth, in that for once, it can't be factually exemplified: without understanding what F minor meant to Haydn, and what he did towards conveying this secret meaning to us, we can't really get to the bottom of the F minor quartets.

Any player or 'mere' reader who has penetrated the secret of another great composer's most personal key will know at once and exactly what I mean – be it Mozart's G minor, or Beethoven's C minor (even if the reader's instinctive understanding of the composer's feelings about that key should be confined to the Fifth Symphony), or Mendelssohn's E minor (in whose orbit the reader will spontaneously include the *Midsummer Night's Dream* Overture, despite its major-mode opening), or Bruckner's D minor (is there another sympho-nist with two major specimens in the same key which, paradoxically, has a deeply personal extrapersonal source – Beethoven's Ninth?), or Schoenberg's own D minor (the only musical character trait he shares with Bruckner?) . . .

And in order to get at the root of Haydn's F minor, more characteristic than which we can't find a single other great composer's personal key, we have to play, and listen to, as much F minor Haydn as possible – confining ourselves, I would suggest, to the mature Haydn's F minor output, for the immature Haydn's F minor is proportionately less characteristic and might even, in certain instances, impede the searcher's understanding by introducing de-characterizing elements of confusion.

By the present stage in this book, the reader will probably believe me when I say that normally, I loathe talking in such abstract terms about what is, when all's played and done, the concretest mode of human thought – music; strictly logically speaking, it is, in fact, the only totally concrete form of thought, for in conceptual thought, as we have seen (p.15), even the concretest notions involve a degree of abstraction, however minimal.

But when one speaks about a greater composer's favourite key, considerations are involved which do not keep within the terms of reference of pure musical thought – psychological considerations which are concerned, not with universal truth, which is the subject matter of great musical thought, but, on the contrary, with musical motivations whose truth is confined to the psyche of a single individual genius. Conceptual, verbal language is not capable of dealing with such motivations, except in terms of abstractions which can't throw any light on them – for the motivations are doubtless as wholly concrete as all musical thought is. In order to get out of this loathsome, but inescapable collection of abstract pointers and reminders, let me simply say that Haydn's F minor can't be fully understood except as *Haydn's* – as opposed to any other, above all Mozart's – F minor (cf.pp.58f.!), and that such understanding inevitably grows with one's instinctive, but none the less certain appreciation of the difference between Haydn's concrete F minor thoughts and his concrete thoughts in any other key: the more mature Haydn we play, the deeper and clearer our instinctive understanding of his very own key will necessarily become; other composers' F minor, too, will help to crystallize Haydn's.

In the English-speaking world, Haydn's second F minor Quartet bears the nickname 'The Razor' – or perhaps only in this country: I have not encountered it amongst North American quartet players. However, it seems that the nickname is actually of historical interest. When the London music publisher Bland visited Haydn at Esterház, the composer happened to be shaving, and exclaimed that he would give his best quartet for a good razor. Bland entered into the bargain, and we enter into its spirit: 'His best'? Maybe not, since there are 45 of them – but there certainly is none more personal, and we are not surprised that Haydn, perhaps half-seriously, considered his second F minor Quartet his best.

Op.55, No.3, in B flat major
(Hoboken III:62)

I have had no closer musical friend in my life than Deryck Cooke: when we agreed with each other, our reasons were identical, as I discovered early on in our friendship, in the course of a night-long session on the Haydn quartets, the like of which I have experienced only with one other person, H.C. Robbins Landon, years ago.

When I joined the BBC in 1959, I started collecting many of the notes Cooke wrote for so-called 'presentation' – the announcers' scripts introducing individual works. Unfortunately, I don't know the date of the only note of his that has ever puzzled me; it must certainly have been written well before the early sixties when I began to coach and promote countless radio productions of the great Haydn quartets (and, incidentally, also of the Mendelssohn quartets which, at that time, were completely unknown, even to quartet players of every description!):

> Haydn composed so many great string quartets that even some of the finest of them are rarely performed; but Op.55, No.3 in B flat major is a particularly unfortunate case – it's hardly ever performed at all. It's difficult to understand why, since it can bear comparison with any of the others . . .

I well remember being absolutely stunned when I first saw this note: where I had grown up, the present B♭ Quartet (whose likely date of composition is, again, 1788) was one of the most popular Haydn quartets altogether, and had been included in all editions of his 'celebrated' quartets – even the one which confined itself to 'Ten Famous' ones, probably in an attempt to allow Haydn as many great quartets as Mozart had written.[1] I personally knew the work intimately by the time I was seven – for the simple reason that amongst the 'famous' ones, it was thought to be one which was relatively accessible, technically speaking, to players with little quartet experience – and hence, of course, to children. And indeed, all its themes confirm my own theory about the reasons for the popularity of certain Haydn quartets which are no

---

[1] In my *Score* article on 'The Interpretation of the Haydn Quartets' written well before I joined the BBC (*op.cit.*), I described the present work as being 'too celebrated for words'.

greater or, for that matter, less great than any of the others from the 45: a cursory inspection of the work will disclose the simple fact that there is thematic symmetry all the way, so that the rhythmic structure of the opening theme – 8 (4 + 4) + 8 (4 + 4) – could itself be described as thematic – cyclically thematic, in fact! For the rest, the extreme popularity and extreme unpopularity of one and the same work in different parts of the world is, I suggest, sufficient proof of the utter musical irrelevance and indeed meaninglessness of a work's popular status – even amongst players, professionals.

A relatively short time of playing study is needed for the realization of the work; a quartet which lives with Haydn won't encounter any difficulties at all, even though, most exceptionally, the initial four-bar model for all the ensuing symmetries is an octave-unison, as is the consequent's corresponding, half-identical opening phrase; each has to stress its *piano*, of course. Did Tost perhaps have the talent of hypnotizing his players, through his tone production and its modulation, into clear and well-blended unison playing? In all these decades, I have known one such leader – Oskar Adler, who was Tost-like, too, in the way he tackled the improvisatory slow movements of the Tost Quartets. In my experience, one other player exerted a Tostian influence on the quartet, improvisatory feats included: he did it from, of all places, the cello's; it was the Austrian composer Franz Schmidt. Adler, incidentally, was able to lead a quartet from the viola – as all the quartet-playing great composers must have done.

Tost emerges more unmistakably in the *adagio*'s variations, especially the first, whose demisemiquaver figurations need all the imaginative finesse in the world, while the second violin need not, on this occasion, save anything up for the first; it will, of course, remember the first's theme, of which its own theme will now be a variation: in most of his variation movements, Haydn lets the theme recur passacaglia-like – in order, it seems to me, to achieve two-dimensional variations, the player's as well as the composer's, and thus to let the string quartet play at its most characteristic, with its own generous creative contribution, which has to take shape by way of improvisation.[2]

The coda succeeding the two variations has to be interpreted with a full understanding of its confirmatory role – whence we have to be able factually and specifically to say what, precisely, it confirms. It's no good saying 'The end of the structure!', for though doubtless true, this type of answer begs the question of what kind of structure we are confronted with. The movement's seeming and deceptive simplicity serves its large-scale, total structural function: what is its exact role in the context of the whole work and, particularly,

[2] I think that my interpretation of Haydn's need for passacaglia-like variation structures receives support from two separate sources. For one thing, that is, the need hardly manifests itself outside his chamber music, and for another, it can be shown not to be congenital – a creative character trait: it grew stronger with the maturity of his quartets, whereas in the works of his early maturity, it is hardly apparent at all; the variation movement of Op.20, No.4 in D major, for instance, gives us little indication of what was to become an almost invariable structural principle.

after what has happened by then, i.e. the first movement? We have pointed out before (see p.51) that the choice of subdominant for the slow movement is, invariably, motivated by the total structure's need for repose, and after the first movement's complexity of development and modified recapitulation with its chromatic harmony and counter-themes, an unconditional demand for repose arises, which both the theme and its variations meet, whereupon the coda points to, and thus intensifies, the repose which has now been achieved. This kind of concrete discussion of what is usually described, perhaps a little misleadingly, as the 'mood' of the music can actually promote the clarity of one's phrasings, whose relaxed character has to impress itself upon the listener, especially the listener amongst one's playing colleagues, as a palpable reaction to the opening movement's tension – which was not altogether relieved by its own recapitulation, but, on the contrary, in places even intensified.

The minuet's simplicity is, again, deceptive: its contrasting ideas, which have to be defined with infinite respect for their individual character and without any respect for the dance rhythm which, if one kept its continuity alive, would destroy – i.e. metrically standardize – them, have to achieve continuity through the way in which they respond to each other, not by way of a superimposed one-two-three; in fact, there are structural junctures, the second bar as opposed to the first being an early example, which would be altogether annihilated by any suspicion of one-two-three. If you want to suspect anything there, it will have to be four-five-six, with an unaccented 'four' to boot: whereas the upbeat phrase makes itself felt as an incomplete $^3/_4$-bar, its resumption in bar 1 introduces the first contradiction of expectation, in that the main beat into which it has led at the beginning is now suppressed in what has become a virtual $^6/_4$-bar, and thus transformed into a continuation of the upbeat which leads to a secondary accent, a not so main beat, in bar 3; the primary accent is deferred until bar 4 – the end of the first four-bar phrase.

The tonical *Trio* has thematic as well as harmonic reason for its refusal to change key; it presents a far-reaching thematic contrast which – yet another innovatory thought here! – overlaps with the principal section. For latently, this contrast happens, not at the beginning of the *Trio*, but at the end of the minuet, whose final cadential figure introduces a brand-new thematic character, though its newness is not obtrusively manifest, hiding as it does behind the discharge of tension which the perfect cadence affords.

Mind you, as the motif becomes the *Trio*'s sole thematic material, it does change character to the extent of replacing its *forte* masculinity with a lyrical, *piano dolce* legato, but the fact remains that despite this mollification, this trans-sexualism as it were, it is not even subjected to variation: much depends on the player's expressive power for the contrast within the contrast, the change of sex while the face remains the same. But if the key had not remained the same, the entire creative adventure – which, for a start, turns a conclusive end into the most preparatory of beginnings – would have gone for nothing.

No doubt Haydn was thinking of Tost's imagination at this transitional change; no doubt the leader-reader of the present lines will, in his turn, except this moment as one of his finest hours.

Mozart possibly did, nor am I letting my grammar slip: I am indeed concerned with one of his, Mozart's, finest hours; of Haydn's we are now sufficiently aware. But we can just feel how this thematic transformation must have tickled Mozart – if, that is to say, the assumed date of the present work's composition is wrong; otherwise, it was Mozart's innovation that tickled Haydn – which again we could feel without difficulty. What am I talking about? The simple fact that much the same thing happens in the first movement of Mozart's Clarinet Trio of 1786. If this B♭ Quartet of Haydn's was, by any chance, composed two-odd years earlier, Mozart had it from Haydn; otherwise, Haydn had it from Mozart. I find this puzzle downright gratifying, for the answer makes sense either way – but only in the case of these two composers, as distinct from any other two, Schumann and Mendelssohn included: Mendelssohn was far more of an inspiration for Schumann than Schumann for Mendelssohn. It is, of course, arguable that Haydn was the stronger inspirer of the two; Mozart would certainly have said so.

What, then, happens in that Mozart movement is that the closing cadential phrase of the first subject becomes the opening, basic phrase of the second. Since Mozart's monothematicism, when it does occur, is almost always stimulated by Haydn's, I feel tempted to suggest that Mozart's own thematic transformation might be evidence of the fact that we got the date of this Haydn quartet wrong. No matter – either way, the innovatory stimulation would be wholly and deeply comprehensible; what is most unlikely is that each of them thought of it alone: their creative and always specifically stimulating friendship urges us to think in terms of a single structural inventor.[3]

There are, of course, a few passages in the *Finale* to which what I said about the work's easy technical accessibility does not altogether apply; they need hardly be pointed out! What they do need is a little attention; though B♭ is not the most comfortable of keys for any of the three instruments, those passages do lie well ('like oil', Mozart would have said or, for all we know, did), and actual technical problems will not arise.

What does need pointing out is that as in the other outer movement, the *Finale*'s recapitulation is vastly enriched as compared with the exposition: the later the stage of Haydn's maturity, the stronger his aversion against mere repetition, and the stronger his desire, so far as his quartet-writing is concerned, to vary in the way we have noted in the case of the slow movement's variation technique – two-dimensionally, that is to say, making the players

[3] I have consulted H.C. Robbins Landon on this intriguing point: his chronological knowledge is unequalled, his musicality unique amongst musicologists. To cut a long story short: my tentatively revised chronology cannot have any foundation in fact, so Haydn had it either from Mozart or from himself.

improvise their side of the variational process, without which the composer's own side would inevitably sound incomplete.

The recapitulation's textural variation accomplished by the middle parts' close imitations will have to show its newness through the *played unexpectedness* of the entries: even somebody who's just come into the room and hasn't heard the exposition will have to gather from the way the entries are phrased that sensational novelty has just occurred. Nor must the cello's little upbeating imitation by inversion be allowed to go under: the upper instruments' *diminuendos* after their *fortes* have to take conscious care of it.

As for the ensuing inversion in the leading part, with the original direction of the theme being confined to the counterpointing second violin and cello, comprehensive textural clarity has to be achieved despite the *presto*, the dynamic level, and the four-part writing; ideally and, if I may say so, realizably, even the viola's little sequential, inverting motifs have to be heard, which means that what has to be audible above all is the rests between them: the ear has to be in a position to appreciate the viola's 'speaking' continuity across the rests, not just the articulation of the motifs themselves. In a word, accompaniment there is none – a rare enough state of textural affairs, extrafugally, in a master quartet!

Op.64, No.1, in C major
(Hoboken III:65)

It may be remembered that Op.33's sequence of keys was B minor, E♭ major, C major ('The Bird'), B♭ major (the quartet we ignored), G major, and D major. For incomprehensible reasons (if any), Op.64 shows a partly different sequence of the same keys: C major, B minor, B♭ major, G major, D major ('The Lark'), and E♭ major. If any: reasons are highly unlikely, motives aren't altogether. With the exception of one key, the two series consist of keys which Haydn used frequently, anyway: there are 7 great C major quartets, 5 B♭ majors (or 6, if you include the 'small' work from Op.33), 5 G majors, and 6 D majors. The exception is, of course, B minor, which occupies a very special position in Haydn's quartet output: we have noted that he introduces 'progressive tonality' into both his B minor quartets (see p.65), starting them in D major. And the B♭ work from the present opus we certainly shan't ignore: it is a supreme and sublime masterpiece.

Not that it is for us to guess the motivation of Haydn's repeat – or rather, his variation. That Op.33 occupied a special place in his mind seems likely, or at least possible, in view of what he said about it to his publisher (see p.64); the association of its keys may have been proportionately strong, as may the motivation of the choice of each single one of them: in the case of B minor, this was palpably the case. One striking fact certainly supports the assumption of motivation, perhaps even musically significant motivation, at least in an autobiographical sense – the fact that the variation includes quite a little repeat performance, for three of the respective six quartets appear in the same order: B♭ major – G major – D major. That G major has the tonic minor's relative major on one side and the dominant on the other – parallel keys in their second-subject and slow-movement functions – does not, in the circumstances, feel like a matter of chance; that, as a matter of sheer intellectual decency, one is hardly entitled to guess any further feels like the frustration of an interrupted cadence without its enjoyment.

Haydn was 58 now: it is fair to say that he had definitely reached the extensive plateau of his ultimate maturity; if we think back to Op.20, we realize that his very maturity covers a developmental span which other important composers' progress from immaturity to maturity cannot remotely rival.

The maturest Haydn was getting ever more conscious of the string quartet's possibilities of extreme textural variation, and the mature Beethoven was going to be grateful to him for ever after, as we notice in every single work of his. In the case of this, the fifth of Haydn's seven great C major quartets, need one say more than that it starts as a normal string trio, which exposes the entire theme of the first movement's first subject, and finishes in stressedly full quartet texture, which yet achieves a concluding *pianissimo* of unprecedented delicacy, the veritable prototype of *'leggiero'*, which is only not printed verbally because the music itself makes it quite clear that there is no conceivable alternative? Except for bad playing, of course: once again, the interpreting quartet has to be deeply conscious of both the structural and indeed the textural significance of Haydn's dynamics, which only make sense if they are heard as an intrinsic part of the musical invention itself.

On the whole, the question of bad playing simply should not arise: the work is still easier than the last quartet of the preceding set, except for one or two tricky passages which soon lose their terror on closer acquaintance. Op.64, No.1 is, in fact, recommended as stepping-stone no.2 into the great Haydn – immediately after the second great D minor Quartet, Op.42.

The opening string trio, then, is easy; all the greater the need to make it great. This time, it isn't one instrument preparing for another's climactic restatement; the first violin has to make its own *piano* version an introduction to its *forte* restatement, whose first phrase will be an octave-unison with the second violin, and hence marginally less free than its *piano* model. Bar 2's upbeating semiquaver motif has to think of its later 'tutti' version (bar 10), too: first violin and viola will allow themselves a jointly characteristic phrasing where the upper three will, inevitably, have to aim at a slightly more quasi-orchestral effect that has to be turned into a full- and well-sounding contrast to bar 2's more acute characterization – which, all-importantly, must not yet give us the remotest inkling of the next bar's *crescendo*.

Bar 2's *sforzato* does not only pin-point the main accent of the phrase, but also serves the negative purpose of removing what might have been accepted as that selfsame accent from bar 1's first beat; without such warning, it can safely be assumed that this first-bar stress would, in fact, explosively occur. Indeed, how often one actually hears it, and in the most distinguished circles too. Notwithstanding Haydn's precautionary measures, if often splits the phrase, now saddled with two principal accents, into meaningless two. Yes, easiness is one thing, ready comprehensibility another.

In due course, that selfsame, upbeating semiquaver motif proves one of the central sources of the movement's essentially monothematic build-up; in the context of the second subject, the second violin will, of course, have to succeed in phrasing it contrastingly, in accordance with the hitherto unexpected and unsuspected lyrical turn of structural events: see Ex.50, bars 6ff.

But the first violin's subordinate part at this stage (*ibid.*) is of quite especial interest. In one respect, Haydn here creates a yet subtler tone-colour melody for the first violin than in the finale of the 'Frog' Quartet, for while the melodic elements of the two are wholly identical, the textural position of the melody isn't: far from its being the principal part, it is the colour melody that raises what would otherwise have been mere accompaniment to the textural status of a prominent subordinate part, which must indeed be played as such; so long as the intrinsic *piano* is heeded, the absence of changes of pitch removes any risk of its being played too obtrusively, of its 'beating' the second violin's principal part – which, to the extent of the colour melody, has to be omitted from the recapitulation: a striking proof, this, if proof were needed, of the colour melody's indispensability. One is tempted to describe it as the most principal subordinate part ever.

On top of it all, Haydn makes structurally sure, too, that the tone-colour melody will receive both the interpretative and the aural attention its textural position demands – by letting it grow, flow out of a principal part that is undisturbed by any subordinate part, simply accompanied by the rest of the quartet, and which consists of a complexly gossamery combination or confluence of normal melodic elements and those of Schoenberg's (and, in the first place, Haydn's) tone-colour melody (Ex.50, p.146).

The second bar of Ex.50 is normal melody, characterized by its leaps on the one hand and their *legato* on the other, but the first combines changes of pitch with changes of colour which thrillingly contradict them and thus create uniquely melodic tension. By inviting normal arpeggio bowing across the strings, Haydn moves his a' (x in Ex.50) down in pitch but, through the open A-string, up in colour, i.e. into emphatic brightness; conversely, as he reaches the $c\#''$ (y in Ex.50), he moves up in pitch but, through reaching the D string from the open A-string, down in colour. The resultant sound is so fascinating, makes such welcome demands on one's powers of differentiating perception, that one asks oneself how it was possible for Schoenberg (see pp.66 and 110ff.) not to think of, compose, and write about conceivable combinations of these different melodic elements; the more urgently does one ask oneself this question since there is not the remotest doubt that he knew the C major Quartet from Op.64 and had, in fact, played it many times at or near the outset of his quartet life, i.e. in his mid-teens. In all likelihood, the diagnosis I have ventured of his repression of Haydn's tone-colour melodies (see p.116) will also serve as an answer to this question: his wholesale repression of Haydn's initiation of this entirely new type of melody simply swallowed up the pitch-*cum*-colour melody too. Its playing, in any case, depends on an extremely smooth *legato* from D- to A- to E-string, and back from E- to A- to D-string; not much right-arm movement, please: the strings lie closer to each other than the visual impression and, alas, also the distinct aural impression of your right arm would make us believe! Difficult the passage definitely is not: full, exclusive concentration ought to be devoted to its ideal sound, which is easily achievable.

Almost nostalgically, we welcome a formal decision which Haydn hasn't made for a long time – to place the minuet second, in the 'old order' of sonata and symphonic events. And the *Trio*, this time, moves to the tonic minor,

Ex.50

since its thematic contrast yields, to some considerable extent, to thematic continuity and surface unity. In my wide experience, it is, in fact, in the *Trio* rather than the principal section that the gravest phrasing offences are committed, chiefly by dance-rhythmically stressing bars which the structure leaves totally unstressed, such as the first (viola, mainly) or the third (violins) – simple continuations of the upbeat before the bar-line, both of them.

Note: Following Haydn's implications, bar 1's fingerings and open strings (as opposed to all later open strings) are, of course, mine, not his.

The slow movement is decidedly not a slow movement and must not be allowed to degenerate into one; its scherzoid components introduce a dance element into symphonic structure which, in due Beethovenian, Brahmsian and Mahlerian course, will make possible the appearance of minuet and scherzo in one and the same work – a formal scheme which this *Allegretto scherzando* does in fact represent in *statu nascendi*, following as it does the minuet that has freed its own place in the total structure for it. Near either end of Beethoven's symphonic life, i.e. in the C minor Quartet and in the Eighth Symphony, we find this scherzoid slow movement which isn't a slow movement combined with the minuet; only, the minuet having become the unexpected movement, it is it that follows the scherzo.

In the interpretation, all depends, of course, on the definition of the tempo character: all will be won or lost with the first eight bars – the more so since Haydn's aforenoteed passacaglia tendency (see, for instance, pp.122 and 139) manifests itself throughout the variations and imposes the creative duty on the theme-resumers to throw imaginative light on different, perhaps even contrasting sides of one and the same tempo character, the strength of whose definition will prove proportionate to the width of its possible interpretative variations!

Character definition is of prime importance for the interpretation of the *Finale* too: with *presto* as with *adagio*, it is far too little realized that any convincing establishment of tempo is largely a matter of character – which might, but need not be rendered faceless by *ricochet* at the end of the first bar and the beginning of the second: much depends on the nature of each player's *ricochet* and, above all, on the leader's phrasing intentions and the other two's adjustability and flexibility; one thing certainly must not happen – the *ricochet* taking over and interrupting the phrasing for the sake of virtuosically delighting the audience (in the main visually, needless to add).

The *piano* is an essential element of the theme's character; it, likewise, one has heard disturbed by an indelicate *ricochet*. A danger stage is reached at what I propose to call the *codetta* theme, first because the turns easily de-characterize the *presto* unless they are taken very fast (but none the less clearly) and before the beat, and secondly because of the second violin's restatement, with the first's counter-melody on top: whereas the first's *mezzoforte* statement has to evince masculine *marcato* character, the second's *piano* restatement, while abandoning none of the theme's outspoken rhythm nor indeed its and the movement's *presto* drive, will have to undergo an utterly unexpected metamorphosis into a *dolce* theme, on top of which what could be described as the first's *simultaneous response* makes perfect sense without losing any of its own graceful, elegant, yet persistent *presto* character; let's face it, contrasting, if not conflicting emotions here have to be expressed within a very short space, and partly even by means of the same thematic characters: not an easy task, though the difficulty is altogether psychological. Four bars from the double bar, relieving unanimity is reached between the fiddles, however, because the first violin lands in the second's basic phrase of the theme, the restatement: this very relief has to express itself through the phrasing of the two – who, at last, proceed in parallel cadential motion, supported by a strong and strongly articulated bass (whose quaver rests are as important as its notes), while the viola helps to clear the air for the duration of this bar by audibly interrupting its own contribution – a structurally functional switch of texture, from quartet to string trio[1] and back. Haydn's

---

[1] Not the normal string trio, though: two violins and cello are recommended as intermittent instrumentation, not for entire works!

structuralization of texture (cf.p.103) pervades all his maturest quartets.

At the very end, the deeply essential dynamic gradation I have touched upon near the outset is virtually never achieved – certainly not in public performance, where the players are preoccupied with 'projecting' the last two bars – a special type of 'bad playing' because it isn't recognized as bad. In necessary musical reality, this final *pianissimo* has to form a downright contrast to the preceding *piano* – both of them, or rather each of them, being firmly structure-bound. In one of Haydn's easiest quartets, then, it is only in the chamber that the end can be heard making sense; in the concert hall, what should be a breath-taking final contrast tends to sound like a tautology, as if Haydn hadn't known where to stop – whereas, in musical fact as it manifests itself through rhythmic structure, the end is a demonstrable and feelable compression, which is why, meaningfully played, it takes your breath away.

Finally, after all our Tost diagnoses, would one have known that this was a Tost quartet? The honest answer is no. But since we do know, there is no logical harm in being wise after the event – in trying to discover characteristics, however secondary, that were aimed at Tost; that way, we might even draw interpretative gain from our enquiry, in that we would inevitably discover, too, where Haydn specially appeals to our own phantasy.

And in this connection, I cannot help developing a little fantasy of my own, whose reality value I leave to the reader to judge. Musically as well as in terms of sheer sound, the work's most novel passage is certainly the tone-colour melody's synthesis with normal melodic progress, and the ensuing, pure colour melody that lifts what would otherwise be mere accompaniment to the musical level of a subordinate part. It is certainly conceivable that Haydn wrote this little succession of textural and structural events for Tost, which is where my historical or biographical fantasy comes in: is it possible that Haydn came to regret not having written the 'Frog' Quartet for Tost, and that this new development of the colour melody is designed to make amends?

The combination of contradictory elements of pitch and colour, in particular, seems to me to be addressed to Tost's unconventional mind and hands, for while Ex.50 is not difficult to play, the fact remains that very often when we hear it, we also hear the overcoming of a conventional, neuro-muscular inhibition which instinctively, spontaneously resists moving up for a lower note and moving down for a higher note. Can we not feel Haydn's glee as he prospectively empathizes with Tost's contempt for this inhibition and enjoys the resultant, smooth and refined *legato* as if nothing untoward had happened, as if the bow were moving the right way for higher and lower notes? Of Haydn's creative empathy with Tost's unconventionality we certainly have noted copious evidence.

Let us, then, in our turn identify with Tost in order to produce playing history's most frictionless, most single-minded, most flowing *legato*!

Op.64, No.2, in B minor
(Hoboken III:68)

And so to Haydn's other B minor Quartet: both of them, we have pointed out more than once, start in D major and are Haydn's only quartets which thus introduce a later age's 'progressive', as opposed to classically normal, 'concentric' tonality. Paul Griffiths[1] turns the G major Quartet from Op.33 into a work starting in the 'wrong key' – by misreading, I suppose, the introductory perfect cadence in G major (see p.77) as a modulation from D major into G major. The 'wrong-key' beginnings, then, are confined to the two B minor quartets.

The texture of the second is problematic – not in the sense that it is badly written, but simply because the originality of the work, exceptional even for Haydn, expresses itself in a most unusual treatment of the medium, which entails a surprising number of pitfalls for the ensemble, whose members are quite often inconsiderately exposed. It has been pointed out by many – Tovey and Rosemary Hughes among them – that this great work is unduly neglected, which remains true today; nevertheless, I would advise any but a very mature Haydn ensemble to treat it as the diametrical opposite of its readily approachable predecessor – in fact, to continue neglecting it: after all, it is better not to play a work than to play it badly. If chamber music survives – and the present book is being written towards this aim – the Haydn quartets will come into their own, or into their own again, and works such as the present one will be discovered, or rediscovered, at the proper stage of interpretative development. Since, however, this book is designed to promote the development of quartet-playing and perhaps even speed it up, its thorough discussion of the second B minor Quartet might, if all goes well, make that proper stage arrive a little earlier – so long as its player-readers will, as it were, meet their side of the artistic contract between us and not tackle the work before they feel confident that on the basis of their deep and wide Haydn experience, and in view of the mature stage they have reached in the development of their own quartet's life, they are ready for it. The date of the work is the same as its predecessor's – 1790.

Once one becomes aware of the fact that the maturer Haydn himself grows, the more does he like to start before the beginning, adopting all

[1] *op.cit.*, p.40.

manner of highly inventive devices towards that end, I mean, that pre-beginning, one realizes that even the D major start of his two B minor quartets (the other being Op.33, No.1: see pp.64ff.) must be heard, amongst other things, as a manifestation of the selfsame structural tendency to widen the arch of his symphonic thought; needless to add, the present beginning seems to owe more to that tendency than the earlier B minor Quartet's – in proportion as Haydn's genius has grown yet maturer. From the point of view of the movement's harmonic structure, at any rate, the beginning proper is not reached before the home key, though from the thematic standpoint we are, by then, in the midst of things. Nevertheless, the interpretation will gain in clarity if its awareness of the proper harmonic beginning becomes tangible – simply audible.

At the age of 58, Haydn had, as we have noted, reached the extended climax of his maturest adventurousness, which his second B minor Quartet betrays with every motif, every phrase, every textural innovation, every modulation. Even with his choice of tonality he succeeds in being exceptionally daring within a self-imposed, seemingly old-fashioned framework, which facilitates the appreciation and assimilation of his creative enterprise: by choosing B minor as his home key and, at the same time, making his total structure homotonal (which he hadn't done in the case of the first B minor Quartet!), he offers an unprecedented (and, for a long time, unequalled) chance to the most unusual and difficult key of B *major*: in it, he casts his *adagio* as well as the *Trio* of the minuet and the concluding, resolving section of the *Finale*, of which much more anon. In the first B minor Quartet, B major was only allowed a look-in for the duration of the *Trio*; the slow movement moved to the violin's own, liberating key of D major, and the last movement finished in the minor. From the playing point of view, it must immediately be emphasized that technically, no audible trace must be left of B major's unusualness: at no point does Haydn invent a composed difficulty, one which is supposed to be heard as difficulty, whose cause is the tonic major.

The delightfully 'false' D major start of the first movement, which extends, like the earlier theme's, over precisely 1⅝ bars, is in fact differently conceived and constructed, notwithstanding this captivating element of identity: it is, throughout, a solo line for the first fiddle, thus intensifying the impression of a beginning before the beginning and, thereafter, of a beginning proper, when, wellnigh shockingly, B minor's dominant seventh enters, as an upbeat, on the last quaver of the second bar – out of the blue, creating not only a sudden change in the weather, but also a downright change of climate. While the first fiddle on the one hand and the three lower instruments on the other are the protagonists of this world-shaking drama, an exaggeration of their chordal contribution would mar or even easily destroy it: they must not forget that after all, the leader had that other hand in it, too, in that what must remain his continuously leading melody throws the dominant seventh's crucial seventh and its resolution into relief.

In the recapitulation, on yet another hand – we know by now that the maturest Haydn despises mere repetitive reprises – the pre-beginning is harmonized, on the viola, by an excerpt from what is both the D major scale and the melodic B minor scale, which latter duly triumphs through the upbeating leading-note of B minor on the second violin – now on the last quaver of the first bar, not the second, as at the outset of the exposition. And in any case, B minor had gained the upper hand from the outset of the recapitulation, owing to the clear B minor implication of the end of the leadback, and of the upbeat phrase introducing the recapitulation. In short, what was the beginning before the beginning has now moved far closer to the actual beginning, overlapping with it, in fact; after all, we are well past the middle of the opening movement's structure, concerned, in topical fact, with the beginning of the end. What I am here verbalizing is the simple feel of the recapitulatory stage, without which it is impossible to phrase it, as opposed to the opening, realistically: far from telling the four players how to phrase it, I am translating their instinctive phrasing impulses into conceptual terms, in an attempt to clarify their minds about their own feelings, without which they shouldn't move anywhere near the present work.

Technically, the *Adagio ma non troppo* is easy – no more difficult, in fact, than the *adagio* of the D minor Quartet, Op.42 (see pp.85). Haydn's love of the passacaglia principle, originally hidden, is coming more and more to the fore, for reasons which seem explicable (see p.122). Only, this time, there are, as it were, two passacaglia themes instead of one, and yet my choice of the term 'passacaglia' is neither wilful nor vaguely metaphorical, for the simple reason that one of the essential features of the structure is the large-scale retention of the two themes throughout; and this retention is so obtrusive that on every single occasion when it is emphatically interrupted, we become alive – in our playing too, I trust! – to a major *melodic* event; for unlike, say, the slow movement of Op.50, No.1 (see pp.87f.), the present *adagio* evinces no *harmonic* interruptions of either theme at all.

The movement, then, is in Haydn's own double variation form, which he not only invented, but developed to a high degree of complexity and subtlety before he handed it on, not only to Beethoven (see p.134), but also, among many other geniuses, to Schoenberg, in whose hands it actually survived the very tonal harmony on which it had seemed to depend. In the interpretation of the two themes' respective rhythmic structures, the contrast introduced by the second theme's asymmetrical five-bar antecedent can be quite naturally stressed – though not, heaven beware, by way of bar accents, but, on the contrary, by means of extremely characteristic phrasing which will depend, not only on the character of this particular rhythmic structure, but also on the character of the particular quartet and its ensemble: the full quartet texture imposes demands on the players' balance and blend which are so clearly defined that I do not wish to insult the reader by detailing them; even the differences between what has to be balanced and what has to be blended, though perhaps unprecedentedly subtle, elate one through their textural clarity, their clearly audible purpose. But one piece of specific advice in this particular respect should be impressed upon the player, each of the four: if, at any stage in the movement, he cannot hear precisely what is happening, spontaneously, without having to think, infer, guess, something has gone wrong – and there actually is some likelihood that he himself is the culprit! 'In the string quartet, the other person is always right' is a maxim whose realism cannot be overrated.

Nor does my pointer to that five-bar antecedent and its asymmetry imply the first theme's symmetry. Admittedly, it seems a regular structure: 4 + 4 bars. But that would be a superficial description, for it has a perfect B major cadence in the middle, where a 'proper' theme would have it at the end – while the end itself is endless, in that its cadence is in, or rather, in Tovey's terminology, 'on' the dominant, F major. The tune therefore asks for a continuation, a consequent – but instead, we get an eight-bar structure composed against the background of a repeat: the first variation of the first theme, which the cello and then, leadingly, the leader has to introduce, naively as it were, as the repeat it isn't, thus making the listening ear aware of the fact that except at the very end of a piece, a great composer never lives down to the listener's expectations. And as the second theme unfolds in response and discloses its aforementioned, asymmetrical structure, 5 + 4 bars, we come to realize that the two themes are really one – split and split off by their first variations; for the second theme, too, or the second part of the solo theme, is immediately followed by its variation, composed against the background of its own repeat, which cello and first violin will again introduce as if nothing had happened: the listener's awareness of the forthcoming contradiction of his expectations is part and parcel of the composer's structure, which consists of expected as well as unexpected contradictions of his expectations. That far extends what we might describe as the exposition: Haydn had developed his double variation form to a degree of complexity which involves what a normal variation movement is, by its very nature, without – an expository part of the structure which goes beyond the mere statement of the theme! From the interpretation's point of view, it is entirely possible to articulate this section in a way which lets its expository function sink in.

From now on, however, the two themes do close up into one: variations succeed each other without implied repeats, as if a theme and variations had been written where the theme has repeats, but the variations haven't. The four variations, or four variations each, include devices both simple and subtle, such as, antichronologically speaking, the Schoenbergian 'octave transposition' at the beginning of the third variation, where we suddenly realize that this conjunct motion, a straight scale from the dominant up to the tonic, is really the 'theme', the basic idea, whereas the leaping sequence of the initial theme is a variation on, or of it. Haydn here notates the only *piano* of the movement: he evidently, and very convincingly, wants a hushed appearance of the theme of the theme; the *piano*, therefore, has to be played climactically, not suppressingly. Quite generally, the highlighting significance of many a *piano* is but rarely realized, with the result that the *piano*'s tone production tends to be negative, denying as it were a *forte*, rather than reservedly, containedly expressive.

The coda, summing up the movement's combined bi-thematicism and monothematicism, is exactly as long as the second theme, i.e. nine bars, but, winding up as it does, it is less pointedly asymmetrical: instead of 5 + 4 bars, it falls into 3 + 6. Having thrown that five-bar structure into relief, the quartet won't find it difficult now to point the difference – not didactically, of course, but as a natural consequence of the new phrasings. Again quite generally, many a logical phrasing is spoilt by its intellectualism, its lack of a natural emotional source, as a result of which natural accents are made to sound artificial, like a lecture on the music in question rather than a performance of it: 'This is how it goes! The proper accent is here, not there!' the player(s) seem to say, rather than play – for which reason the effect is even more boring and depressing than an essentially pleonastic lecture would have been.

Asymmetry, too, is one of the most fertile elements of the minuet, whose first part reveals a 5 + 9-bar scheme: the most regular of dance forms transformed into a veritable orgy of irregularity! But this time, most surprisingly, it actually seems that the passionately irregular Haydn 'had it' from the often passionately symmetrical Mozart – though once again, the stimulation could have gone either way, for the Mozart quartet in question was composed in the same year as the present work. It is not, then, one of his Haydn quartets, but his very last quartet, the F major 'Solo', whose minuet one is immediately reminded of in aural view of the present minuet – though characteristically, Mozart, as opposed to Haydn, makes a regular virtue of his vice of irregularity: both the principal section and the trio evince symmetrical asymmetry, 7 + 7 bars and 5 + 5 bars respectively. Whichever way one or the other admired friend's inspiration went, it must have gone one of them: that the two quartets containing Haydn's and Mozart's most asymmetrical minuets should have been written, independently, in the same year is a bit too much to ask of the God of Coincidence! For the rest, is it still necessary to point out that there is no accent, none at all, on the principal section's first main beat? Rarely in the history of main beats, strong beats, has there been one that is less main, weaker.

In their respective *Trios*, on the other hand, the two out-Mozart and out-Haydn each other, for while Mozart sticks to his Haydnesque asymmetry (albeit in Mozartian guise), Haydn produces a relaxing *dolce* contrast in the technically not so relaxing tonic major, which balances the asymmetry of the principal section by imperfect symmetry: 4 + 4 bars in the first part, but 4 + 4 + 4 bars in the second, which therefore is less symmetrical, in that the middle four are a compression – composed, that is to say, against the background of eight bars. Significantly, Haydn marks them *dolce* again, expressing the compression's tension with the relaxing sweetness of the opening phrase, with which they are identical, and of which the leader will have to remind us without, of course, aping his original phrasing.

The *Finale* rivals the slow movement in originality: Haydn may not have invented the sonata rondo, but nothing comparable to this combination of sonata form and rondo form can be found in any other composer's work, or indeed in any other work of his own. As for the textbook concept of the sonata rondo, it is, entertainingly, far further removed from this movement than either the sonata or the rondo itself.

We start out from what seems like a rondo theme, as which it can, therefore, easily be played with proportionate conviction. But we are at once persuaded that it isn't: sonata procedures take over, to the extent of the music's movement to the relative major and indeed to a second subject proper, or rather improper – for needless to add, we are once again confronted with a monothematic structure, the second subject being built out of the material of the first.

The sonata train of thought appears to pursue its course, more distinctly even than is Haydn's wont: there is an unambiguous codetta, sharply articulated, and further emphasized by the first violin being requested, to begin with, to confine itself to the G-string. The changes to and from the fifth position have to occur at pronounced articulation points: Haydn quite evidently wanted to leave it to Tost and to you whether to employ am-biguous *glissandos*, or one of them, in the service of both continuity and your intervening articulation; the possible alternative, *glissando* or no, must have played its part in his actual invention; for this particular change of position could doubtless be managed without the chin-rest (cf.p.129). My guess is that Tost, after an extended *a* crotchet, did slide up with a tasteful *diminuendo*, but contradicted the listener's expectation of a corresponding slide back, thus intensifying this second, very particular, i.e. stronger articu-lation point. What you are going to do is not for me to say – the less so since I'm not familiar with the neurotic complications which may surround your *portamento*, and for which our time, rather than your esteemed self, would be to blame in the first place; all I can say is that if they exist, I'd leave well alone.

The normal repeat of the exposition is followed by a development over-flowing with capricious invention, interruptions by general pauses included; and by the time the recapitulation arrives, separated from the leadback by one of those general rests (as they should be called, pauses being fermatas), any suspicion of rondo we might have harboured to begin with is dispelled for ever – or rather, for, a few bars.

For the reprise of the theme proceeds to behave like a rondo return: it shows no desire to move on to the second subject; and what happens instead of the second subject is, in fact – the first again! Now in B major, the concluding key of the work, it firmly, if belatedly, establishes a rondo context – which, in its turn, is quickly contradicted by an equally belated reversion to the second-subject stage: it is the codetta that leads us into the coda, as if we were in the recapitulation of a sonata structure after all. Well, so we are: the one doesn't exclude the other, though it never included it more contradictorily and, at the same time, more harmoniously, logically. That is the essence of great art.

I would submit that it follows that the interpretation of the *Finale* has to show Tost-like, almost impish, mischievous freedom, largely on the part of the first violin, which has to be firmly assured of instinctively empathetic support – one of the chief reasons, this, why the work should only be approached by a grown-up quartet which knows its Haydn, and which, preferably, has grown up together. Op.64, No.2 is one of those master quartets which, in private as well as public performance, at once reveal the slightest tensions between players, let alone long-standing ambivalences. For an ensemble's Golden Wedding-day, on the other hand, it is the ideal celebration piece – even if, at that age, the players' B major intonation should be a little erratic. But then, the only listeners admitted would be equally free of any ambivalences towards any of the players or the quartet as a whole. In the ideal chamber, that is to say, the listener 'follows' too: one can almost hear him listen.

Op.64, No.3, in B flat major
(Hoboken III:67)

As sublime and perfect a masterpiece as any, the B♭ Quartet from Op.64 (1790 again) provides negative confirmation of my little theory that Haydn's popular and much-played quartets owe their fame, ultimately, to their symmetrical structures: from the opening five-bar phrase, asymmetry abounds in this work which, consequently, never made it as one of the 'celebrated' Haydn quartets and, in fact, continues to be neglected; it is truly astonishing how few of the world's – rightly or wrongly – leading quartets have incorporated it in their regular Haydn repertory; quite honestly, at the time of writing these lines, I can't think of any!

In the opening movement, the first, highly unusual thematic contrast is an *ostinato* motif of a short quaver and two *legato* semiquavers; in order to emphasize its rhythmic meaning which gives it its character, I would suggest starting the passage off with an imperceptible metrical distortion – a marginal extension of the break between the quaver and the semiquavers, whence their value will of course be very slightly reduced. (I realize, alas, that as soon as one verbalizes such advice instead of playing, singing or whistling it, it tends to be exaggerated.) The cello can, of course, please itself at the outset, so long as it doesn't forget its dynamics; but with the entry of the middle parts, improvisation has to yield to structure which, at the same time, will establish a natural continuation of whatever the cello's fanciful rhythm introduced to begin with: now the two have to sound like the one instrument we have heard so far, perfectly blended rather than balanced, and including in their utterly natural continuation the *character* of the cello's *piano* – its colour, or rather, a natural, recognizable variation of its colour, whose identity cannot, of course, be retained. At the same time, there is no need now to revert pedantically to the metrical values: my cautious advice applies to the middle parts too – the more so since the cello now underpins the *ostinato* with its quavers on the beat.

A different, very perceptibly varying approach will have to be adopted as from the 9th bar of the development, whence the textural situation and the mounting course of events is emphatically identical with the exposition's, but only in order to throw into relief this *tertium comparationis* – and thus the downright polarity between the expositive, B♭ appearance and the developmental, A♭ reappearance of the *ostinato* passage, which the recapitulation, meaningfully enough, leaves clear and undisturbed, unaffected even: against almost certain expectation, the reprise simply ignores this striking, well-remembered event. The interpretation will have to vary its developmental resumption yet more drastically than it would have varied its recapitulation – in proportion as it points differences which are glaringly obvious from the very outset: where the exposition continues the opening B♭ major, the developmental A♭ resumption grows out of its own relative minor. One possibility for the cellist, as well as presently for the others, is to do as if nothing had happened – to the extent of making it at first appear as if the exposition had really been a variation of what now emerges as the more ordinarily played *ostinato*, with less, yet less contradiction of its metre! However, this is but one possibility amongst countless ways in which the musical imagination can make sense of this polarity on the basis of a clearly perceived identity.

In the *Adagio*, the second violin has to listen to its balance very carefully: it mustn't forget that its solo bars in the principal section proceed under the first's *held* notes, in aural view of which textural relation there is no need whatever to force the dynamics (*mezza voce*) – the less so since the lower two play a purely accompanimental role too, entirely supportive. They as well as the leading second fiddle won't, I trust, fall into what one might describe as the all too frequent first-bar trap: the aim of the first bar's respective phrases is – needless to add by now, one hopes – the second. The antecedent-consequent relationship between the two fiddles is rendered more complex and subtle by the leader not being silent while the second violin speaks, while the second, together with the lower instruments, observes at least partial, respectful silence during the more flowering responses of the first – though carefully considered, the silences don't cover the actual answers, but the ensuing upbeat phrases, which the three lower instruments should be heard to be glad to leave in peace; it is up to the first violin's free phrasing thus to convey the lower instruments' happiness! The silences should not, however, encourage the leader to indulge in unusual liberties; what one hopes are his usual liberties will be quite enough.

The middle section is simply, or rather complexly, a variation of the theme in the tonic minor – which, however, happens to be E♭ minor; it can, perhaps, best be characterized negatively, by pointing out that Mozart would never have dreamt of doing such a thing – not only because of the six flats, which only lead us to the relative (G♭) major, but also because he'd have preferred a contrasting theme to an equally contrasting variation: it was left to Haydn to invent the paradox of paradoxes – monothematic ternary form. Admittedly, Mozart took it up, respectfully and a little half-heartedly, in a single movement – the second of, naturally enough, his second Haydn quartet, where four bars of the central contrast are a variation on the movement's theme, whereas the other, consequential four bars are newly invented melody! In the present movement, the first violin will please inventively revel in the contrast: the fact that it is but a variation would even make itself felt against his will – if 'but' is the word: the contrast is as far-reaching as Mozart's unthematic (read: sub-thematic) contrast would have been.

The recapitulation is, of course, varied too: in particular, the triplet rhythm will have to be brought out, or rather, in, as a new and utterly unforehearable element; both fiddles have to express their delighted astonishment at the news – the more so since it will prove the recapitulation's leading event, in that *not a single bar* will be without this rhythm or its own variation, to wit, the suppressed first notes of the triplets. Show me a recapitulation by any other composer whose principal feature is something that never happened in the exposition, or the development, or the middle section, and forms a veritable contrast to all that has happened before! It will therefore have to be played as a new thematic contrast at a stage where thematic contrasts are no longer expected – nor do its intermittent accompanimental guises detract from its newness, which almost lends those mere accompaniments the appearance of subordinate parts, as which they will have to be played – almost!

It is in this conrete way that one will be able to realize, characterize and define Haydn's style, rather than through historical authenticity which, while it unsuccessfully tries to recreate the sounds of Haydn's time in physical and psychological conditions which cannot help being vastly different from his own, makes barely any difference between the sound of his music and that of Boccherini's or Dittersdorf's. In artistic reality, the difference is not only world-shaking, but we actually understand it better, hear it more clearly, than did the ears of Haydn's own time, Mozart's apart. In this all-important sense, then, our approach to his style, to his manner of expression and to the underlying, all-determining matter, is actually more direct, more knowing, quicker of hearing, than was his contemporaries' – aside from the Tosts, a tiny minority, of whom, accordingly, he made a gigantic fuss. The direct route to Haydn's style is through his creative character.

Though the opening miniature phrase of the minuet has its accent on the first bar's first beat, a really delicate interpretation will succeed in investing this stress with temporary significance, forehearing the immediate reiteration and extension of the phrase, whose previously accented beat will now prove wholly accentless. The three lower instruments can help, in that their two first-bar beats, likewise, are temporary, and can be phrased in a way which forehears the third beat when their own phrase is repeated and extended. When they come to imitate the leader's 2-3-1 in bars 8 – 9, they, and above all the now leading second violin, will have to show echoing wit, starting and continuing on as low a dynamic level as the first violin's *diminuendo* has reached with the last note of its own phrase.

The viola's imitating, accented trills after the double-bar are more difficult technically than the first violin's before it, so much so that they frequently sound quite embarrassing, especially on a relatively ill-sounding C-string and without the purposive support of the cello. It won't do the player any harm to have a few minutes' preliminary look at the passage, not in order to arrive at a firm picture of how he wants, and is able to play it, but, on the contrary, in order to give himself a broad, secure basis for various types of continuity-conscious execution, from which he will choose, in the event, the one which provides, again, the wittiest comment on the first violin's cadential pseudo-conclusion, which now gives way to the viola's (and cello's) leg-pulling continuation.

The *Trio*'s rhythmic contrast between the syncopating antecedent and the resolving ³/₄ of the consequent cannot be made too much of: it is and remains the section's basic, dominating idea, and produces one of those many contrasts with the principal section which the *Trio*'s unchanging key only serves to throw into relief. There is, of course, no contrast without unity: there is no contrast between you and an apple, but there is contrast between you and me. Nor is the unity of minuet and *Trio* confined to the harmonic dimension; unity never is. Themes belong together or they don't, and in masterpieces they invariably do. The unity between the minuet's and the *Trio*'s themes operates on the basis of what I have called the principle of reversed and postponed antecedents and consequents: the *Trio*'s aforementioned antecedent forms a natural consequent to the minuet's antecedent, at the bottom of the sharp contrast between the two build-ups (Ex.51). The *Trio*'s own consequent, moreover, can be made to follow on naturally:

Ex.51

The interpretation of the respective themes won't lose through the players' consciousness of this intimate, complementary relationship, though I won't go so far as to maintain that interpretative gain can be derived from my observation – unless, of course, it merely articulates what the players had been feeling in the first place, a condition which would, in any case, constitute the ideal relationship between analyst and recipient, the only one which is wholly musical and nothing but musical.

At all events, a combination of the two themes will be heard to lie, or rather move, at the back of the finale's theme, whose insistent semiquaver upbeat phrases will be recognized as the progeny of the minuet's quaver upbeat phrases, while the *Trio*'s syncopations now follow without our post-ponement (*cf*.Ex.51). Here, the interpretative value of this recognized unity need not be negligible: the most emphatic characterization of each theme will, at the same time and of necessity, bring out their character resemblances. Since in either case, the insistent upbeat phrase will form part of the character-ization, it ought perhaps to be pointed out that insistence all too easily produces wrong accents – on the first note of what the composer insists upon; the upbeats will lose none of their character if they are kept rigorously free of accentuation – on the contrary: the more distinctly their played shapes convey their meaning, the more characteristic and indeed insistent they will sound.

This insistence reaches its numerical culmination in the *Finale*'s leadback which, together with the opening of the recapitulation, consists of no fewer than six consecutive repetitions of the little motif of two semiquavers and a quaver. In the recapitulated theme itself, the melody looks after some part of (though by no means all) the necessary variation of the motif, but the end of the leadback consists of actual, also melodically literal repetitions of the original motif, whose diminished fifth with its dominant (seventh) function frees the line of harmonic support which, in the circumstances, would be wholly tautological: the dominant seventh chord has been sounded anyway. It's all up to the leader, then, who can invent his variations, express his changing attitude towards the motif, along countless alternative lines, so long as a truly back-leading single line is both his basic motive and the result; a steady *diminuendo* is a possibility, but only if the ensuing *mezzoforte* on the actual upbeat of the recapitulation doesn't unleash an accent: generally, universally speaking, the ability to switch to a higher dynamic level without automatically investing its first note with an accent is an absolute musico-technical requirement no string or keyboard player should be unable to meet. It isn't enough for the listener to realize retrospectively, after he has heard further notes, that the first wasn't meant to have an accent; on a bowed instrument, at any rate, its accentlessness has to be clearly audible at the moment of its enunciation, as the effect of its pronunciation – its tone production.

Towards the end of the recapitulation, the selfsame motif enjoys an event unprecedented in the exposition – an interplay between the inner parts against the syncopations in the first violin on the one hand and straight three-crotchet phrases in the cello on the other; the passage is remarkable for its four-part writing without either counterpoint or accompaniment: string-quartet writing at its most characteristic. The syncopations are, and must remain, the leading, principal part, while the other three are subordinate parts, marking the normal beat in their own way which, unless the players are careful, easily lends itself to exaggeration: the middle parts, particularly, what with the brevity of the motif and the staccato dot on the quaver, often whip themselves into incisive accents on each beat of the bar, outbeating each other in their constant alternation, which remains unaware that every single beat is audibly available quite apart from their own contribution: where the cello rests, the first violin itself marks the beat with its own staccato quavers before it resumes its syncopations. Nor indeed have I heard many leaders and viola players who were aware of their joint *staccato* quavers, two of them – which, though elements of vastly different lines, have to produce a well-blended *and* well-balanced sound; the balance is needed on top of the blend since, at these particular points, an unaccented violin-note meets the aim of the viola's phrase, and hence an accented viola-note – yet it is the violin's that is the principal part! With an explosive accent from the viola, the violin line will, of course, be lost altogether. The passage presents, in short, an ideal practice for the natural assimilation of that type of true quartet sound which can't be found in any textural situation outside the string quartet.

Op.64, No.4, in G major
(Hoboken III:66)

With the G major Quartet from Op.64, we return to the other end of the regrettable scale – to 'celebrated' symmetry – but let no one, in view of that fact, underestimate either the mastery or the sheer inspiration of the work! Asymmetry was Haydn's natural inclination, but when, for some semi-musical reason or other, he decided to impose the limitations of symmetry upon his imagination, the very limitations turned into an inspiring stimulus. The work still dates from 1790: the entire *opus* does. And we are still in the middle of the Tost quartets, which comprise Opp.54, 55 and 64, so that this is their second G major quartet, the first being the very first Tost quartet, before which Haydn only wrote one great G major quartet – in the *opus* whose keys are the same as the present one's – Op.33, No.5. Two further G major masterpieces were to follow: five altogether in this characteristic quartet key are, perhaps, surprisingly few.

As if to poke fun at whatever may have been the symmetrical requirements for this work, the opening theme out-symmetricizes its own symmetry, as it were: both the four-bar antecedent and the four-bar consequent fall, in their turn, into two-bar antecedents and two-bar consequents, and the second two-bar antecedent is near-identical with the first, the only – inspired – difference being the responsive variation of the first bar's upbeat to the second. In the circumstances, these semiquavers will have to be played with arresting significance – without losing their upbeating drive: what they do have to lose is any trace of an accent which the player's desire to play it with significance may have produced behind his back!

As for the accompaniment of the basic phrase, whose last note covers that upbeat and whose last two notes cover its variation, Op.20, No.5 (see p. 59f.), Op.33, No.2 (see p.69) and, most recently, Op.55, No.1 (see p.129) have taught us enough for the middle parts actually to listen forward to this opportunity of making sense of what is frequently presented with very little of it; the only additional observation I would allow myself is that rather gratifyingly, the second violin can choose between two fruitful alternatives in the respective second halves of the bar, which, when played on the A-string, will facilitate the tone-production vis-à-vis the first violin's principal part, whereas the D-string will facilitate the accompanimental blend with the viola. The actual choice will, of course, depend on the particular quartet's and its instruments' colorific circumstances.

The melody itself aims at the second bar and recedes, falls off, after the accent on the third. At the end of the sentence, Haydn utilizes the symmetry towards taking his revenge upon it: without it, he couldn't have added his blatantly anti-symmetrical epilogue, which turns into the transition to the transition! It has to be played as wittily as it is composed; a very light touch of irony will clarify the joke on the rhythmic structure, but anything heavy-handed will, on the contrary, destroy it. One has to express the smile one can see on the composer's face as he went from bar 8 into bars 9 and 10.

Haydn takes harmonic revenge, too: after demonstratively establishing the dominant, he side-steps it with his actual second subject, whose body he doesn't allow to settle in any key, and whose syncopations will therefore be played questioningly, i.e. ever further forward-urgingly, rather than asser-tively; it is only after the second subject's melody is over and we're back in continuous, *forte* semiquavers that the dominant is re-established – not without a flat sixth, though, a hangover from the subject's initial, labile stage, at which we had three tonical implications, the dominant minor and, to begin with, its relative major with its own subdominant. Again, the opening stage of the second subject will have to be played as developmentally, as un-'state-ment'-like, as it is composed.

For the firm and final establishment of the second-subject level is not reached before the codetta, whose *sopra una corda* (as well as, of course, the coda's) invites of hesitation on the upbeat prior to the first *glissando* ('B-portamento': see p.92).

Likewise, the contrasting *piano* character of the minuet's – once again the second movement's! – consequent can hardly materialize without a little lingering over the upbeat: the ensuing melody is of course much calmer than the more rhythmic antecedent. It is absolutely essential that after the double-bar, as a miniature development section begins (whose instability is confined to a modulation to the dominant), the second violin continues at *piano* level.

Attention need hardly be drawn to the extreme contrast which the *Trio* achieves within the tonical framework. The leader must, of course, be made to feel as free as Tost doubtless wanted to be. He should even be allowed to hasten somewhat at the beginning of model and sequence in the *Trio*'s own mini-development (whose instability is confined to a wink at the sub-dominant), and to hesitate over the leadback, as well as – is it necessary to make this point? – over the opening upbeat.

For the accompaniment of the *Adagio*'s principal section, the opening movement of Op.55, No.2 (see p.131) has taught us all there is to heed. The movement is a doubly characteristic Haydn structure – another mono-thematic ternary paradox whose tonic minor middle section contains its own paradoxical solution, to wit, a frictionless amalgam of what is normally poles apart – variation and development. It is up to the interpretation to contrast this labile harmonic structure with the stability of the principal section, though it should not be automatically assumed that the middle section will need proportionately more agogical attention: it isn't only harmony that invites freedom from metre! In fact, the principal section's own variations don't make sense without the interpretation's collaboration: once again, they quite obviously address themselves to Tost's imagination. In fact, is there any instrumentalist who has been as clearly characterized by any composer as Tost was by Haydn? Three, perhaps: Mozart by Mozart, Beethoven by Beethoven, and Chopin by Chopin. But Haydn's characterization is astound-ingly specific: fiddlers will agree that one can glean details of Tost's technique. And, more important, its musical inspiration.

The *Finale* does not show any interpretative problems, so long as unthink-ing bar accents – or, for that matter, half-bar accents! – are avoided. I must be the record-holder, so far as having heard history's stupidest accents is concerned: I even once heard a bar accent in bar 5, where the sole stress is, of course, the b''. In fact, the *presto* character is only realizable without the remotest bar accents; otherwise, however fast the actual pace, the tempo will never sound fast.

As for that famous bar 5 and its recapitulation, its phrasing has to be individual, characteristic, it can't be the result of a committee meeting, but, on the contrary, presupposes the second violin's successful, total subordination to the first: these semiquavers as well as the duration and weight of their crotchet aim really have to sound as if they came from a single player. With a vengeance, the same is, of course, true of bar 13, which is not recapitulated. For the rest, the movement's dynamics are a crucial part of its structure, from whose shaping they have to grow: they must never be superimposed – as, unfortunately, they often are.

Op.64, No.5, in D major
(Hoboken III:63)

The 'Lark' Quartet, the fifth of Haydn's great six quartets in the violin's own key (the record-holders are the seven C majors), is probably the one universally popular amongst all his works for the medium – so what has it got, or not got, on top of its seemingly blatant, but actually deceptive symmetries (as we shall see in two paragraphs' time) that is responsible for its singular status? I would suggest that its most important qualification is that the *Finale* satisfies listeners and leaders alike on a fairly superficial level which, needless to add, hides its considerable musical substance. It is the virtuoso aspect of this so-miscalled *moto perpetuo* which is giving great, two-sided satisfaction. (How can one thus describe a complex, monothematic ternary form with a fugal middle section wherein the brilliant, stressedly homophonic theme suddenly discloses its contrapuntal potentialities?)

The listener's joy is not in need of explanation, while the leader's springs from his having it both ways – virtuosically and easily: his part (and, of course, not only his) lies so wonderfully that one is almost tempted to call the movement a beginner's virtuoso piece, whereas what the listener hears is brilliant technical achievement. One particular spot apart (which will be discussed when we come to consider the *Finale* in detail), it can in fact be claimed that the movement sounds as difficult to play as it's easy: we here see one of the reasons for Haydn's choice of key.

What about those deceptive symmetries, then? If we examine the opening themes more closely, we find that Haydn actually smuggles polyrhythmic structures and textures into them. For the rhythmic structure of the opening tune does not correspond to the 'Lark's' song, to which the opening tune forms the virtual accompaniment through having turned itself into a mere subordinate part.

The interpretation of this polyrhythmic structure and texture is therefore quite a task: as a virtual accompaniment, the opening melody has to be phrased differently from its first appearance – yet not so differently that the polyrhythm is destroyed! In simpler words, where bar 2 has formed a definite phrase-ending, bar 10, while still disclosing, if by way of a less emphatic stress, the end of the 'accompaniment's' opening phrase, has to help the leader along – not to bar 11, but to bar 12, which is his own phrase-ending. The easiest role in this context is the cello's, for it, as opposed to the middle parts, had to lead on to bar 3 in the first place – though now, in bar 10, it will have to follow the middle parts' less emphatic accent by simply playing its phrase as an upbeat, whose opening D, however, will have to retain sufficient bass weight naturally to blend the chord, the more so since its quaver will have to suffice to support the middle parts' crotchets.

If the cellist-reader protests that I have hardly given a description of the easiest textural role in the world, my rejoinder is that the easiness I've been talking about is clearly relative – to the middle parts new-born difficulties. For the rest, what has been said about bars 2 and 10 is of course true of bars 4 and 14 too, so that the selfsame phrase, the middle parts' bars 11–12, will have to be quite differently shaped in bars 13–14! Such clearly defined ambiguity we definitely haven't encountered before – all part and parcel of what, superficially, seems Haydn's simple symmetry.

Nor is this the end of the story of Haydn's highly innovatory first subject. Its very transformation of a leading melody into the accompaniment of another, unpredictable and, in fact, differently organized melody gave later geniuses an idea they might well not have had without the help of musical history's innovator-in-chief. Mozart took it up for concerto purposes, turning an orchestral exposition's leading melody into the accompaniment of the solo exposition's entirely new melodic thought; the first time he did it was, it will be remembered without recourse to the score, in his A major Violin Concerto, whose orchestral first subject becomes the accompaniment of the soloist's. Mendelssohn, in his own Violin Concerto, went one step further – or, if you like, inverted both Haydn's and Mozart's steps: in the last movement, it is the soloist's theme that becomes the 'mere' accompaniment to a new melody that has grown out of the development section. In both these instances, the fiddler-reader will agree that again, the phrasing of the tune-turned-accompaniment has to be significantly altered according to its new context, which changes its rhythmic structure.

While Haydn's polyrhythmic approach continues into the second-subject stage, it will be musically convenient, at this point, to examine the opening of the development section, which is one of Haydn's beloved pseudo-identities with the opening of the exposition, though this time, the harmonic difference is immediately apparent, for while the middle parts proceed as at the beginning, the F♯ bass prepares for the reinterpretation in the subdominant, which will prompt the momentarily leading second violin to shape the phrase differently from either bar 1 or bar 9; how to reflect the new harmonic context is a matter for the second fiddler's imagination, whom the viola will have to follow. But the more outspoken, in fact, the extreme variation starts, of course, with the *legato* version of the theme that had gone accompanimental at the beginning, to wit, in the third bar of the development; Haydn's *mezzo-forte* throws it into relief as against the *piano* of the preceding hint at the original version. Without forgetting the first violin's leading role, which has, in fact, started with its (equally *mezzoforte*) upbeat phrase three crotchets before the event, the second violin, together with the viola, will make the most, the utmost, of the *legato* contrast and the differences it produces in the actual construction of the melody itself. This veritable sensation starting in bar 3 of the development section is the most illuminating lesson I know in Haydn's characteristic monothematicism and its equally sensational success – even though the present movement is not, of course, monothematic. But what the *legato* version of the theme shows our naked ears with overpowering clarity is how Haydn actually intensifies contrast by making it aspects of the same idea, rather than different ideas. With him it is, in fact, true to say that the stronger and more immediately obvious the *tertium comparationis*, the stronger, deeper, and wider the contrast: he avails himself of the natural and simple cognitive fact that the same thing seeming utterly different creates a far intenser experience of contrast than do different things. The middle parts will therefore not confine their contrasting attention to the actual melodic differences but will, underneath it all, give – under the second's leadership – full expression to their own, inevitably overpowering experience of the contrast.

It isn't only the spicy, scherzoid, essentially instrumental character of the original theme that changes into its opposite, a lyrical, essentially songlike flow in the development: another aspect of the theme, too, is replaced with its opposite and thus paradoxically aims at extreme relaxation at the high point of harmonic tension – the theme's relation to what was its polyrhythmic partner. The polyrhythm is resolved and the two rhythmic structures unfold alike; the entire quartet will, of course, have to celebrate this structural unison by its subtle and unanimous distribution of accents.

We have touched upon the entire structure's central paradox: from the point of view of rhythmic structure, it is only at the beginning of the development that complete relaxation from tension is achieved. For at the second-subject stage, too, what now proves the movement's basic motive (as distinct from its basic motif), i.e. polyrhythm, continues to manifest itself behind the popular style and its symmetrical pretexts. In fact, the syncopations of the second subject can easily be misphrased: they really have to be played as if the bar-lines had been displaced. *Sforzatos*, that is to say, continue to displace the bar-accent where it would otherwise threaten to return altogether to normal; nevertheless, enough metrical normality comes to the fore to turn the more usual polyrhythmic struggle between foreground and background into an acute, manifest conflict in the foreground itself – which is eventually resolved *subito piano*, by way of the three-crotchet upbeat which must, therefore, be clearly articulated *as against* its immediately preceding model: a slight comma after the model is what is needed in order to restore the rhythmic balance.

After the recapitulation of the two themes rolled into one, there is yet another variation of the rhythmic structure – another reconciliation, in fact, though in the opposite direction: instead of the opening theme becoming a melodious melody whose shape concurs, rhythmically, with the shape of what is no longer the counter-melody, it resolves itself into the ex-counter-melody's accompaniment, the remaining traces of its own independence being confined to the subordinate viola and cello parts. Nothing would be more nonsensical for the second fiddler than to try and save the melody from the accompaniment it has now become: the whole point of the texture is this successful metamorphosis, and it has to be played as such; unfortunately, it isn't very often. For the rest, the very fact that I have had to devote an exceptional amount of space to this 'simple' and popular Haydn movement is a measure of the hidden complexity in which he will almost invariably and successfully indulge within the limitations of his self-imposed straightforwardness, his deceptive squareness.

From the interpretative standpoint at least, to be sure, the *Adagio cantabile* is simpler and hence easier, though its complexity from the point of view of its total structure stands in direct ratio to the number of forms which – with the utmost, and ever-surprising clarity – it compresses into its structure: no fewer than four! At the same time, Haydn alternates between them with such pointed certitude that there really is no need to describe this unique build-up beyond listing them – ternary, sonata, variation, rondo. Only of one danger the players have to be warned – of not making the theme's *adagio* character sufficiently clear: many are the occasions when the movement is decharacterized by a restless tempo.

The minuet and the tonic minor *Trio* start with a $c\#''$–d upbeat which is yet another example of Haydn's monothematic extreme contrasts, of the 'same thing' being almost shockingly different. It is of the profoundest importance for the players, and above all for the leader in action in either case, to be deeply, comprehensively, unreservedly conscious of this very fact: the remotest trace of resemblance between the two upbeats, beyond the actual notes and their harmonic degrees, and beyond the fact that each of the two occupies the space of the third crotchet in a $^3/_4$ bar, would have a devastating effect on the character of the principal section's upbeat – an effect one hears all too often, though one is never quite sure whether it is actually the *Trio* that has decharacterized the minuet. The conventional approach to an upbeat is, after all, purely negative: don't stress it, don't make it sound important, don't displace on to it the main beat's weight. But avoidance never communicates; besides, each of these self-instructions is likely to change or, more often, reduce the character of the minuet's upbeat, *which has to be as unlike the* Trio's as superhumanly possible, notwithstanding the underlying identity between the two – indeed because of it.

The contrast between these two 'identical', identically unaccompanied upbeats, then, is exclusively rhythmical: any approximation to their common metre would be disastrous. For while the *Trio*'s consists of two quavers which are but the first two notes of an extended upbeat phrase, any leaning the minuet's *acciaccatura* might show towards an *appoggiatura*, towards a quaver, would simply destroy its entire function, which is that of a weighty, single-note upbeat whose very weight is indicated, and must indeed be produced, by the *acciaccatura*, which therefore has to be distinct on the one hand and as close as at all possible to the dominant to which it leads on the other.

Its downright jocular character demands, in fact, that it be stressed, receive the weight due to it, without detracting from its upbeating function, its clearly audible upbeating sound. This admittedly unusual requirement means not only theat the ensuing main beat has to receive yet more weight, but that the upbeating function, the upbeating sound must be heard before the main beat is. How do we realize this aim? Easily – by inserting a breath between upbeat and main beat: however weighty, the upbeat will now sound gravely and rightly incomplete, since it is not immediately continued; and it will thus unmistakably establish its identity and function well before the next note is heard.

The next upbeat, at the end of bar 1, cannot, of course, ape this pause, which will now emerge in a shorter version – though still long enough to form an element of definition of both the upbeat itself and indeed the tempo character of the principal section. Then, at the end of bar 2, it is resolved into the two quavers which start the *Trio* – retaining here, at the same time, an essential, characterological contrast: the minuet's are *legato*, the Trio's *staccato* (as Haydn would have said), or *spiccato* (as we are inclined to say). The opening upbeat, therefore, has to form an extreme contrast to *both* the Trio's and the minuet's own in bar 2 – which, likewise, is but the opening of an extended upbeat phrase. I'd go so far as to say that in order weightily to establish both its own character and at least one side of the minuet's, the opening upbeat has to border, however tastefully, on vulgarity, on playful heaviness.

If I am absolutely honest, with a single, ever-varying exception, and so far as performances which I haven't coached, directed, or advised have been concerned, I have only heard more or less characterless versions of this minuet – dozens and dozens of them. The exception occurred, most fortunately, very early in my life – in the quartet which Oskar Adler led and Franz Schmidt played the cello in. Until this day I remember the grins on Schmidt's face as Adler threw in entirely different, ever wittier versions of this heavy upbeat on the six occasions he had to play it within a single performance; needless to add, both the three expository and the three recapitulatory versions had something in common which contrasted them with each other in their turn.

The *Finale* is not in need of extended advice, so long as both balance and blend are well-listeningly heeded throughout: the sharpest possible listening concentration is an absolute requirement all the way; when, you might well ask, isn't it? But in the present instance, it has to be accompanied, induced by *spontaneous* knowledge, and indeed foreknowledge, of what each of the others is playing, or isn't. The leader's single awkward spot, which I mentioned at the outset, is, of course, his flying visit to the fifth position in the recapitulation's bar 22 (bar 101 from the beginning), for which a variety of fingerings is possible; your choice entirely depends, if I may so put it, on your fingering character.

In any case, three conditions have to be met: the leader has to practise the passage a little, he has to be precisely aware of the role of the others, especially the viola and cello, and they in their turn have to have a complete advance picture of the crucial bar's texture, with particular reference to the cello's first and only quaver in the bar and, conversely, the viola's ongoing semiquavers. For three-quarters of the bar, there is, in fact, a string trio of semiquavers, and the cello's opening quaver makes the necessary retention of the tempo character yet more difficult; the three passages of total *tutti*, likewise, have to retain the movement's essential lightness.

As for the actual bowing, Haydn's '*p e sempre staccato*' shows us how far we have moved in our technical terminology; *pace* Leopold Mozart (see pp.103f.), Haydn must have had something *spiccato*-like in mind, for without wanting the slightest shade of *spiccato*, he needn't have bothered to issue any instructions: at that speed (*vivace*), there would only have been one type of bowing possible if he had intended the bow to remain firmly, *détaché*-like, on the string.

When, eventually, the soft, three-part four-semiquaver *legato*s arrive, they shouldn't be allowed to interrupt the phrasing through unintentional accents on the first of each four: a little joint string-trio practice with firm phrasing intentions will do wonders. What is important at this point, too, is the *subito piano* after the *fortissimo*, which has to be heard as from the second violin's emergence from the D major chord at the beginning of bar 120.

In the last *tutti* bars, i.e. the movement's conclusion, the first fiddler must be given the chance, against heavy textural odds, to permit himself a marginal *accelerando*, which the others have to be able to follow without the slightest friction; in particular, the second violin's penultimate $a-g'$ at the culmination of the mini-*accelerando* has to be carefully watched.

Op.64, No.6, in E flat major
(Hoboken III:64)

The last of the 1790 quartets, the last of the Tost quartets, and the last of the present *opus* is, once again, one whose history in different cultures seems strikingly unalike (cf. pp.138f.). On Radio 3, one heard an introductory note by the supremely musical and well-informed Misha Donat, according to which the work 'belongs among the least performed of Haydn's great string quartets. Its neglect is perhaps due to the reflective character of its first three movements . . .'

Where I grew up, on the other hand, the fourth of Haydn's six great E flat quartets was by far the most popular and the most widely played; it was included in all the 'celebrated' volumes of my childhood – and, rather ironically, I wondered as a child what its extreme popularity was due to. Not that I disliked it – but its slightly uncomfortable key figured a little more prominently in my assessment than it does today, when I would warn players not to counteract the key's opaque colour: it is part of the music's character, of what Donat describes as its reflectiveness. Are we to suppose, then, that it is in the United Kingdom that reflective music is 'out'? I certainly knew the quartet backwards by the time I went to school: I remember, on one of my first school days, drawing a musical mate's attention to the slow movement's B♭ minor middle section; in this respect, my assessment hasn't changed at all, so will the reader kindly take the place of my school pal? He won't regret it.

The work is the 'easy' type of great masterpiece – easy to understand, that is, and, key a little apart, easy to play. At this stage in our investigations, I am almost sure it is no longer necessary to assert that bar 1 is an upbeat bar – though not the only one: it may still be necessary to point out that the first two bars are an upbeat to bar 3, whose two-note phrases are an unexpected contrast to the preceding build-up and have to be articulated very distinctly; there is well-defined articulation in the middle of this third bar, as opposed to the middle of the fourth, whose two-note motifs lead the phrase to the third beat. In the middle of this fourth bar, therefore, there is the opposite of articulation.

What is highly characteristic of the opening movement and deserves the interpreters' central attention is its textural contrasts, which drive Haydn's normal textural variety to one of its extremes – quite consciously so, it seems. Not only are the quartet's various ensembles contrastingly explored, but Haydn makes a feature of the minimal ensembles – no fewer than four duos, with special concentration on the contrast between the two upper and the two lower instruments, which distinguishes, *inter alia*, the opening of the development section, where the pairs overlap to the extent of a bar's *tutti*. After the lower duo has replaced the upper duo, the texture grows through the normal string trio and an intervening duo between the middle parts into a full quartet, at first (and only at first) relieved by rests.

The reason why I am going into such textural detail, however selective, is that it is impossible to do this textural variety and these textural contrasts full justice without a clear consciousness, at any given stage, of the precise instrumental combination one forms part of: obviously, the sound one has to produce as a member of a particular duo is quite different from one's tone production in any specific trio, as distinct again from the full quartet. Many are the performances one hears in which the players indulge in unchanging tone production and tone modulation, regardless of the ever-changing textural context, with the result that the moments of natural sound, of realistic balance and blend, are confined to the full quartet texture, and the composer's structuralization of his textural contrasts goes for nought. Your entire central musicality has to concentrate on the particular duo or trio sound the composition expects you to produce at any given structural point.

That afore-praised middle section of the *Andante* is quite clearly Haydn's last personal offering to Tost, whose imagination and freedom of phrasing the leader will once again emulate; to describe it as I have described it is really doubly misleading, for 'Fantasy' would be a far more realistic description for what happens in the middle of this movement, the more so since its key signature and my key description are a vast oversimplification: within six bars, we become aware that we haven't just turned to the tonic minor, but that an intense modulatory process is about to commence which will endow this fantasy with the nature of a development section; once again, we are confronted with a combination of forms – ternary and sonata – second-subject-less, to be sure! The modulatory drive leads the section's own theme through D♭ major, A♭ minor, E♭ minor, and an implication of F minor, to the latter's tonic major, which is both the principal section's and the early middle section's dominant: the leadback has been reached, the recapitulation is expected to be expected; for the meeting of this expectation is part and parcel of the music's meaning, its drastic relaxation of tension at a pivotal juncture.

The first violin, then, has to have maximal freedom in the middle; the three lower instruments' contribution to the rhythmic definition of this fantasy is, must be, nil, even though they have four semiquavers during the leader's first crotchet – which, in view of the *subito piano* on the second of them, cannot partake in the section's rhythmic characterization, since the *subito piano* imposes a brake (if not indeed a break) on the first semiquaver. More importantly, these and all the succeeding, continuous semiquavers have to be produced without rhythmic articulation, and with the greatest restraint – almost inarticulately, one is tempted to say. The one exception (which, however, should not be noticed as such) is the *diminuendo* bar – the 8th of the fantasy, the 39th of the movement – where there is a certain degree and amount of articulate motion from quaver value to quaver value, and at one point (the second violin's second, third, and fourth semiquavers) even from semiquaver to semiquaver. But the bowing of this exceptional bar will not, of course, differ from the accompanimental bowing of the rest of the middle section; it is, as the reader will forehear by now, the most restrained variety of Carmirelli bowing (see p.42) that is here required. At no point must there be the remotest rhythmic friction between the first violin and the rest, however freely, even outrageously, the leader imaginatively decides to behave; his freedom, including its more outrageous aspects, will be characterized by the necessary, divinable logic, for the very essence of successful improvisation is its approximate predictability from stage to stage – not because something conventional is coming, but because the outrageousness of what's coming has to be proportionate to its determining logic the bar, or phrase, or motif, before.

As in the case of 'The Lark', but in an extremely different manner, the minuet's upbeat is lent weight by and through its ornament; this time, however, the upbeating crotchet is but part of an upbeat phrase that extends over 2⅓ bars and must be heard to lead straight to the third bar, whose *sforzato* has to be immediately followed by, in fact, audibly result in, a *diminuendo* that dominates the rest of the phrase, the principal accent of which is now past.

What that first note of the upbeat phrase requires, as opposed to all its other notes, is, again, audible recognition of the fact that it is not, after all, a single note – even less so than the corresponding upbeat in the minuet of 'The Lark'. No fewer than three ornamental notes precede it which, together with the main note, constitute a turn, so far as the actual constituents of this group are concerned; at the same time, a turn is both the last thing that Haydn wants and, alas, both the first and last thing that springs to many a leader's mind. Why don't they stop to think that if Haydn had wanted a turn, he'd have notated it, as he did on so many occasions upon which we have already remarked?

No, his notation is quite unmistakable: he wants three quick, very quick, notes to precede the main note, whose main-ness, and corresponding relative weight, has to be as clearly articulated as what we might describe as the upbeat's upbeat – the three turning notes. It follows as a matter of logical course that in order for this articulation properly to precede the crucial main note, there will have to be the slightest of commas after the upbeat and before the first $e^{b''}$; for the comma itself will easily lend the upbeat the necessary weight and will, if short enough, lead to, make us urgently expect, the main beat at the same time. In order to make a colorific contribution to this leading function and its effect, the first violinist is advised not to start the movement in the first position, but in the third or fourth: the darker, D-string colour will than naturally precede the brighter A-string $e^{b''}$. The fourth position is preferable, in order for the non-turn to roll off as fast as possible, which it will if it is started with the third rather than the fourth finger.

Five bars further along, the question of fingering introduces considerations that could be of a more personal nature: speaking 'personally' on the basis of our firm identification with Tost, we can hear him increase the urgency of the second phrase's upbeat (which, this time, is confined to this single c'') by an audible downward plunge – a *glissando* to the $e^{b'}$ that will, ideally, carry a tasteful *espressivo*. The alternative change to the G-string and the change of colour involved in it would, of course, make its own sense, which would smoothly correspond to the shape of the phrase. Still, to me it seems as if Haydn might well have composed this contrasting, single-note upbeat with a view to what he could expect to be Tost's *glissando*.

As always in the case of such thematic extreme contrasts, Haydn retains the minuet's key for the *Trio* in order to throw the contrast into relief, to rub in the vast difference of 'the same thing', i.e. E^b major. The *Trio*'s grace notes are meant to be the starting-points for graceful *portamentos* (cf. Op.20, No.3, p.50); in other words, both first and, later, second violin have to play the theme on the A-string throughout. The quaver accompaniment, meanwhile, has to adjust itself most tactfully, unobtrusively, and flexibly: there is no need to 'do' anything 'about' the slurs; just play them with both your ears and your whole mind deep inside the first-violin part.

The *Finale* is, perhaps, the work's strongest contrast, as which it will have to be realized: its intermittently explosive joy is unprecedented in the entire quartet, and contradicts any conceivable expectation. It is, in fact, the one movement whose E♭ colour and mood is by no means manifest and need not, therefore, be brought to the fore. Its combination of rondo and sonata, however, its developmental, modulatory drives, make it weightier than it would or could otherwise be: a flippant, facile performance, such as one often hears, is out of the question.

The *presto* character will be immediately established, not by the conventional, musically meaningless or, at any rate, vague 'one in a bar' which only produces bar accents, in fact one per bar, but by driving the *piano* antecedent up to its highest note; while it does, of course, consist of two one-bar phrases and one two-bar phrase, the intervening articulations are – should be – as nothing compared to the forceful articulations of the consequent's two two-bar phrases.

From the point of view of the movement's clearly defined ambiguity, its simultaneous gaiety and wit, nothing is more fascinating than the penultimate joke – which, unfortunately, is almost always played as nothing but a joke; ironically enough, the joke itself is missed if you do nothing but try to turn it into one.

Let me explain. The comic effect stands or falls by the precise augmentation of the theme (the new dotted rhythm apart) – precise in the sense that according to the player's and listener's pulse, it has to be spontaneously felt to be twice as slow. In order to be as jocular as possible, however, the usual interpretation doesn't care over-much about the augmentation; it concentrates on an allegedly funny, slow tempo, any old tempo.

Without the change in the rhythm of the upbeat, both the joke and its serious substance would have been far weaker: in order for the *presto* upbeat not to lose character in augmentation, it has to be re-rhythmicized. The character has not, of course, remained the same – which, however, is true of the entire augmentation, including its remaining, exact part, i.e. the repeated quavers at a quaver's and a crotchet's distance respectively. My pointer is designed to alert the reader to the fact that the exact part of the augmentation isn't all that exact either: if it were, the quavers would have had to change into crotchets.

In other words, while Haydn aims at the experience of an augmentation, he does not wish to be silly: he re-rhythmicizes and hence re-characterizes his theme in order for it to make full sense at the slow pace. That sense intensifies the joke on the one hand and lends it serious weight on the other: if it wants to come off, the theme has to be seriously phrased; and at the slow pace, what were the two one-bar phrases turn into two well-articulated two-bar phrases which aim at the principal accent of the second; the first's must be weaker!

With the resumption of the *presto*, the original phrasing has to be resumed – with, if I may say so, a vengeance, if possible. That is to say, the joke is over; there is no need, therefore, for the experience of a precise diminution. For the purpose of seriously returning to the mood of gaiety, which now climaxes in veritable ebullience, a *poco più mosso*, a suspicion of *prestissimo*, would be experience as entirely logical, in which case the drive up to the $b^b{''}$ must be all the more determined.

It remains to be said that Beethoven's structural habit of slowing up before the end, and of thus emphasizing the concluding discharge of tension, may well originally have been inspired by this most Beethovenian Haydn coda, the only example, prior to Beethoven, of what was to become a structural character trait of his – one which had a powerful effect on later composers. Another innovation, then, which can be traced back to Haydn.

Op.71, No.1, in B flat major
(Hoboken III:69)

At the age of 61, at the protracted climax of his creative life, Haydn returns, from now on almost equally protractedly, to a creative question that has always fascinated him – the beginning before the beginning (cf.pp.150f.), which can, *inter alia*, take the shape of an introduction, however short and seemingly inessential. The opening of the *Eroica* has been known as an innovation not only in countless history books, but even in one of Zubin Mehta's masterclasses. The chordal introduction which replaces an introductory section Beethoven has, of course, from Haydn, who explored and exploited all possibilities of its relation to the body of the movement, nowhere more subtly so than in his penultimate great B♭ Quartet; there are five of them altogether, if we don't accept the Op.33 work as great (see p.7).

Since the present cadential, chordal call to attention falls outside the repeat of the exposition and does not, of course, play any role in the leadback, it might be argued that far from subtle, the introductory chords could not be more conventionally separate from the first movement proper – but nobody who is actually familiar with the movement's build-up would dream of arguing thus. And since the question how to take these chords is intimately bound up with their role in the further evolution of the structure, this role had better be examined in all its aspects, intriguingly latent as well as manifest. For the fact is that demonstrably, none of the structure's crucial stages – repeat, beginning of development, leadback *cum* recapitulation, and the end – would be the same, could conceivably be the same if the chords weren't there.

The question why they aren't included in the repeat is the easiest to answer: strictly speaking, they are. Not, however, in their original form: a dominant variation replaces them at the end of the exposition. On the one hand, it produces a new, contrasting context for the opening, while on the other, it integrates the beginning of the development into the context of the beginning of the movement.

At the leadback stage, we are confronted with a cello motif (Ex.52, p.176) which is as pseudo-conventional as are the introductory chords themselves: nothing which is composed in a way that retains its expressive value can be considered a mere *cliché*. This one Haydn last heard in a similarly expressive context – in fact, at a similarly 'back-leading' stage, back to the theme, that is: in

Ex.52

the finale of his first Haydn Quartet, Mozart leads back thus from the end of the exposition to the beginning of the movement (Ex.53):

Ex.53

The pseudo-conventionality of both the introductory chords and this chromatic motif is an absolute condition for the motif's function in its capacity as the end of the leadback: it functions as another, more drastic variation of the chords. As against them, it is instinctively heard as a diminution, now preceded by an additional, upbeating note, the need for which arises through its overlap with the theme, whereas the chords haven't overlapped, either at the beginning or at the end of the exposition. I am describing the end of the leadback as a latent variation, not because it wouldn't be manifest to any 7-year-old if sung or played immediately after the chords, but because the means by which it spontaneously establishes itself as a variation cannot be considered part and parcel of normal variation technique. A chromatic motif instead of the chords: this is the intended experience, and a rich experience it is.

At the end, the introductory chords are, of course, compressed into the two forte chords after the *pianissimo*, but if we don't confine ourselves to this manifest part of the variation and listen to its antecedent, which starts a bar earlier, i.e. at the preceding half-bar, we suddenly become conscious of yet another complete variation, more than half of it latent, less than half manifest.

Only after having felt and thought through these three variations of the seemingly isolated chordal introduction are we in a clear-eared position to decide how to play it. The possibilities are many, but they all share one absolute condition, a negative one: this introduction is quite certainly not the place for the definition of the movement's tempo character; whatever the chords do, they mustn't be in time – just as their variations occur at stages in need of an agogical contribution. For the rest, a little *ritardando* can be made just as meaningfully as a little *accelerando*; either will be played in audible preparation of the tempo definition. The way in which one will hit the triple stoppings (none of which is a real triple stopping, since an open string is always involved) will depend on the nature of one's phrasing; the possibility of sounding the three strings together, as an unbroken chord, should not be neglected if one's phrasing would make this sound the ideal solution.

We shall, of course, return to the subject of what we might describe as Haydn's multitudinous, exhaustive, and highly contrasting variations on the theme of the introduction to a sonata structure. Needless to add, they are not confined to his string quartets; in fact, the analytically interested reader will, I promise, deeply enjoy a comparison between Haydn's treatment of this theme in the present movement and in the opening movement of the A major Piano Trio he wrote in 1794, shortly after his Op.74 quartets and, in fact, not long after the present work (a year or so). There, likewise, the structure starts with a chordal two-bar call to attention, whose further fate discloses both striking similarities with, and significant differences from, the function of our present introduction: the comparison will fascinate the thoughtful reader throughout, and will further illuminate each relevant structural stage in either work. It is, of course, the afore-discussed stages which deserve his prime attention.

The work as a whole is in what one might describe as Haydn's 'grand' style; technical difficulties apart, it is comparatively unproblematic. But at the beginning, a heavy responsibility falls on the middle parts: the leader won't be able to escape from their tempo implications in bar 3! However, inasmuch as what he does with the introductory chords will clearly foreshadow the tempo that logically flows from them, the responsibility for putting the middle parts in the right, rhythmical frame of mind will, after all, be his. In any case, the contrast between the opening *fortissimo* and the theme's *mezza voce* cannot possibly be exaggerated. For the rest, the first movement's grand style means a great deal of full quartet texture, with its textural variations unfolding all the more subtly within it: what is needed from the playing point of view is more, rather than less, finesse of blend and balance than ever.

In no fewer than three places, the *Adagio*'s full quartet texture is contrasted with its opposite, the unaccompanied leader; only once is the transition gradual, by way of a normal string trio. Many are the occasions, even in public performance, when one can still hear the leader's recollections of his surprise, his delayed or remembered trauma, at being left alone, when he does not naturally adjust to these opposite textural circumstances – or rather, the absence of any textural circumstances. There is absolutely no problem here – just the question how well the first violinist knows the movement, and how well he can produce and modulate his tone without help or hindrance: one impression he must avoid at all costs – that he doesn't seem to know what to do with his freedom, which he is heard to find rather intimidating. The only possible source of realistic fear in such circumstances is his own lack – or repression – of imagination.

The minuet's textural contrasts between the quartet and, chiefly, the cello-less type of string trio should be playingly noted with audible certitude:

their structural function is so clear that it need not be explained. The *Trio*'s and the minuet's identical key once again serves to emphasize the thematic contrast between them, of which the players should be over-conscious. Thematically, this is indeed one of those none too rare Haydn Trios[1] which unconditionally need free, inventive interpretation on the part of the first fiddler. Characteristically enough, Mozart wrote only one of them – in his second Haydn quartet, the D minor one with its D major *Trio*; the work altogether thinks a great deal of its dedicatee and addressee.

In the present *Trio*, it is, of course, the other sections and particularly the first part to which this requirement applies: if the opening, 8-bar antecedent and consequent were played at any pace approaching metrical regularity, they would lose their entire sense and only sound embarrassing. The initial, two-quaver upbeat, that is to say, already has to define, *via* its arresting hesitation, the free agogics that are going to dominate the movement – not with the implication that everything will be in the tempo of the upbeat, but, on the contrary, with the clear indication that the temporal contrast between the upbeat and, say, the first bar's gradually accelerating quavers will be typical of the section's agogical range; any parallelism between an initial hesitation and one over the first bar's corresponding quavers would certainly be ridiculous – though the second bar's will, of course, allude to whatever happened in the opening upbeat: here as anywhere else, the phrasing, however free, has to recognize, and be determined by, the structure – or rather, the player's imaginative understanding of it.

The second fiddler will, of course, forehear bar 3's agogics in view of both the initial upbeat's and bar 1's, which is why Haydn there gives him the first part's only chance himself to go with the leader's quavers in quavers rather than crotchets.

At the recapitulatory stage, however, everybody is successively drawn in quaver-wise: the expository model now facilitates the lower instruments' task, though the leader should not, of course, copy his own exposition in order to make life easier for the lower instruments, or indeed for any other reason. Many are the leaders who do just that – for no reason at all, whatever their motivation. One cannot be reminded too often that in meaningful music, there simply is no repetition. That goes for the recapitulation of the principal section too, the present one or any other: interpretatively, it will always have to be a variation.

Repetitive phrasings should likewise be avoided in such quasi-sequential and sequential structures as start off the finale. Quite apart from the meaninglessness of repetition, they would, at best, sacrifice continuity to articulation: in order to make model and sequence hang together, the two have to be differently phrased, the sequence climaxing on the model, which has inevitably aimed at it; in normal structural circumstances, any end of any

---

[1] Cf. the *Trios* from *opera* 20, No.6, 33, No.2, 55, No.3, 64, Nos.2, 4, and 6 – and, forthcomingly, 74, Nos.1 and 3, and 76, No.1.

(quasi-) sequence will therefore always be more sharply articulated than the end of the model – as can be heard in the finale's bars 4 and 2 respectively, or in its bars 8 and 6 respectively.

A frequent misphrasing occurs at the imitative beginning of the development section, whose subject is a codetta phrase that may, in fact, have been misphrased before the double-bar, in which case the cellist is thrown into an insoluble dilemma: should he continue the wrong phrasing or contradict the leader? The point about the phrase is, of course, that it aims beyond the semiquavers at its own end, whereas in the excitement of the cello's solo entry and of the ascending counterpoint which, step by step, fills the entire quartet texture, an explosive accent is often placed immediately after the upbeat, on the first semiquaver. Correctly shaped, on the other hand, the phrase will suddenly disclose its textural function and the texture itself will gain in communicative subtlety, in that each aim, each accent coincides with the next entry's de-accentuation on that first semiquaver; even the accent of the last entry, the first violin's, coincides with both the cello's and the second violin's renewed de-accentuation: Haydn was careful consistently to retain this subtle state of contrapuntal affairs.

Above all, however, the *Vivace* has to be played with ever-renewed wit, of whose implications such aspects as the just-mentioned contrapuntal opening of the development are nowise free. It would be ridiculous, or rather, most depressing for the player-reader if I now proceeded to instruct him how to be witty: if he doesn't hear the immediate, winking smile on the movement's face, he had better not move near it. But a point of principle can be made about interpretative wit: where it doesn't disclose additional musical meaning, it has gone wrong and will not even strike the musical listener as funny; if anything it is likely to embarrass him. We only have to stop and think about how we react to compositional wit, real and phoney – on the part of Haydn or Beethoven on the one hand and many a Hollywoodian joker on the other – in order to realize the truth of this proposition, which applies to both creative areas, the composer's and the player's, with equal force. What is important clearly to realize about this finale is that wit, irony, even a touch of parody lie at the very source of both the movement's mood and, therefore, its actual rhythmic structures; we only have to imagine, for a moment, a series of solemn opening phrasings in order to become alive to the high, or rather, deep degree to which Haydn succeeded in musicalizing fun, or in discovering possibilities of purely musical fun such as Mozart's profound and affecting humour would never have dreamt of.

When he, Mozart, decided on musical jokes, such as, pre-eminently, in *A Musical Joke*, they weren't all that musical nor, therefore, all that funny. Is it not most striking that what was no doubt intended as a universally popular piece has become one of the very few works of the mature Mozart which wouldn't fill a recital room, let alone a concert hall? I think it is in contrast to Mozart's unrivalled sense of musical humour that Haydn's, or for that matter Beethoven's – may I say? – sense of musical wit, their sense *for* thoroughly musical jokes, is most clearly understood.

And it is important to understand this side of Haydn's creative character, because its effects are not, of course, confined to our present finale. In this book, and specific, localizable jokes apart, I have been fighting shy of going into the funny side of many of Haydn's movements and thoughts: perhaps more than anything else, it goes without saying, and if you say too much about it there is always the risk of your words resulting in unmusical or downright extra-musical exaggerations. Conceivably, the present movement is the ideal instance in view of which to raise this self-evident subject: it is, in every possible respect, the diametrical opposite of Mozart's *Musical Joke*, because its ultra-musical jokes are so essential a part of its musical substance that without them, that very substance couldn't have been communicated.

Even as I write, however, I can feel my fear of obtrusively jocular performances for which my words here may be to blame, and which could reduce this music to the level of Mozart's effort. In order to forestall any such course of anti-musical action, let us now have a concrete look at the opening 12-bar sentence, its fun, which will be part of the basis of the entire structure, and at any interpretative implications or inhibitions arising from our inspection of the structural consequences of Haydn's comic approach: there won't be any advice as to how to be witty!

The melody's early return to the tonic in bar 2 and the subsequent, over-emphasized tonics are a clear joke on conventional, short-winded melodic 'ideas', whose parodistic aspect is immediately counteracted by the cello's tonic (in perfect tune, please!) being the perfect cadential resolution's sole support; the middle parts, at first most unconventionally led by the viola, confirm and the viola proceeds on the off-beat. The interpretation will have to let the joke make its own effect, conscious as the leader has to be, not only of the queue of tonics, but also of Haydn's counter-measures, which should prompt him to confine himself to the music's meaningful compensation and over-compensation, and prevent him, for instance, from playing his Bb in bar 2 funnily, i.e. conclusively.

Both harmonically and with its downright rhythmic aping, the responsive phrase of bars 3–4 continues the joke on conventionality – which, this time, the leader can support if he feels so inclined, the more so since what, in that case, would be his slightly over-stressed F in bar 4 would also contribute, by way of sharp particulation, to Haydn's serious counter-measures which, needless to add, have their funny side too.[1] In itself, in fact, the second violin's confirmation is tonically, pleonastically funny, but as a thematic response to the viola's continuation in bar 2, it is a major inspiration: what was single-minded continuation turns into equally single-minded conclusion! A mature second fiddler's phrasing will be able to combine confirmatory articulation with a refined recollection of whatever the viola had been doing in bar 2.

[1] I am harping on those counter-measures because *A Musical Joke* is totally without them.

The fun of the ensuing, obtrusively regular sequence is contradicted by the middle parts' irregularity: here the quartet's, or rather, topically, the Dvořák-like string trio's, complex task turns out to be at its easiest, for the ambiguity of fun on the one hand and serious substance on the other is neatly divided between the leader, who can let himself go ironically if that's the way he feels, and the other two, who have to look after the contrast between what they do to the model and what, again inspiredly, Haydn invites them to do to, and about, not to say against, the sequence.

The octave-unison B♭ at the end of the sentence, whose realization has nothing to do with our present discussion, needs especial consideration nevertheless: rarely has this note been heard 'in tune', i.e. well blended. First violin and viola have the same B♭, while the cello has it at the octave below. Now, ironically, experience shows that if the upper two take the note on the same (A-) string, the blend which, after all, has to sound the leader's B♭ in a leading role, i.e. at the end of his melody, is more difficult to achieve than when the viola decides upon the darker D-string, which can produce an ideal combination of blend and balance: listeningly speaking, the viola's and cello's blend has not only to be blended with, but also balanced against, the first violin!

What has everything to do with our present discussion is the second violin's renewed confirmation in bar 12 which, identical with the first, lands, a beat later, on the selfsame B♭, whose colour will easily be relatable, on the A-string, to the first violin's.

All we can do now is put the second violinist in full possession of the facts which his provisionally concluding joke, his phrasing of the reconfirmation, whatever it's going to be, will have to take into account. What happens after it is relevant: it is wittily identical with what happened after it the first time over. In fact, when I said that there was no repetition in meaningful music, I assumed as a matter of course the reader's awareness that I was speaking apart from jocular repetitions, whose joke is precisely that normally, musically, repetitions don't exist; the second violin's re-confirmation is indeed an example. As for the repetition of its continuation, the only immediate differences are re-instrumentation and a full quartet texture at the end of the first violin's model; neither will or need affect the second violin's phrasing of the reconfirmation. What could affect it, on the other hand, is a new precedent in the viola part (bars 10–11), which may seem remote enough to be ignored, though any trace it left in the second violin's joke would fill it with serious meaning. The second fiddler might even wish to repeat precisely whatever he had done before: we have just explicitly accepted the possibility of jocular repetitions. If his creative desires or needs move in that direction, his original phrasing will have had to be sufficiently characteristic to be identifiable upon re-introduction – for otherwise, the joke is condemned to go for nought. A characteristic phrasing, on the other hand, can be musically developed and so accumulate new musical meaning while still acting a 'precise' repetition – so long as its outstanding character traits recur.

Every Haydn (or Beethoven) joke, then, has a serious counterbalance, which the interpreter ignores at his and the music's and, yes, the joke's own peril: in and outside music, the more serious a joke's substance, the greater and more lasting its fun, its effect.

Op.71, No.2, in D major
(Hoboken III:70)

The penultimate work (1793) amongst Haydn's six mature D major quartets shares one feature with all of them, another with one of them, while a third, striking feature cannot be encountered in any other great Haydn quartet.

What all the great D major quartets have in common is, of course, the very conscious brilliance of their key, which is invariably explored as widely and as consistently as possible: as one sits down to play this work, I think it is good to know about the desired brilliance of sound, without which much of the actual sense of the music would be lost. Mood and tone-colour are intimately related, and while we can't easily speak of a brilliant mood, we immediately identify the kind of mood that manifests itself through brilliant sound.

With the D major Quartet from Op.33 (see pp.80f.) the present work shares – I almost said, 'the finale', which would have been a profound insult to the very essence of Haydn's creative character, since its most outstanding trait is that it never allows itself to repeat itself, always develops what even a Mozart (not to speak of a Bruckner) might have repeated. But when we reach the *Finale* of the present D major quartet, we shall hear what my thoughtless observation would have meant: it would have been relevant to the background of the two finales, certainly not their foregrounds – or, to put it yet more conscientiously, some of the very foreground of the last movement of Op.33, No.6 has meanwhile become background, so that in order fully to understand the rich implications of the present *Finale*, one really has to know the other one too. I am raising an interesting question here: does Haydn's communication presuppose knowledge of the other *Finale*? The answer is, of course, no – but not a simple no: if we know the other *Finale*, we are granted insight into private, purely musical thought – into autobiographical musical reflections which yield musical truths we would otherwise have to go without. And far from objecting to our intrusion into this autobiographical area, Haydn would doubtless have been delighted at it. Had they played the quartet together, Mozart's insight would thus have intruded – but Mozart, having contributed quite a little to Haydn's D *minor* (see pp.19f. and 85f.), was dead.

Now for that third feature, a basic structural one, which is unique to the present quartet, which many another Haydn work but no other great Haydn quartet evinces. It is, of course, Haydn's new, violently contrasting 'variation on the theme of the introduction to a sonata structure' (see p.177) – the quartet's *slow* introduction, in Haydn's own characteristic *adagio* tempo, in fact. A sobering thought: how many quartet players, how many quartet 'experts' are there who would immediately respond to the question, 'How many slow introductions are there amongst all the great Haydn and Mozart quartets?' with the answer, 'One each'? (Mozart's is, of course, the *adagio* he addressed to Haydn at the beginning of 'The Dissonance' – his last Haydn quartet.) The thought is sobering because in a minimally educated quartet society, everybody should have this answer ready, whereas I am convinced that in ours, nobody has, literally nobody.

This new variation on the theme means that unlike the introduction to the present *opus'* first quartet, our *adagio* introduction won't itself turn out to be a theme for variations at crucial junctures of the sonata structure. But the fact that it won't be a theme for variations doesn't make it unthematic, for it can be a theme for something else – in Schoenberg's language, for the kind of 'developing variation' which he considered at the root of all musical thought.

And indeed, from the outset, the players, above all the leader, should be alive to a basic fact to which, to my knowledge, not a single observer on this slow introduction has yet drawn attention – that both the first subject's fundamental octave leaps (Ex.55) and the minuet's less leaping, i.e. triadically filled-in octaves (Ex.56) are clearly (thematically rather than sub-thematically) foreshadowed by the introduction's opening octave and its sequence:

Ex.54

in fact, in all three instances, the octave is the opening thought, though the introduction hides it behind, and so establishes the continuity between, two successive motifs, whose first is a single note (chord); they have to be sharply articulated against each other, with the result that the opening of the *Allegro* will be played as an overpowering contrast – 'the same thing', the octave, again making a more different impression than different things could: where there was weight on the upper octave, whereas the lower octave, as the first quaver of a three-quaver upbeat phrase, couldn't have been more weightless, and where the two couldn't have been more separate, the two couldn't belong

Ex.55

Ex.56

more intimately together, in that the weightlessness of the upper octave leads straight down to the lower octave's weight.

I cannot hear any objection to starting the *Adagio* in a grand, broad structural style, as if half an hour's very slow rhetorical music were ahead: that, after all, is the style in which the opening sequence is composed, and its gradual transformation into a short introduction constitutes much of its musical meaning – so far as one can do verbal justice to it. The interpretation will clearly have to illuminate the paradox of the fermata on the end of the model rather than the end of the sequence: at the end of the model, we still feel in terms of a short introduction, and nothing could be further from our expectations than a sequence. When it intriguingly ensues, our feeling of and for an extended structure has started, and no interpretative articulation must now rival the decisiveness of the two opening definitions of entities – the breath between the *forte* and the *piano*, and what will have to be a lavish pause, in utter contradiction of the continuity it is succeeded by, and which will have to shorten the breath between the *forte* and the *piano* in the sequence.

Like the preceding work, the present one poses few musical problems to spontaneous music-making: in most of the quartets he wrote with an eye on London, Haydn seemed either to avoid esotericism or (as we shall hear in the case of the *Finale*) plunge for the Mozartian kind of esotericism – in a distinctive exoteric garb.

Ideally, the *Allegro*'s imitative octaves, I mean the lower three, will all be different, yet audibly successive, each logically following from its predecessor – until the first violin enters with a drastic transformation of the motif, which no longer consists of two *forte* notes, but has changed, equally *forte*, into a radically disjunct three-quaver upbeat phrase, as whose model, just as radically contrasting, one should still be able to hear the conjunct three-quaver upbeat phrase in the very first model, that of the first sequence. Let us not forget that the two basic thoughts, that of the introduction and that of the body of the movement, share an easily discernible background: the first three octave entries, two of them imitative, correspond to the opening chord, which is followed by the 'same' three-quaver upbeat to a stressed, long note. I think consciousness of this relation will clarify both the unity of, and the contrast between the two openings; in fact, palpable unity will intensify the contrast, and a tangibly defined contrast will automatically increase the unity.

Superficially, and only superficially, the texture of this first movement may often seem quasi-orchestral, but nothing would endanger its very nature more gravely than an orchestral playing style, for as soon as every player listens as carefully as is his wont in thinner textures, he will discover that throughout, Haydn's quartet-writing is just as subtle and, yes, as transparent as it is in them; every bar is intrinsically string quartet and would be crudified beyond toleration, sometimes even beyond comprehension, if one tackled it orchestrally. Indeed, the movement's very brilliance depends on its realization as an intrinsic string quartet; in the whole of mature Haydn, there are only two movements whose texture shows, intermittently, slight orchestral corruption – the outer movements of 'The Emperor' (see p.216). Everything else is part of the extreme variability of Haydn's always deeply essential quartet textures.

The *Adagio cantabile* has often been called an aria for the first violin; well, that depends on what you mean by aria. If you just mean '*cantabile*', I don't see any need for the synonym, but if you mean that the principal part is quasi-vocal, I'd like to hear the human voice which doesn't make a mess of the semiquaver triplets, not to speak of the dotted semiquavers. There is a type of instrumental song of which the human voice is incapable and which evinces melodic characters that are crassly unvocal without ceasing to be *cantabile*: the combination of different instrumental implications, or of instrumental and vocal implications, can yield as much musical meaning as the combination of forms; after all, meaningfully speaking, instrumentation, scoring, is but an aspect of form – or rather, the sources of sound are, instrumental and vocal; what the composer's texture does with, about, and against them corresponds to what his structure does with, about and against form.

Sing by all means, I say to the first violin, quite especially where a singer couldn't; your instrument, as distinct from, or even opposed to his, can combine the most lucid rhythmic characterization with undiminished melodic purpose and decisiveness.

But above all, improvise! The movement may seem simple, but where another composer, even another great composer, would have *stated*, Haydn often *develops*, and where another composer would have restated or repeated, he emphatically varies; it is, particularly at these junctures, either developmental or variational, that the music would fall flat without what I'd like to describe as your strict rhythmic freedom. Bowingly, there is a vast range of variation at your disposal: I am thinking, especially, of the triplets and their contrasting contexts, dynamic contrasts included; compare, for instance, bar 7 with bars 51 ff.!

Nor am I addressing myself to the leader alone: the others have those highly characteristic triplets too, but there is only a single bar where, by way of concluding, relaxing climax, two of you – the middle parts – have them together – three bars from the end.

In a well-definable way, it, together with the penultimate bar, is the most difficult spot, and here goes my definition: concentration has to operate multidimensionally in that (1) your own as well as (2) the first violin's *diminuendo* has to be continued; (3) your triplets have to flow naturally from his; (4) his melody has to be perfectly balanced, remembering that it may well involve him in a little *crescendo* on and even beyond the first crotchet value (his first two quavers), before he joins your *diminuendo*, which really ought to be at his service; (5) you upper three have to arrive at a finely judged *pianissimo* blend on the first beat of the penultimate bar, which (6) enables the cello, at the same time, to balance the two opening notes of its own, final *pianissimo* triplets against you, and (7) to make his triplets a natural continuation of yours, middle parts, as yours were of the leader's. (8) Last but first, there has to be utter, *spontaneous* unanimity between all of you, for the foregoing factors will, must, should vary from performance to performance. In the bar before the cello's triplets, the second violin will lead the middle parts' largely instinctive operation: its in the principal subordinate part.

A word, finally, on the *Adagio*'s key: it does not, as is the 'normal' *adagio*'s wont, relax into the reposeful subdominant, but, on the contrary, increases the level of tonal tension by ascending to the dominant – an entirely natural course of harmonic events, it will be agreed, in view of the unusual degree of variational and especially developmental tension which the structure accumulates. Again, I'd say that it can only be an emotional and hence architectonic advantage for the ensemble and especially the leader to be clearly conscious of this relatively rare state of large-scale tonal affairs; vague consciousness there would be, anyway.

For the interpreter and especially the leader, the unusual structure of the minuet's beginning opens up possibilities which we won't readily encounter in any other work, any other movement. But then, the minuet itself starts unlike any other movement you might care to think of. There are, in other words, two types of beginning – upbeating phrases (most of them in the Austro-German symphonic tradition as opposed to the musico-cultural orbit of, say, the Stravinsky fiddle Concerto, which not only starts with, but virtually consists of, downbeat phrases – for the upbeating instrument *par excellence!*), and downbeating opening phrases or chords, such as, for instance, in the *Kleine Nachtmusik*. Now, where a movement starts with an upbeat or, still better, an upbeating phrase, there often is an opportunity for the player of the principal part to exercise a degree of freedom he is unlikely to be able to equal in the rest of the movement: the introductory phrase, that is to say, offers him a chance to creep, slide into his tempo definition by way of initial, persuasive hesitation – to approach, as it were, the tempo definition cautiously, searchingly; never again in the course of the movement will he easily encounter any opportunity to behave as freely as he naturally did before any tempo character has been established.

And so to the present minuet's exceptional beginning: though it starts with the cello's triadic assertion which makes sense as either a downbeat phrase or an upbeat phrase down to the D of its second bar, the triadic assertiveness as well as the metrical rhythm of the phrase would, in either case, make any hesitation sound like a bad joke, whereas Haydn's actual beginning is a good one: a playfully solemn arpeggio of the tonic triad's root position.

Overlapping with this introductory gesture, however, is the first violin's real, unambiguous upbeat phrase that is the opening of the minuet's tune; we could almost call the cello's opening an 'introduction', for the simple reason that nobody would have noticed anything amiss if the minuet had started without it. Through the rhythmicization of the tune's second and the minuet's third bar, as well as by dint of the fact that the arpeggio has now changed into one of the $\frac{6}{4}$-chord, the first violin's has become a real pronounced upbeat phrase, and the $\frac{6}{4}$-chord makes sure that far from being conclusively assertive (as the cello was, ironically, at the beginning), it leads, urges somewhere, searches for its aim – which is, paradigmatically and in actual fact, the completion of the arpeggio, the bass on top.

I suggest that it is this singular structural situation which places the moment of greatest rhythmic freedom not at the beginning, but immediately after the beginning: the cello's ironically metrical rhythm would make perfect sense, whereafter the leader could enter with a rich variety of alternative liberties, all of them well 'under' the tempo which the cello has provisionally defined. Personally, in order to stress and maybe even define the structural comedy of the situation, I'd recommend a touch of vulgarity to both cellist and leader, in which case a little climax of vulgarity, the leader beating the cellist to it, would have to be tastefully executed: by way of changing the cello's down- and upbeat phrase rolled into one gesture of assertion into an upbeat to both the full quartet texture and indeed the first principal accent of the melody, the leader could be heard to pull the cello's leg with a much slower, wilfully assertive upbeat phrase whose every beat could, in fact, be taken on an ironic downbow, whereafter the main beat will, of course, have to be played on a downbow too. In such rhythmic circumstances, it would be down to the lower three in bar 3 to establish the main tempo, and even the basic contrast with the, once again, tonical *Trio* would thus have been immediately established. In a word, whichever way you tackle the beginning, it's bar 2 that is the moment of greatest agogic freedom, and a 'reasonable' upbeat will still be at the leader's disposal at the recapitulatory stage.

In any case, to make, after the principal section's introductory and upbeating orgy, the *Trio* stunningly upbeatless was a major inspiration, however simple the incisive thematic contrast thus achieved may sound after the creative event – and to me, it doesn't sound simple at all; rather, clearly complex. When did we last have an upbeatless Trio? I'm only asking the question in order to give an approximate measure of the creatively intended – and indeed realized – unexpectedness of this *Trio*'s exceptional structure; no wonder Haydn sticks to the tonic.

The *Trio* of Op.64, No.3 in B♭ turns the syncopated and tied upbeat into an accented note, as does the *Trio* of the F♯ minor Quartet (Op.50, No.4), at any rate in the second fiddle, against which the viola has a real upbeat. The Trio of the D minor quartet 'for beginners', Op.42, starts with a whole bar's solo upbeat phrase, because the minuet had started on the bar too: for obvious reasons, and as in the present instance, Haydn always coordinates trio and minuet purely metrically. The *Trio* of the B♭ work from Op.33 which we have ignored does start upbeatlessly, as does, of course, the Scherzo. The *Trio* of the A major work from Op.20 starts with a two-bar solo upbeat phrase. But the last time anything like the present situation obtained was in the first F minor Quartet, that from Op.20 – except that that *Trio* overlapped with the principal section. That was 28 quartets and 21 years ago. Before that, in the C major Quartet from Op.20, we do get close to the present situation – except that the principal section doesn't hide an upbeating orgy behind starting on the bar! The same is true of the minuet and *Trio* of the very first great quartet – Op.9, No.4 in D minor.

In sum, the present contrast is literally unique in Haydn's output, and playingly, one simply can't make too much of it: my suggested opening of the principal section puts it into the clearest possible perspective. It is for the viola to characterize the *Trio* thematically and indeed rhythmically; the first violin's consequent will not only respond to the viola's phrasing (rather than ape it), but will take the textural contrast between antecedent and consequent into account: the full quartet is concluding the first part of the *Trio* by replying to the texturally weakest type of string trio, two violins and viola (the ill-judged instrumentation of the otherwise inspired Dvořák *Terzetto*: see pp.36f.). In the *Trio*'s second part, statements and responses get intenser and proportionately shorter in the quasi-developmental middle; they are now between the middle parts on the one hand and second fiddle and cello on the other, and it is the *piano* whose colour has to contribute to the expression of increased tension. Thereafter the original rhythmic structures of antecedent and consequent are resumed, now as between the successive lower instruments on the one hand and the first fiddle on the other; ideally, they will do what Haydn did – create a variation, in their case phrasingly, on the first part.

Of the *Finale* I wrongly said that the present work shared it with that of the D major Quartet from Op.33; then I said they shared backgrounds, and finally I said that the Op.33 finale had become background (see p.182). What does all this mean? Simple truths – if, as I hope, Op.33, No.6, is well remembered, playingly remembered, in which case the finale's combination of variation form, rondo, and Haydn's own new double-variation will still be alive in the reader (*cf*. p.80). While they are all still identifiable, down to the basic alternation between D major and D minor, they have now been pushed into the background by another additional element – sonata, which introduces the further, elemental contrast between statement and development (cf.p.124), and thus turns the 'other', minor-mode theme into a developmental middle section,[1] while the final return, and variation, of the 'rondo' theme becomes an extended *allegro* coda, which is of overriding importance for the interpreter's definition of the tempo character of the body of the movement – a characterization that has to keep the ultimate *Allegro* firmly in mind. In order to stress this contrast, again from the outset, as well as to establish 'the' theme's character in no uncertain manner, it is strongly advisable – almost necessary, it seems to me – to creep into the theme at the beginning by way of a two-quaver upbeat expressing astonished reluctance (the theme is surprising enough in all conscience). The initial hesitation has to smile – at things the phrasing is aware of, whereas the listener (including, in the first round, the listening player) isn't: he has to feel able to extend a credit account of trust to the leader's opening agogics. The further development of the structure and its phrasing can be relied upon to reimburse the listener with interest – so much so that he will expect further and different agogics at the recapitulatory stage, for which Haydn has furnished a secure basis with his almost laughing accent on the first note of the upbeat: since, in the leadback, we've heard this upbeat, successively, no fewer than 10 times, Haydn allows himself a jocular overarticulation of the one – the 11th – which, at last, counts.

Thus the only point at which the listener will expect an *a tempo* upbeat will be at the last appearance of the theme, where, however, his expectations will

[1] In fact, Haydn grew fond of contradicting expectations created by his own, new double-variation form: in the slow A minor movement of his aforementioned, homotonal A major Trio, he creates the same impression of 'another' theme in the tonic major which, likewise, retrospectively turns into a middle section, because its expected first variation is replaced with the finale which, significantly enough, becomes, as it were, part of the slow movement's structure, in that it follows *attacca*. That, it will be remembered, happened a year later.

be contradicted – not, this time, by the leader's rhythmic liberties, but by Haydn's *Allegro*, whose tempo must be immediately and clearly defined, from the upbeat's word 'Go!' For the rest, in order to let the rich complexity of this structure sink in, it will, for once, prove enjoyable to play two works in the same key in succession – to play Op.33, No.6 and Op.71, No.2 in order of composition. If a pianist is around, the session's homotonality could be meaningfully interrupted by a relevant work in the dominant – the afore-mentioned A major Trio, whose slow movement would complete what would have turned into the richest possible structural experience, a grand view of Haydn's development of a form which he invented.

Op.71, No.3, in E flat major
(Hoboken III:71)

Both *opera* 71 and 74 were written in 1793, between the two London visits, which has prompted many observers to suggest that they were written with a view to larger halls, and larger audiences who needed introductory calls to attention. In my opinion, with the exception of the previously mentioned outer movements of 'The Emperor' (see pp.41, 185, and 216), which isn't Op.71 or 74 anyway, there is no evidence to suggest that Haydn went by anything but his own creative urges: his preoccupation with the beginning before the beginning we have noted well before his London visits (see pp.75ff. and 87.), and as for his textural approach, the present quartet has the withdrawn quality typical of Haydn's E♭, and which always goes together with a highly economical texture, as opposed to the brilliant, often full textures which have prompted those observations – and which, let us hasten to remember, can be found as often outside *opera* 71 and 74 as within.

The introduction before the exposition proper is certainly not the shortest ever: a single E♭ chord together with an equally expressive, lavishly extended bar's rest constitutes at least as long an introduction as, say, the first work's in this *opus* – not to speak of the two E♭ (!) chords at the beginning of the *Eroica* (cf.p.175), no doubt the children of the present introduction, among other Haydn parents.

Even though there are no obvious references to the introduction at any of the relevant stages of the structure – the end of the exposition, the leadback, the end of the recapitulation, and the very end – it would be quite wrong to suggest that this time, the beginning before the beginning is not an organic part of the sonata movement, that it is no more than a call to the London audiences' attention. But before we consider its significance for the total structure, its local structural significance has to be concretely examined – and a concrete examination is a playing examination: how long is the fermata? Any old length, many a performance seems to imply, most unsatisfactorily: unless you decide that the chord is utterly unrelated to the movement, in which case you might just as well omit it, its rhythmic relation to the beginning of the first subject must have a bearing on the movement's tempo character – or rather, to put the horse before the cart, the tempo, however unknown as yet, will determine the duration of the rest, for in music, as opposed to jurisdiction, there is retrospective law, which is audible not only at the moment of retrospection, but also at the moment of its object, its past effect.

The witty asides or off-stage effects of bars 5 and 6 (cf.Op.20, No.3, p.47) are pre-conditioned by the subject's early turn to the dominant, which usually invites a beginning before the beginning (*cf.*, e.g., Op.33, No.5, p.78), and whose comic effect is intensified by the introductory E♭ chord that drives the home-key home. The player-reader will note that the relation between the pseudo-separate introduction and the body of the movement is getting closer and closer, the fermata's required length ever more tangible. In part, it must depend on the articulation of the chord itself and cannot, therefore, be prescribed. But assuming that the chord will be enunciated broadly, rather than by way of an orchestral 'attack', the pause's duration becomes palpable in rhythmic view of the following opening phrase's pace. So far as sheer speed is concerned, we do know, after all, how long the silence is supposed to be – approximately twice the normal value of this minim rest, as it will define itself with the first minim of the *Vivace*. Or do we? The *Vivace* starts at the double-bar, not before, so that notationally speaking, our only guide, our only measure, is the duration of the chord. But musically speaking, the duration of that first minim is just as operative; only, we mustn't subject it to the rules that govern the notation of a pause.

I would suggest that with a real, concrete feel for the broad opening chord, and an equally concrete, if prospective feel for your particular *vivace* character, the pause will in its turn feel organic if it isn't twice, but approximately thrice the *vivace*'s minim value. In this way, the extended bar's silence will feel part of the piece both while it happens, i.e. consequent upon the chord, and after it has happened, retrospectively, in view of the *Vivace*'s tempo character.

We have devoted quite a little space to the beginning before the beginning, especially its silent part – but quite apart from the fact that every beginning needs utmost concentration, clarity, and persuasion, this particular beginning has to prove, not a call to a distracted audience's attention but, on the contrary, the immediate centre of attention, as integral part of both the serious and especially the witty side of the opening subject and its pointedly premature turn to the very dominant with which it has tonically started, and to which it immediately returns quasi-sequentially – the 'quasi' referring to the sequence's diminution of the model, which turns the process into a sub-thematic rather than a thematic one. And sure enough, the opening tonic triad's 12 notes allow the dominant only $1/12$ of its total sound – the only $B^{\flat}$, which is the first violin's!

The repeat is experienced as an elemental contrast to the initial exposition of the theme; and as such it is pointedly composed, as is the modified recapitulation. But the end, by way of final resolution and relaxation, returns to the introductory chord in triplicate, the concluding chord compensating for the theme's dominant misbehaviour by confining itself to the other two notes of the tonic triad.

The interpretation of the off-stage joke will – should ideally – vary from player to player, or rather, from players to players, but everybody will fruitfully bear two considerations in mind; first, that the 'aside' returns at the end of not only the consequent, but also the restatement's antecedent. As a result, one hears many a boring, unimaginative repetition of what, originally, may have been a witty and logical phrasing. If repetition is intended to be part of the second and third aside's joke, it will have to be played, as it were, in inverted commas; sheer, mere repetition will never sound intentional, invariably either accidental or downright embarrassing, as if the interpreters couldn't think of anything else.

Secondly, there has to be a high degree of unanimity between the members of the trio and the quartet which have to execute the 'aside'; its modified recapitulation, in particular, what with its *tutti* texture, its jocular, additional acciacccaturas and, below all, its very pronounced *piano* level in spite of everything, will only come off if what is heard is a sharply characterized, single joke rather than four of them, however, diverging, mildly so. The recapitulation's *piano* acciaccaturas in particular are a challenge to the four players' unanimous subtlety. Nothing is more easily possible than that one or the other members of the quartet might slightly disagree with the form the joke is taking – and there is no other textural situation in which one ought to subscribe more unreservedly, more passionately, to what, in quartet-playing, should be one's constant maxim anyway: 'the other person is always right'.

The slow movement, a lively *andante*, is a particularly subtle combination of Haydn's own double variation form with normal variation form and rondo form. The structure does not, however, impose the slightest problems on the interpretation. As in most of his other double variation movements, the 'other' theme (a) is in the tonic minor (or, in a movement in the minor mode, in the tonic major) and (b) can itself be regarded as a variation of the basic theme, whose own interpretation should, perhaps, be approached with a little more caution, circumspection, inasmuch as the wellnigh successive accents and the eventual *sforzato* at the end of the antecedent will have be carefully graded: the *sforzato* is, of course, by far the strongest stress which, however, only makes sense if the dotted crotchet accommodates an immediate *diminuendo* thereafter; in the preceding bar, the player-reader may agree that in order to shape the motion of the phrase, a difference between the equally notated accents will have to be made, the second being the stronger – still weak enough, however, to leave plenty of dynamic room for the ensuing *sforzato*! There aren't all that many phrases in this world which contain three prominent accents in short succession, and which oblige the interpreter to clarify the function of each of them as it is heard: when we hear the first two, we must be made to grasp immediately, quasi-instinctively, that neither is yet the principal stress of the phrase – that rather paradoxically, both of them prepare for it. So maybe my contention of the movement's problemlessness is a little hasty, but if you want to turn these accents into a problem, you had better first play the phrase without any accents at all: the three only emphasize what, logically, you would be doing anyway.

That bar with the two accents contains a curious inscription: '*licenza*'. Is the reader's ear and/or musical education up to what Haydn means thereby? It is a sweet remark, nowise addressed to the players, and thus unique in Haydn's entire output. If I may translate it as clearly as possible, it means, 'I know!' For what happens in this bar between the violins is consecutive octaves, which I was strictly forbidden, of course, at my L.R.A.M. exam. Brahms once planned a little book, of which I saw a few pages, on consecutives in the great masters, and why they committed these crimes, of which there is a wonderfully concealed instance in Schoenberg's *Transfigured Night*; whereas Haydn, less conservative than Schoenberg, makes no attempt at acoustic concealment. But that he really deemed it necessary to point out that he knew what he'd done and proposed to take this liberty, that it hadn't happened unconsciously or unintentionally as in a failing L.R.A.M. paper, goes to show that what I suggested on p.158 was to the point – that we understand him better than 'they' did!

Minuet and *Trio* once again share the tonic key and thus give us no inkling of the revolution that was soon going to happen to the key relationship between principal section and *Trio* – nor do I wish to give any advance notice of what, the reader will agree when the time comes, is going to be experienced as a downright sensation; but readers who are too curious about what's going to happen to Haydn's approach to the tonal structure of the minuet – as I would be – are advised to interrupt perusal of the present page and turn, instead and for a minute or two, to p.199.

As is his wont, Haydn throws the contrast between minuet and *Trio* into relief by making them in many respects the 'same' – not only keywise, nor just, inevitably, upbeatwise. In fact, both sections start with an unaccompanied upbeat phrase – the minuet's extending over 1⅓ bars of the leader's part, the *Trio*'s over 2 complete bars of the cello's. But what overpowering contrast develops between the two, which the respective interpretations have to define and characterize with emphatic polarity! The minuet's upbeat phrase would make just as much sense without the first bar-line, which a twentieth-century composer would have omitted, whereas the *Trio*'s crotchet upbeat is real, leading as it does to the first-beat crotchet which concludes the first of the upbeat phrase's two sharply articulated motifs: the cellist has to be conscious of doing the opposite of what the leader had been doing, for which articulating purpose, as against the flow of the first violin's upbeat phrase, he will need a distinctly more relaxed tempo.

The *Finale*'s *Vivace* imposes, again, clear tempo restrictions on the interpretation; and as in the *Trio* though for entirely different reasons, the danger of too fast a tempo must be avoided. But as we have remarked before on more than one occasion, avoidance never communicates: the *Finale*'s tempo definition has to spring from positive characterization. Of what?

Of the refined wit implied in the theme with its absolutely literal repetition of the bar-long opening phrase, and with what we could have described as its waltzlike accompaniment if the waltz had yet existed at the time: it is fascinating to observe how both Haydn and Mozart anticipated the quick waltz before the normal waltz had come into being, though the yet slower ländler had already been born; Mozart did it in the first, *presto* (!) movement of his very early G major String Quartet, K.156 – one of the only two early Mozart quartets which deserve our playing attention (the other being the neighbouring C major work, K.157).

In order for Haydn's witty articulation to succeed, the melody's rest between the model and the repetition has to be outspoken – which characterization will, at the same time, enable the middle parts' quaver accompaniment to keep the necessary distance between the two quavers; the *Vivace* will nevertheless make itself felt so long as the tempo is faster than would be that of a danceable ländler or even that of the future's normal waltz. Once the tempo definition has truly succeeded in deriving from the opening structure and its unmistakable smile, the further course of the movement will not present the remotest tempo problems; on the contrary, what the playing quartet will find, perhaps to its surprise, is that its characteristic opening tempo will provide solutions in the most unlikely places, such as the semiquavers played against the theme: their phrasing will naturally happen, whereas at a faster pace, they would have been rolled off rather than phrased. Even the final, *tutti* semiquaver climax, not an easy octave unison in all conscience, will fall into characteristic place, where otherwise, the semiquavers would have resulted in a disintegrated, or gradually disintegrating, mad and meaningless rush.

Op.74. No.1, in C major
(Hoboken III:72)

With the whole of Op.71 and Op.74, we are in 1793, between Haydn's two visits to London. I quite deliberately did not make this announcement solemnly at the beginning of Op.71, No.1 because, as I indicated in my introduction to Op.71, No.3, so many conclusions have been drawn from the historical position of these works, so many illusory characteristics have been attributed to them, that I thought it would make a nice change to examine these masterpieces where they belong – not in their historical or geographical context, that is to say, but in the general context of Haydn's development as a quartet composer at its extended, maturest stage and, in particular, in the contexts of his successive variations on the theme of the introduction, of which the penultimate of his seven great C major quartets – only 'The Emperor' was to follow in that key – is again a novel and deeply thoughtful example. In its style, the work can be described as the string quartet at its most brilliant; in fact, in the *Finale*, the lower instruments have the time of their lowly lives, producing virtuosity with ease, and with enough energy left to send messages of good-will right across to the finale of Beethoven's Rasumovsky Quartet in the same key.

After what has been said, apropos of Op.33, No.1, about the most realistic approach to dynamic marks (see p.67), the first movement should be fairly plain sailing; Haydn here clarifies his structural intentions very carefully. One of the quartet's most fascinating features is, once again, the introduction. By now we are, I submit, entitled to ask: what is new about it?

Like the preceding one, it is tempo-less. But unlike the single chord, it consists of a perfect cadence, thus harking back as far as Op.33, No.5 (see p.78), at which stage the commentators don't say anything about an opening call to attention! In that quartet, however, the perfect cadence underpinned a melodic motif which played a crucial role in the body of the movement and, accordingly, the movement's tempo and character started *with* this cadence, not after it. The present cadence's role in the body of the movement is far subtler, its musical distance from the body of the movement far greater. In order to increase the urgency of the resolution which is tantalizingly delayed by a pause, Haydn does not, as in that earlier G major quartet, content himself with the dominant chord, but intensifies it through the seventh. The melodic motif which the cadence seems to engender rather than being engendered by it

– simply leading-note to tonic – is, for the moment, nothing to write home about; one's attention is caught by the cadential movement, the harmony, rather than by what happens on top of it.

All inevitable expectations thus aroused could not be more sorely mistaken: together with the harmony but very much as the principal determining agent, the pseudo-conventional melodic motif immediately, and most unconventionally, proves not merely thematic, but actually the movement's omnipotent basic motif. Not only does it assume its proper – if, of course, varied – place in the actual *Allegro moderato*'s second bar, where it retains its rhythmic proportions, the long leading-note and the short tonic, but it is, in unlikely fact, responsible for the highly chromatic antecedent's every single melodic interval but two, since apart from the opening sequential structure and the antecedent's articulation of its own cadence, the entire four-bar antecedent proceeds stepwise and consists, moreover, of *six* semitones as against two whole tones and two minor thirds, the latter happening articulatingly between melodic motifs rather than within them! Innocent as it sounds, then, this tempo-less introduction proves closely integrated thematically, to the extent of being the thematic basis of the movement. The end of both the exposition and the entire movement refers to it, of course, and the two-bar leadback's circumlocution of the dominant seventh is so obtrusive a variation on it that one is almost surprised when the resolution doesn't *precede* the recapitulation according to the model at the introductory stage, but *is* the opening of the recapitulation.

The rhythmic build-up (yes, the word is justified notwithstanding the two chords) of the introduction is very much a matter for the individual interpreter, so long as he meets three conditions, two negative and one positive, and all of them pretty self-evident. The duration of his fermata must, of course, be well outside any perceptible extension of a semibreve in his forthcoming *Allegro moderato*, and the tonic chord, though a mere crotchet, has to come across unaggressively, without a trace of the kind of attack the same player might well employ when leading an orchestra in such chords: the sound has to be determined but well-blended, well-rounded. The positive requirement is equally obvious: however far outside the *Allegro moderato*, the emphatically free tempo of this introductory cadence has yet to bear a tangible relation to it, has to be felt as an introduction to it – an easily achievable task so long as the forthcoming *Allegro moderato* is firmly in the leader's (and the cellist's!) mind at the time of the introduction.

The eventual definition of the movement's tempo character will indeed depend on the cello's quavers in the first half of the body of the movement's first bar, though experience shows that any uncertainty in the cellist's mind or any mild discrepancy between his tempo and the leader's will quickly be adjusted once the leader gets a chance to phrase his melody; after all, the cello's characterizing role is only accompanimental, whereas the leader's must be principal despite the cellist's chronological precedence. Yet again it should be possible for the leader to adjust his character picture to the metre of the cellist's opening quavers, at least to the extent of avoiding palpable contradiction or an equally palpable margin of discomfort.

For the rest, is our reaction, or rather, our lack of reaction to this downright sensational theme not a depressing sign of our *blasé* attitude towards music, our current state of relative insensitivity produced by over-feeding or, in any case, over-availability? It is, the reader will admit, quite an extraordinary theme, the like of which cannot be found anywhere else, either at Haydn's time or before or after: not even Bach's *Chromatic Fantasy and Fugue* is able to present its extraordinary thematic structures as if nothing had happened; on the contrary, they still sound weird at the present stage in the history of listening (including, of course, the player's own listening). Why does this Haydn theme not endanger our composure? Why do we, I mean many of us, play it as if it were any old theme, whereas an ideal interpretation would, I suggest, be able to express the almost shocked astonishment at, as it were, the chromatic scale turning into a sublimely characterized theme, as well as the player's enthusiastic understanding of how it was possible for this to happen? I do hope that the fuss I am making will prompt the reader to wake up and play this theme for what it's worth, in which case the rest of the movement which, second subject included, is dominated by it, will prove an ever newly exciting experience, and an unproblematic experience to boot.

Haydn's dynamics are, of course, an intrinsic part of the opening revelation; at the risk of repeating myself, I have to draw attention to their all-importance – for one hardly ever hears a performance wherein they aren't underplayed. The *forte* of the introduction does not exclude but, on the contrary, necessitates a *crescendo* on the endless semibreve: the full *forte* sound will be reached with the crotchet, which will thus, one hopes, avoid any nasty noises. With the theme and the (i.e. its) tempo, a *piano* has to set in which, if it is sufficiently positive, sufficiently characteristic, will sound *subito* despite the intervening, extended rest, during which the tonic chord's well-rounded *forte* sound will still be in the listener's (including the playing listener's) ears. The *crescendo* of bar 2 must not start before the end of the resumed basic motif, which is now melodically integrated; the *crescendo* in its turn does not exclude but, on the contrary, necessitates an infinitesimal *diminuendo* at the end of the antecedent, down from its top note. The reaching of the *forte* level, which coincides with the opening of the consequent and, again, does not exclude but, on the contrary, necessitates a clear dynamic definition of its opening upbeat phrase (bar 5 of the body of the movement with upbeat), will thus be clarified and express its structural function. The aim of the *forte* upbeat phrase is inhibited by the *sforzato* on the upbeat that follows the downbeat phrase: it is of supreme importance that the thus inhibited accent must make the listening ear expect the forthcoming cause of the inhibition! All meaningful phrasing, that is to say, throws light, not only on the shape one hears, but also on the future: thus contrasting articulation is harmoniously combined with continuity.

Both the diminutive noun and the adjective of the *Andantino grazioso* seem to stress the fact that it is not a slow movement proper – as does its dance-rhythmical (almost waltzlike, or rather, ländler-like) background (see p.194). For this very reason, the movement represents yet another drastic innovation of which Beethoven was to avail himself in such works as the C minor Quartet or, near the other end of his creative life, the Eighth Symphony – the four-movement symphonic structure without a real slow movement, and with two dance movements in the middle instead, one of them playing the role of the slow movement only to stress, at every corner, that it isn't one, and that any slow-movement interpretation would be a fatal misinterpretation.

So far as tone quality is concerned, there is a nasty bar for the viola – the fifth. Consistency with – rather than any copying of – the first violin's opening, which is magnificently placed on the G-string, has to be the prime consideration. Unless the viola player's instrument can boast a very good C-string (the rarest of occurrences), however, he will find that the c' and a had better be played on the G-string, which will move the sound quality nearer the first violin's own G-string. If handled carefully, the difference in colour of the first $f\sharp$ on the C-string needn't matter too much, because the note is the leading-note in a normal, close root position of the dominant seventh, and the second $f\sharp$, which admittedly is solo, doesn't matter all that much either, because a corresponding contrast is remembered from the first violin's progress from b to the open G-string. Of course, if you start vibrating furiously on the $f\sharp$ in order to hide your embarrassment over the change of string (how shaming to play this unaccompanied solo in the first position!), everything is lost, in that the corresponding contrast turns into its opposite. It must be realized that in any case, an even and none too vibrato tone is required for this upbeat phrase. In order for the movement not to degenerate into a danceable dance, the first phrase's upbeating function must be treated as antecedent to the responsive upbeat phrase's continuation: the grace notes in bar 3 show unambiguously where the first principal accent lies; we here have an antecedent and a consequent each of which consists of an antecedent and a consequent, with the result that the viola is not involved in principal accentuation at all: the consequent's consequent is – which is, again, the responsibility of the leader.

The minuet is a movement of exceptional weight – which is not the only exceptional thing about it, for exceptional weight needs quite a few exceptional means of communication to make itself felt. The principal section – and therefore also the *Trio* – starts without an upbeat – which is not to say, however, that either starts without an upbeat phrase, as the upbeatless minuet and *Trio* of the D major Quartet from Op.71 did (see p.187); there, the first violin's upbeat phrase ensued, as it were, belatedly – after the cello's introductory phrase. The three opening *sforzatos* of the present minuet do not imply successive equal accents: how could they? There is, after all, an opening phrase, and any phrasing with three successive equal stresses would be impossible – would cut the phrase asunder. No, the first two bars lead to the third, whose *sforzato* therefore receives the strongest accent: a *crescendo* of *sforzatos* will be the most natural solution. Without *sforzatos* and near the other end of the dynamic scale, the *Trio*, likewise, opens with a two-bar upbeat phrase whose aim, the third bar, can be felt to parallel, in a spirit of resolution or at least relaxation, the minuet's third-bar aim.

Resolution? Relaxation? The question is of the utmost importance to the interpreter, for if he doesn't know, doesn't feel the knowledge of whether to accumulate or relax tension, he is, as a communicative player, wholly paralysed. Something has happened with the *Trio*'s change of key which is altogether unprecedented, either in Haydn's own work or anywhere else: the distant key of A major has been chosen as contrasting key – the dominant of the dominant's dominant, which therefore ought to give us a feeling of multiply increased tension, not of relaxation.

But it doesn't. Haydn achieves the opposite – with an innovation with which Beethoven is invariably credited, a key-relationship for which English (as opposed to German or American) musicology hasn't even yet found a name. In German and American, it is called *Terzverwandtschaft*, third-relationship, except that the American translation doesn't clearly express the fact that keys whose tonics are related by a third are suddenly regarded as close relatives; the only such relation we are aware of prior to the introduction of 'third-relationships' is that between major and minor keys bearing the same key signature.

I think I have the answer, not yet given in any treatise on diatonic harmony, to the question how Haydn (ever more so in the last decade of his life) and Beethoven succeeded in turning, overnight as it were, 'third-related' keys into close relatives. The usual answer is in triadic terms which, in themselves, are demonstrably unsatisfactory: you don't feel, experience the closeness of the present *Trio*'s A major to the minuet's C major as a relation of the two notes of the A minor triad (or, for that matter, the F major triad) which, as such, isn't anywhere near your listening mind as the change from C major to A major happens. What, however, is jolly close to your mind is *the leading pull of the mediant*; I'd go so far as to say that if the term 'leading-note' hadn't happened to be chosen for the seventh degree, nobody would object if the mediant were called the leading-note: innumerable melodies testify to its powerful pull towards the tonic. You only have to sing, inside your head, mediant – tonic in any key to convince yourself of the instinctive truth of my submission. It is because from the moment of the *Trio*'s opening A major, the minuet's C is retrospectively felt as a 'leading-note' that paradoxically, the *Trio* (sensitively thus constructed in both the melodic and the harmonic dimension) is felt as resolution; it is for the same reason that that notorious F in bar 23 of the first movment of the G major Quartet, Op.64, No.4 (see p.162) is experienced as a natural event which, in fact, can now be heard to have foreshadowed Haydn's later preoccupation with third-relationships, and that the multiplicity of third-relationships by Haydn, Beethoven, and all later geniuses is immediately accepted as organic.

The interpreter, then, is fully justified in treating the *Trio* as of old as central relaxation, and as if to prove my contention, Haydn, again exceptionally, broadens out into a coda whose A minor rubs in my pull from C to A three times over (bars 101–102, 104, and 106), before he lands on the dominant, E major – whence the E pulls us, 'leads' us, back to the minuet's C as the minuet's C had pulled us, 'led' us, to the *Trio*'s A!

I am confident that my explanation will be of interpretative help: at last, the *Trio*'s A major won't be played artificially, as something strange, remote, but naturally, as something familiar, indeed familial – as a close relative whom Haydn was the first to discover, as he was the first to discover everything else, atonality (as we shall hear) included.

As for the lower instruments' time of their lives in the *Finale*, no listener suspects that the brilliant semiquaver passages in the *fugato* development are really very easy to play. The second violin, in particular, coming (chronologically speaking) on top of the lower two and turning into a D minor that would play itself if anything could, for once outshines everybody – maybe even the first violin which, when it finally takes over, doesn't find things all that easy. But don't force the pleasure, or you'll spoil it (amongst other things, because you are going to use too much bow). For the rest, every player with experience of contemporary quartet-writing will agree with my suggestion that this is one of the sections which it should be obligatory for contemporary composers to study if they are thinking of indulging in a bit of brilliant quartet-writing.

Op.74, No.2, in F major
(Hoboken III:73)

In deference to the playing student's point of view, I have to get my introductory remarks on the second of Haydn's three great F major quartets out of proportion, for from the student's standpoint, the most important feature about this popular work, included in all the 'celebrated' editions, is that it is a well-tried, eminently suitable introduction to the greatest Haydn for an inexperienced second fiddler, even though – or rather, partly because – in the second variation of the *Andante grazioso*, he will have to cope with an exquisite solo in B♭ minor which, however, does not lie badly. More about it when we reach it in the course of our detailed discussion of the work, whose variation on the theme of the beginning before the beginning reveals, again, an utterly new approach to the question of the introduction, an answer to it so natural that one accepts it thoughtlessly as a conventional device, unalive to the fact that nobody had ever done anything comparable – or has meanwhile, for that matter. As for Haydn himself, the only introduction which can at least be compared in one respect to the present one is, interestingly enough, the next one, 'The Rider's' (see pp.205f.) which, however, evinces more dissimilarities than similarities.

For one thing, we are to play the beginning before the beginning in tempo – in principle, anyway, if not pedantically in character. For another, it consists of an eight-bar period in octave unison for the entire quartet, with an implied modulation to the dominant and a dominant end; the only sign of its preceding the exposition is the pause and the eventual dominant resting point. The melody is, however, itself amazing, for it gives an elementary preview of things to come, elementary enough to consist of the tonic triad and the dominant triad and not much else; in fact, literally the only other thing is the dominant's leading-note, which confirms the dominant end beyond any possible doubt. The rhythm of the first three bars, moreover, is identical with that of the first subject's first three bars. For the first time, the chronic, conventional description of a 'call to attention' is not without musical meaning, in view of the fanfare-like character of the introduction – which, at the same time, takes care not to disclose too much, to make a forceful opening statement without the force of prediction: after the introduction's *forte*, the body of the movement starts, in fact, *subito piano* – an unobtrusive contradiction of expectation, but all the more touching for that.

At this stage in our investigations, the player-reader will not be surprised to learn that the usual murder of this introduction is achieved by bar accents, eight of them. How gripping the period can become if one actually phrases it – just because its deceptively simple triadic outline does not let the listener suspect that there's much of a shape there: the phrasing must uncover the shape and progressive shapliness of what, when it's all over, will no longer seem an elementary tune! For the purpose, notwithstanding its triadic assertion, the first bar has to 'beat up' to the second, while the third, as a variation of the second, will receive a stronger accent on its first beat than the second – less strong, at the same time, than the aim of the background antecedent: bar 4. The identical bars 5 and 6 must not, of course, be played identically; together, they have to prepare for the contrasting rhythmic culmination, which sets in with bar 7, whose semiquaver, and thus implied dotted rhythm, seem the introduction's only unthematic element. Seem.

For the one introduction which we will never expect to return in the structure it introduces does come back at the leadback stage, some of it, in combination with its contrasting replacement at, or rather after, the end of the exposition; and it is then, before the leadback's modified return of the end of the exposition, that the dotted rhythm of the introduction's end has to reappear, sharply articulating the end of the developmental stage, and followed by a G.P. which, corresponding as it does to the silence that has marked the actual end of the exposition, prepares the way for the final unison transition to the recapitulation, whose model is the unison transition to the repeat. For this crucial purpose the dotted rhythm had to be saved up, in order to coordinate the end of the introduction and the start of the body of the movement with the end of the development and the start of the recapitulation, as well as with the end of the exposition and the start of the development, which was preceded by its own version of the unison transition. As for the actual end of the exposition, it was a mitigated, de-dotted version of the dotted rhythm: recognition is facilitated by the fact that the introduction finished in (or rather, 'on') the dominant too. The players will have to be clearly aware of these connections, for emphatic connections are composed for the purpose of being played, thrown into relief; unplayed, with no more, therefore, than the notated relations, their effect varies between that of an embarrassment and that of a disaster: the interpretation will always have to refer to what the composer refers to; it is as simple as that. The clarification of the introduction's newly subtle role in the main structure is really the only 'task' the interpretation of the first movement has to set itself; otherwise, it is a movement which will be found to impress both its phrasings, and its textures, sharply contrasting in one or two places, crystal-clearly upon the playing mind, which will also find that a great deal of imagination is needed for the purpose of meeting Haydn's requirements – imagination whose nature and range he indicates just as clearly, if one can read, not between the staves, but between the notes. There are, in other words, plenty of metrical traps (such as the aforementioned bar accents), whose only victims will be players who lack rhythmic imagination.

In what is once again the not so very slow variation movement (cf. pp.197f.), the only trace of Haydn's double variation form is, this time, the B♭ minor variation which, sure enough, assumes the position and function of a middle section, whereas the principle section indulges in Haydn's passacaglia-like approach (cf. p.122), with the theme's repeats submitting to variation in what, in the structural circumstances, is experienced as a recapitulation: variation form and ternary form are again combined (cf. pp.80, 124, 167, 189).

The B♭ minor variation's middle-section-like contrast is promoted by its harmonic structure, which doesn't retain that of the theme. The theme's first part finishes in the dominant, the minor-mode variation's in the relative major; and where the theme's quasi-developmental middle modulates to the subdominant's relative minor, the B♭ minor variation's modulates to the subdominant – differences of which the experienced second fiddler had better be aware. But we promised advice to the newcomer: it is he for whom the present work is a wellnigh ideal introduction to the maturest Haydn. The third position will be found eminently suitable for the B♭ minor variation's antecedent and much of the consequent; the jump from the D-string to the E-string in bar 2 happens to occur at a stage where a natural break is required anyway, and more than the break produced by the staccato dot. For the last two bars, or at least the very last phrase before the double-bar, I recommend the fifth position. Back into the third after the double-bar, back into the fifth you know where. The rest of the fingerings explain themselves on the basis of what I've said; it so happens that the ends of both parts work wonderfully on the D-string, whatever your specific phrasing intentions. Even the inexperienced second fiddler will agree that Haydn invented in terms of a well-lying melody in this unwell-lying key; he had plenty of second-violin experience to draw on, though the quartet in which he played second and Mozart viola was a thing of the past: Mozart, we must keep reminding ourselves, was dead, had been dead for two years.

As for the phrasing of the theme itself, and hence the character of the movement and its tempo, it is the slow-movement trap into which most quartets fall, with an utter disregard for the *grazioso* nature of the theme, whose double dotted quavers and dotted semiquavers characterize both its almost scherzoid nature and its dance background so clearly that one fails to understand how the *adagio* one usually hears has come about; what is certain is that any such characterless tempo is the result of its sheer pace having been imposed on the rhythmic structure, rather than the tempo character having been derived from the extremely well defined rhythm of the theme. I think this warning is enough: within the range of possible *andante grazioso* tempos there is enough variety to satisfy any leader's musical personality; the real slow-movement elements of the theme will have to be contrasted, of course, with its playful side – a contrast which will easily realize itself so long as none of the rhythmic motifs is weakened, de-characterized.

Rhythm returns with a deeply gratifying vengeance in the minuet as distinct from its third-related D♭ major (!) *Trio (cf.* the minuet of the *opus'* first work, pp.198ff.), which merely retains a single rhythmic element – the motif which starts with an acciaccatura whose relation to the minuet's demisemiquaver motifs is immediately feelable: the demisemiquavers can't be played fast enough in order to emphasize their acciaccatura-like significance, for which purpose the single, complete motifs will have to be sharply articulated; personally, I don't think this possible without the tiniest of commas after the dotted quavers. But in the heat of this articulation, the ultimate aim of the antecedent must not be forgotten – not by the listener either, who, in the course of bar 2, has to be kept aware of the fact that the phrase's centre of gravity is further ahead; it wouldn't be enough for him to realize the fact when bar 4's *sforzato* is reached, for in that case, he would have misunderstood bar 2, however temporarily. And what an aim it is! No less than the relative minor's dominant seventh, and at the beginning of the consequent, D minor is strikingly touched upon for a moment, on the way to the dominant.

The 'leading' tendency of the mediant (*cf.* p.199) is, as it were, incorporated in the contrast and continuity between minuet and *Trio*: the mood of the *Trio* really 'hits it off' in that it conveys precisely the relaxation we feel when we 'resolve' the mediant on to the tonic, in our inner ear. This spirit of relaxation has to permeate the *Trio*'s second-violin tune as well as the first violin's playing around it until it actually takes over the leading role.

In the case of both *Trios* of the first two works of Op.74, then, there is this utterly unexpected 'resolution' to the third below, minor in one case, major in the other – it doesn't matter: both leaping 'steps' are, in fact, steplike in their intense dis-tensioning effect. Thus the traditional, relaxing role of the trio is not only retained in this revolutionary step, but in fact emphasized and harmonically supported as never before – not even in the change from tonic minor to tonic major, a sovereign example of which is the *Trio* of Mozart's only great quartet in the minor mode – his second Haydn quartet.

The *Finale* is so real a *presto* that its thematic structures continually characterize its nature – except that 'characterize' is too static a verb for what they do: it is urgent movement, motion whose urgency they define and constantly redefine. The reader will bear with me if I offer a single example – the more easily, perhaps, since clear consciousness of such examples affect one's interpretation, even emotionally: clarification of one's motives results in their intensification. The antecedent of the theme (*a* in Ex.57) aims, ultimately, at the unprecedented semiquaver figure in bar 4 (*x* in Ex.57), together with the ensuing quaver F; the principal accent, that is to say, will be

Ex.57

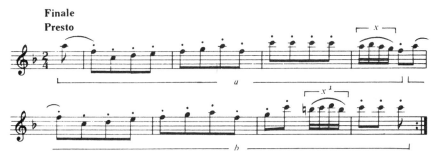

on its first note, the A. This relatively static role of the semiquaver figure turns into its opposite at the end of the consequent (*b* in Ex.57), where it – now precedented – has become the most urgent upbeat phrase (*x*[1]) leading to the end of the sentence, with the result that the principal accent, the first semiquaver, has now become the least accented note altogether: what was relatively static has become as dynamic, as forward-urging as at all possible in the circumstances. The interpretation will aim at a clearly expressed resting-point at *x*, and aim at the opposite at *x*[1], retaining, at the same time, sufficient background unity of contrasting phrasings to throw the close relation between the motifs into relief. Everything proves mobile, even the relatively immobile; this is the structural principle behind Haydn's ever-renewed and -renewing definition of the *presto* character. In view of it, the player-reader will be thoroughly fascinated by the further fate of the semiquaver figure throughout the movement, until at the end, before the syncopations which intensify the motion yet more urgently, it reaches maximal mobility by having become the central element of a two-bar phrase (Ex.58):

Ex.58

Op.74, No.3, in G
(Hoboken III:74)

'The Rider' is the last of the six quartets composed in 1793, the relatively quiet year in Vienna – between the two strenuous London concert seasons. No, my title is no misprint, for the Quartet's most forward-looking innovation, though by no means its only one, is its tonality, of which we have had a premonition as early as the finale of Op.33, No.6: to say that the work is in G minor is a vast over-simplification. The outer movements, that is to say, turn to the major mode, not by way of the usual, composed and extended Picardy third, but well before the final stage of their respective structures – at the recapitulation's second-subject stage, in fact. And the third of the normal tonical movements, i.e. the minuet, isn't in G minor either, but, again, in G major: it is only for the *Trio* that Haydn turns to the tonic minor – where, in a normal G minor work, the opposite might well have happened: the principal section would have been in the tonic, and the trio might have turned to the tonic major (compare, for instance, Mozart's oft-mentioned D minor Quartet). In short, 'The Rider' is really musical history's first work centred on a home tonality rather than a home key: it is, in fact, in G – or, should you have accepted the stupid habit of saying 'in G' when you mean 'in G major', you'd have to say that it's in G minor-major. The interpreter had better be aware of this new approach to tonal structure: all his G minors are aiming at G major.

The other wellnigh revolutionary innovation is, of course, the new, unprecedented, unforehearable variation on the beginning before the beginning – all the newer since, as in the preceding F major Quartet, it starts with an octave unison in the tempo of the movement; this time, however, the unison doesn't extend over the entire introduction but, in and with the consequent, yields to a movingly contrasting harmonic texture. It is, however, again an eight-bar period moving to the dominant, whence the unknowing player could be forgiven if he thought that it would play the same role as the preceding quartet's introduction – or at least a similar role. Haydn could not contradict his expectations more violently, for while there is no trace of the introduction in the leadback, it actually, and almost unbelievably, forms the development's central subject, in view of which astonishing fact we seriously have to ask ourselves whether we are indeed justified in describing it as an introduction! In the circumstances, 'an introduction which proves not to be one' would be the most realistic description – and one which would immediately remind us of this structural function's influence on Beethoven: compare, for example, the opening movement of his frequently mentioned, late B♭ Quartet.

The players will have to be audibly alive to the introduction's central role in the movement's total structure; to put it bluntly and realistically, the opening octave unison has to be phrased: it rarely is. The low notes define the basic line; the others have to recede despite their *acciaccaturas* and their continued *forte* level.

The viola entry responding to the cello's triadic opening of the first subject will be played in the close second position, which there is plenty of time to make sure of. It must start with a clear upbeat phrase: it hardly ever does – and the same goes, of course, for the upper instruments.

Stem the flow of the music – with a playful hesitation, perhaps – as you come up against the same upbeat's new meaning at the beginning of the second subject which, incidentally, can hardly be played very fast if the *glissandos* (cf. Op.20, No.3, p.50) are not to become tasteless; in a word, it bears *grazioso* character. This particular contrast between the subjects is resumed in the 'riding' Finale, whose recapitulatory metamorphosis into the tonic major it makes indeed possible.

In between, the middle movements teem, likewise, with innovations; in fact, the key of the *Largo assai* represents a veritable revolution, though what we know by now about its third-relationship makes its E major far less remote than its tonic's tritonal distance from the work's tonic would indicate – its polar, diametrically opposite position in the circle of fifths. In order to make this musical revolution a living reality, I would suggest avoiding an overlong pause between the first two movements: the 'leading' impulse (cf.p.199) of the first movement's final G should still be in the listener's ear.

In the slow movement itself, the rhythm of bar 14's upbeat phrase should not be allowed to conceal its metre – which can, in fact, be clarified by a free approach. In bars 49–50, the unfortunately usual *tremolo pp* must be shunned at all costs: these are real demisemiquavers, and indeed thematic as such; their continuity from the preceding *ff* must be audible in order for the *ff–pp* contrast to make itself fully felt.

Haydn's progress, or regress, from the slow movement's E major to the minuet's exceptional and utterly unprecedented tonic major strikingly confirms my highly empirical theory about the real musical significance of third-relationships: he does not, as he would have to if he followed his invariable, normal procedure, return to G minor for the minuet, though he could easily if there were any musical reality behind the accepted explanation of third-relationships; the two tonics would remain triadic notes. But whereas

G 'led' to E, E doesn't 'lead' to G, and so he 'merely' lets the dominant of the dominant's dominant resolve, relax on to the tonic major.

In performance, the interval between these two movements will, ideally, be about the same as that between the first two: the listener (including the playing listener) should be given a chance emotionally to compare the two contrasts, and surprisedly to note that the first is actually the lesser – though theoretically, it is maximal!

Thus, the minuet's revolution is, of course, likewise its key, which has to be played, as it were, with the converted person's exaggerated conviction: he has to convert too! The usual murder of the minuet happens almost at once – by halving the antecedent, unalive to bar 3's upbeat phrase, which postpones its expected accent to bar 4: the expectation of a $2\frac{1}{3}$-bar upbeat phrase is contradicted by a $3\frac{1}{3}$ one. And not even the consequent's *forte* should become the phrase's principal accent, which is bar 8: the *forte* level has to be reached *within* the upbeating motion.

Exceptionally, the *Trio*'s relation to the principal section is a tensing one, even though it does retain the playfulness of its normal relaxation: another drastic innovation, this, and one which only real musical understanding will bring to light. For the *Trio*'s octave leaps, see the minuet of Op.50, No.2, p.92: a great deal of interpretative variation can, of course, be employed – *should* be; mere aping would result in another murder.

The *Finale*'s single danger is two tempos instead of one; one for the ride, another for the semiquavers. The contrast between the theme's *fortes* and *pianos* will have to be as incisive as possible – but must not, on the other hand, hide the opening upbeat's upbeating drive. The work's introduction is often considered 'riding' music too; I don't think we need bother about visual or extra-musical acoustic associations: the interpretation will gain nothing from them.

Op.76, No.1, in G
(Hoboken III:75)

With the first quartet (started, probably, in 1796 and completed in 1797) of the Op.76 set Haydn continues his exploration of novel tonal structures; in fact, he makes harmonic life more difficult for himself than ever before. Once again, that is to say, he replaces the expected home key with a mere home tonality – which problem, however, he tackles the hard way, i.e. the opposite way of the one he had pursued in the preceding quartet. For there, the deliberate tonal confusion – the flowing together of the home tonality's minor and major modes – had, straightforwardly, followed the natural resolving tendency of the Picardy third: tonic minor had aimed at, urged towards, and thus been relaxingly replaced with, tonic major.

Now, however, against the heaviest possible odds, Haydn brilliantly succeeds in a reversal of this procedure: the bulk of the so-miscalled G major work's finale is in G minor, though he does heed the Picardy third to the extent of ending in the major – well after the dramatic onset of the recapitulation, which is thus expected to run its 'normal' G minor course, at least until the second subject. He was to resume the selfsame approach, which started an utterly new chapter in the history of symphonic thought, in the C major 'Emperor' (Op.76, No.3: see p.216), but meanwhile, it is truly fascinating to observe that just as he had chosen B minor for his introduction of progressive tonality (see pp.64ff. and 150ff.), so he now chose G for his first two quartets in a tonality rather than a key – Op.74, No.3 in G minor → major and Op.76, No.1 in G major → minor (→ major).

For the interpreter, the new structural departure is of the utmost importance: he is aiming not only at the finale's tensing G minor but, ultimately, at one of the most liberating major-mode resolutions in the history of music; unexpected tension needs unprecedented discharge.

The history of composition did indeed pay attention to Haydn's innovation – which, at the same time, did not result in a broad formal development. Nor indeed would we expect it to do so: while his replacement of key with tonality was taken up on a broad front, his minor-mode finale after a major-mode opening movement introduced *an element of concluding tension*, or, at any rate, of far-reaching tension at a structure's penultimate stage, which few geniuses were prepared to face – two, to be precise: Mendelssohn and Brahms, the former in his 'Italian' Symphony, the latter in his not so F major

Symphony, his first Violin Sonata, and his not so B major Trio. String quartets of this kind, on the other hand, there are, Haydn apart, none: perhaps we would have needed another Haydn, another genius with a veritable passion for turning things upside down, in order to continue this potential tradition in the string quartet; Schoenberg might well have done it, had he continued tonally. But at the reception end, the unexpected minor-mode finale certainly has not proved an obstacle: both the present work and the 'Emperor' are amongst the composer's most 'celebrated' quartets, nor do the aforementioned works of Mendelssohn and Brahms suffer neglect.

The present Quartet offers Haydn's concluding variation (or perhaps, as we shall see in due course, two concluding variations) on the theme of the introduction – and a highly contrasting variation it is again in all conscience, not only in view of its own, novel variations at the end of both the exposition and the entire movement, nor indeed in view of its equally novel, more distant treatment by the leadback. No, its elemental contrast as against the other variations is the contrast it produces itself within the work, and immediately too: its nonet texture on the *forte* level gives rise to a solo line, *subito piano* – an unprecedented textural contrast in Haydn's entire quartet output, which has to be played for all it's worth, whereas one often hears, on the contrary, mitigation at either end: thin chords on the one hand and the cello's utility *mezzoforte* on the other. Nor can the tempo of the chords be metrically identical with the theme's. These are contrasting characters, whose common tempo has to emerge from the phrasing of their common elements: as the first bar is an upbeat to the second, so the theme's first bar, together with its own upbeat, is an upbeat phrase to its second, as a result of which bars 1 and 3 correspond to each other contrastingly; the *legato* upbeating motion of the one has to be experienced as against the *staccato* upbeating motion of the other. The original *staccato* upbeat and the eventual octave *legato* synthesize the antithesis, which the viola proceeds to obliterate with its *legatos* in bar 9.

Duos for violin and cello and violin and viola form the transition – itself a transition composed of contrasts – to the full quartet texture, which is retained for most of the exposition, at whose very end it is resumed after a bar's interruption: throughout, the players have to remain aware of such textural contrasts and their structural role, which is at its most incisive at the beginning of both the movement and the development section, in that the latter again throws up duos. In fact, with due attention to both all upbeat phrases and, if I may so put it, all upbeat textures, the movement should not present any major difficulties: though highly original, its build-up makes itself crystal-clear from stage to stage.

Nor does the *adagio* evince any musical problems, so long – an all-important condition! – as its *sostenuto* character is immediately realized, towards which end the semiquaver in bar 2 has to become a real and expressive (though certainly not over-burdened) part of the melody, rather than a mere means of rhythmic definition. The texture is full again: blend and balance have to be carefully and continually watched; such motifs as bar 3's viola diminution of that selfsame dotted quaver rhythm in bar 2 have to be clearly audible without at the same time endangering the leading role of the principal part; needless to add, the viola has to be forehearingly aware at this point of the cello's sudden octave on the one hand and the second violin's *e'* on the other – which, with the viola's own *e*, produces another octave. The situation will be different in bar 11, where nothing would be more harmful than the often-heard, thoughtless, mechanical resumption of bar 3's tone production: though the second fiddle again doubles the viola's E (the texture having moved up an octave), the cello's octave now is a thing of the past, the most recent past – the bar's first quaver! Textural subtleties of this kind invariably abound in Haydn's full quartet textures and just as invariably preclude the remotest sign of a thick texture – if, that is, they are identified, playingly recognized and flexibly adjusted to what happens in the other parts, not only the principal part.

With the minuet, we overtly reach Haydn's actual, musical wish-fulfilment which he had merely put into the titles of his Op.33 works: see pp.64f. Now that he writes real scherzos, he doesn't mind calling them minuets – rather ironically so: try and dance to a *presto* minuet! He was, of course, the first to push the minuet into the background and thus inspire the early Beethoven towards his scherzos. But as with Mozart, there may have been reciprocal stimulation: Haydn had meanwhile heard Beethoven's three Piano Trios, Op.1, as well as the Piano Sonatas Op.2, which Beethoven had dedicated to him; Haydn's decision openly to defy the minuet's characteristic tempos, to contradict the minuet not only rhythmically, but even metrically (and hence, of course, verbally), may well have been made with the help of Beethoven's scherzos and their tempo directions. In view of not only the present movement's *presto* pace, but also its asymmetrical theme, it is difficult, in any case, to find the '*Menuetto*' which, as a title graces the present scherzo, even in the structure's background; the title approaches, in short, complete meaninglessness, except, if you like, as a historical reminder.

The music, on the other, meaningful hand, is an entirely new – very fast – type of Haydn scherzo, a masterpiece at the first attempt – though 'attempt' is hardly a realistic description of the aged master's achievement, which is without a trace of experimentation.

It can be played as the first example of its kind, though – with the spirit that underlies surprising, even shocking newness, stunning innovation. At the same time, it is this movement which is most frequently misinterpreted – with flat disregard of its sharply defined *presto* character: compare, knowingly, the usual interpretations of as early a minuet as that of Op.20, No.1 (pp.36f.)! For the rest, an articulating breath, thought rather than played, after the four-bar antecedent and before the six-bar consequent is, of course, a natural requirement.

The *Trio*, on the other hand, is often taken faster than the principal section, whereas it is in fact markedly slower, and not tempo giusto either: the structure is wholly pointless without emphatic agogic freedom of melody.

The pizzicato accompaniment may well have been inspired not so much by that Haydn Serenade which probably isn't by Haydn (*cf.* p.9) as by the selfsame texture in most of the *Trio* of Mozart's oft-mentioned D minor Quartet (the second of his two quartets in that key, i.e. the second Haydn quartet). In either case, the leader must be made to feel absolutely free, able to depend on extremely empathetic pizzicatos, whatever his antics; the plucks will have to be two-dimensionally on the dot, of course – together both internally and with the leader as if he had told them what he was going to do, which he audibly won't have, if only because each time, he'll be doing different things anyway. The constants in his variable interpretations will be *a* the hesitating first phrase, and *b* the 'catching up' of Ex.59. The further

Ex.59

course of agogic events will be determined by *a*'s and *b*'s interpretive thematicism; not that they will be imitable models of future behaviour – which, however, will have to make sense in regard to them. Ideally, the pizzicatos will express responsive appreciation of the leader's phantasy: it all will sound as if the others were so well together, both with him and with each other, because they fully understand him; their applause will, as it were, take the form of unanimous pizzicatos.

It must be admitted upon reflection that the octave unison with which the finale starts is itself an introduction; it has gone entirely unobserved, because nobody has expected Haydn to extend his variations on the theme of the introduction to the last movement. Why not? The unison is, it will be conceded, not unlike 'The Rider's' introduction – a relationship which is inevitably strengthened by the identity of key. And here as there, the mediant and the submediant are emphasized – in the 'Rider's' case in order clearly to define the key, in the present case in order just as clearly to redefine it with a vengeance, to rub it in: G minor is, quite literally, the last thing that anyone would expect, for it has never happened before, and what *has* happened before would have seemed to exclude this sensational event from the realm of mere possibility, of conceivability.

So when it happens, it has to be played as what it is – a downright structural miracle. It is, of course, strictly and overtly thematic – so much so that countless so-called analysts have described it as the first subject which, in reality, starts after the introduction is over, with the viola's upbeat to bar 7. Not even the fact that this is the very place where the recapitulation starts has made anybody think in terms of an introduction – a paradoxical one, to be sure, for nothing could be more central to the movement than its opening, basic motif. It and its continuation will have to be played with unqualified insistence on the minor mode which it represents – for in undue course, it will be used for the movement's, if not indeed the entire work's, most over-powering contrast, the movement's liberation by the major mode, which will reinterpret the basic motif in what we now know to be a characteristically Haydnian way: the same thing will sound more overwhelmingly different than different things could have done (*cf.* pp.172, 183f. and 193f.). For the interpretation, this moment is the whole quartet's supreme test: everything can be gained or lost from or with it.

I almost feel too respectful towards the first fiddler's imagination to tell him how to handle this juncture, but there are a few basic musical facts which his invention, however free otherwise, will fruitfully take into account – freeingly, in fact.

First, the acciaccatura added to the triplet upbeat – the first note to be heard – lends the newly unfolding, now lyrical theme just the right, minimal tinge of an unsentimental *grazioso* character. Secondly, from the word *acciaccatura* it is clear that the tempo will have to be imperceptibly slower, at any rate to begin with, and in order to throw, thirdly, the contrast into relief which the singing *legato* crotchets represent as against the original phrase's masculine staccato crotchets; what has, as it were, given birth to the *legato* is, of course, its first crotchet – the major third, which will have to receive loving, though nowise exaggerated emphasis – a demi-semi-*tenuto*, perhaps.

Is it the first time in the history of composition that a work's undoubted and unforehearable climax, its utterly unexpected culmination, ensues at this late stage in the development of its structure – a stage which, normally, is deliberately predictable in that it is concerned with dis-tension, the natural result of one's expectations having been met? Haydn once again achieves the impossible, a pure paradox – an explosive discharge of tension by way – if not by means – of a total contradiction of expectation! Thoughts such as these won't do the interpreter any harm before he faces the finale – before, mind you, not during it, and not before he's played the work: such thoughts only assume musical reality as a result, a function of one's understanding experi-ence of the music.

Op.76, No.2, in D minor
(Hoboken III:76)

For reasons which, I am genuinely ashamed to confess, I am unable to discern, 'The Fifths' is one of the least misinterpreted of Haydn's great quartets. It can, of course, be shown that the composer makes his intentions so unmistakably clear that possibilities of misunderstanding simply do not arise – but if one is honest, one can undertake the same demonstration in the case of works which continue to be misunderstood and misinterpreted, even by leading quartets which would win any libel or slander case against a musician who had described them as misleading quartets. Personally, I'd plead justification, but I doubt that any jury would accept my analytic evidence as objective – which would teach us a thing or two about the demonstrability of objectivity: the expert witnesses I would call would be laughed out of court by a legion of expert witnesses for the plaintiffs.

Why do I raise this issue in the present context? Because analytically as distinct from interpretatively, our experts, all of them so far as I know them, have made an indescribable mess of the 'Fifths' – whose nickname, incidentally, is for once functional, though not quite functional enough, since it ignores the intervals into which Haydn transforms the basic fifth.

In a recent doctoral thesis on Haydn's motivic work in his late symphonic compositions, which was subsequently published by no less a firm than Bärenreiter,[1] Raimund Bard notes that the basic fifth is 'modified' to become not only a perfect fourth but even as imperfect an interval as a tritone. He doesn't as much as realize that with infinite subtlety, Haydn also transforms the basic motif into a minor third, a minor second, a minor sixth, a major sixth, and so – or rather differently – on. The afore-implied, respectable interpretations of the work, on the other hand, have realized these facts, at least instinctively, without the slightest difficulty. Proof: they realized them, in the other sense of the word, in performance.

The present work, which was completed in 1797, is the third and last of the composer's surprisingly few complete D minor quartets, nor indeed is it all that D minor: as we should expect, Haydn's exploration of the replacement of home key with home tonality continues, and though he does finish the first movement in the minor, he doesn't, as so often on other occasions, stick to the home key for the *Trio*, into which he injects major-mode relaxation, and as for the last movement's retro-active Picardy third, it radiates back well beyond the transition to the second subject (retrogradely speaking): it is the first subject which the tonic major turns into a wellnigh lyrical theme! I should not, therefore, blame any future quartet for describing the work in their programme as a 'String Quartet in D': the ultimate climax of the work is the finale's unexpected, decided, and irrevocable turn to the major – a fact of which any ensemble has to be conscious from the outset. At the same time, the quartet's minor-mode aspects and, above all, the opening movement, show the influence of Mozart's second Haydn quartet in the same key, which the composer – with Haydn's help, to be sure – had turned into his own most tragic one (not, that is to say, G minor). The problem of the theme's

[1] Raimund Bard, *Untersuchungen zur motivischen Arbeit in Haydns sinfonischem Spätwerk*, Kassel/Basle/London, 1982.

accompaniment, incidentally, is the same in both first movements: *cf.* Op.33, No.2, p.69, and the references there given.

There is, however, a single exception to what I described as the least misinterpreted great Haydn quartet, to wit, the first movement's coda, whose lower-part syncopations I have not yet, in fact, ever heard played correctly in public performance. Viola and cello must be heard to interrupt the second fiddle and *vice versa*, and the interrupted instruments must, with their *crescendos*, help as much towards the audibility of each interruption as the interrupting ones. The first violin, finally, has to have a precise idea of what's going on below; there is, for instance, no time to recover from the shock of it all in the third bar of the coda, where the beats, half-beats (off-beats), and de-accentuated semiquaver upbeat phrases (second violin and cello) have to ensue in the strictest rhythm in order to introduce the upward-drive towards what is surely the compressed emotional climax of the entire movement. Ideally – dare I suggest it for once on the basis of bitter, lifelong experience? – these few bars might be memorized in score.

The, again, not so slow movement is as overtly monothematic as the first: undoubtedly, Haydn is musical history's greatest thematic economist, and we have recognized monothematic ternary form, like monothematic sonata form, as a typically Haydnian paradox. The middle section, that is to say, is a development, in the technical sense, of a fragment of the theme, and is followed by a modified recapitulation: once again, Haydn achieves a strict and clear combination of no fewer than three forms, i.e. ternary, sonata, and variation form; with the 'exposition's' first repeat resolved into a variation in the recapitulation, this reprise achieves two variations of the theme's first part for the value of one. There are great opportunities here for the leader's imagination, including, of course, his agogical finesse: Haydn's variations would be sadly incomplete without those of the quartet, which the first violin will lead even more individualistically in this movement than in the outer movements.

The minuet is an infinite canon, with a *Trio* from which Beethoven can be heard to have learnt quite a little. In performance, the canon only works on two conditions – that each pair's phrasing remains utterly unaffected by the other pair's main and subordinate accents at any given point, and that not-withstanding the *forte* level, each pair's intonation is not only spotless, but listens to, and does let itself be affected by, the other pair's intonation.

In the *Trio*, the *forte* and *fortissimo* upbeats will easily be clarified by minute breaths preceding them, the one before the *fortissimo* climaxing on the one before the *forte*, and neither *forte* nor *fortissimo* robbing the upbeats themselves of their audible upbeating function. The tempo of the *Trio* will naturally relax that of the principal section, whose '*ma non troppo*' is itself crucial.

If, once in a lifetime, Haydn repeats himself, it is really and exclusively himself that he is repeating – an ultra-Haydnian, revolutionary step, that is to say, such as nobody else, not a Mozart and not even a Beethoven, would have dreamt of. In both the finale of the preceding quartet and the present finale it is the theme itself, a characteristically minor-mode theme, that appears, shortly after it has been recapitulated, in a vastly contrasting, unforeseeable major-mode guise, and thus introduces a climactic structural stage in the major, wherein the movement ends.

At the same time, it is not altogether fair to speak of a repetition, or indeed of a new 'guise': after all, the minor-mode finale of what has seemed a major-mode work is something very different from a 'normal' minor-mode finale, and as for the contrasting 'guise', it turns out to be as characteristically major as the model was characteristically minor.

These reflections will convey the all-importance of bars 180ff. to the player-reader, though Haydn makes his intentions – the singularity of the event – so abundantly clear that little need be said by way of additional advice. The *pianissimo* – strikingly the movement's first! – has to be heard as the new dynamic development it is: the listener has to be conscious of it as the movement's first. While the rhythmic characterization of the syncopated bars must not be allowed to suffer in any way, the characterization of the lyrical *legato* bars, their cantilena, will probably necessitate an infinitesimal *meno mosso* as from the opening of the D major stage, at any rate to begin with. I say 'probably' because much depends, of course, on the character of the leaders' initial *Vivace assai* – but if the original tempo definition does prove profoundly characteristic, the *pochissimo meno mosso* will follow quite naturally. In the end, the listener (including the playing listener) will be brought to realize spontaneously that that crucial *pianissimo* was not only the movement's first, but also, equally importantly, its last.

The quartet's popularity confirms, again, my little theory about both the public's and indeed the players' 'celebration' of symmetrical structures; at the same time, the true musician is pleased to note that at least thematic economy and monothematicism do not prevent a work from becoming a popular favourite – a lesson which the first movement of Beethoven's Fifth taught him in the first place. At the same time, it remains true to say that Mozart's master quartets and quintets are more popular than any of 'the 45', and there is little doubt that Mozart's wealth of melodic invention has a wider appeal than Haydn's wealth of harmonic invention: don't even serious music lovers consider Mozart a greater composer than Haydn, a more inventive, more moving one?

Op.76, No.3, in C
(Hoboken III:77)

The fame of 'The Emperor' is not, perhaps, quite commensurate with its greatness: it certainly is not among the greatest of the great, and its outer movements are Haydn's only great quartet movements which realize, however successfully, a brilliant quasi-orchestral texture rather than intrinsic quartet thought. Its only searching aspect lies in Haydn's continued exploration of a home tonality, instead of a home key: the *Finale*, largely in the minor, turns the 'C major' title of the work into a bit of a misnomer – which would make it the last of Haydn's seven great quartets in that key, one more than his great D majors: no other key reaches either 7 or 6 great quartets. Otherwise, in any quartet's study of all the great Haydn quartets, the work will assume an isolated position, inasmuch as nothing new about Haydn's quartet thought can be learnt from it: any quartet which knows all the great Haydn quartets with the exception of this one may justly claim that it has made a complete study of Haydn, the quartet composer; personally, I wouldn't blame any quartet which never got round to studying this particular work, though, it would certainly miss the miracle of the eminently final minor-mode *Finale*.

One only has to consider that so far as the expositions and recapitulations of the outer movements are concerned, well over half of the music is written in double or multiple stoppings and/or octaves, in order to realize that on this occasion, it was actually Haydn's intention orchestrally to crudify the texture and rob it of the string quartet's characteristic subtlety and finesse – which, significantly enough, he retains to a considerable extent in the respective development sections; on top of the elemental contrast between statement and development (see pp.124 and 189), they thus offer a new type of textural contrast, unparalleled in any other quartet. And that all the double and multiple stoppings lie supremely well and sound brilliantly resonant goes without saying; the *Finale*, incidentally, starts as a nonet.

According to its nature, then, the first movement's texture explains itself; its realization does not stand in need of advice. What ought to be clearly heard is obvious, as are the sheer accompaniments – which, nevertheless, when they unfold on the *forte* or *fortissimo* level, in semiquavers and double-stoppings, can quite often be heard as an unholy row obscuring the principal part, especially where it, too, consists of semiquaver motion.

The theme of the second movement's variations is what it is all about – the national anthem Haydn had composed a few months earlier (stimulated, it is said, by 'God Save the King'). It has remained a national anthem ever since – of Germany, or of Austria, or of both, with utterly dissimilar texts, of course. The fact that the movement is the climax of the work expresses itself in its key too – or rather in its key relationship vis-à-vis the home tonality: from C major, we are ascending to the tensing dominant, rather than receding into the reposeful subdominant. As for the structure of the movement, not since Op.20, No.4 had Haydn written such simple variations; in fact, the present structure is markedly simpler than that of a quarter of a century earlier. We have seen that normally, variation form always excites his spirit of creative adventure, whether he combines it with other forms or not, whether he introduces his own double variation form or not. That was true, too, of the variation movement of Op.20, No.4: together with the work's homotonality went a 'coda' of extreme harmonic enterprise, really a development section instead of a coda – in a form which normally shuns all development in the technical sense. No such adventure is noticeable in the present movement. In fact, nowhere is it more obvious than in the present slow movement that for once, Haydn was consciously aiming at a popular masterpiece, and while we may regret the concessions to popularity he made on this single occasion, we have to concede that, nevertheless, it does remain a masterpiece.

I would go so far as to suggest that Haydn even remembered, perhaps quite consciously, the slow movement of Op.20, No.4 when he set about this one: the parallels are too close on the one hand, too unlike any other variation movement he had meanwhile written on the other. Both structures, that is to say, consist of three variations and a modified recapitulation, which Haydn here describes as the fourth variation, whereas in the earlier work, he left it without title, not only because of its recapitulatory function, but also because it develops into the aforementioned development, whereas the present, so-called fourth variation, really the fullest and richest statement of the theme, contents itself with a short coda of, intriguingly, indefinite rhythmic structure: only the first three bars are rhythmically defined, and the ensuing two pauses represent, not an extension of a four-bar phrase but, on the contrary, a compression of an eight-bar phrase; in terms of its sheer duration, the coda is, in fact, seven bars long or seven and a bit, since a sensitive conclusion will, I trust, extend the second pause beyond the duration of the first. In terms of rhythmic invention, the end is indeed the most original part of the movement, whose relation to its model at the other end of the composer's creative life as a quartet master we shall now examine stage by stage – together, of course, with the necessary interpretative implications. In the earlier variation movement, the first variation is, it will be remembered, the second violin's. In our present movement, the second violin has a comparable solo role in the first variation, though it is the theme itself which the second fiddle here enunciates: throughout the variations, Haydn adheres to his beloved passacaglia principle, in that the theme is continually repeated. But texturally, this first variation is the most original: it is a duo for two violins, with the first's subordinate part, its semiquaver figuration of and around the theme, representing the variation – which has, of course, to be played as a duo, with a clear consciousness of the desirable sound quality. Older violinists amongst my readers may not have played duos for ages, but from their student years they may remember the sound of some outstanding Spohr duos or of some less outstanding Mazas duos; in any case, they will now be aware of enjoying the greatest duo for two violins they have ever played (even though the *Trio* from 'The Bird', Op.33, No.3 may rank as a close second in their memory, if it is at all comparable!). What is important for the leading second fiddler to realize is that the first has not altogether abrogated his leading role: the very fact that his subordinate part *is* the variation imposes a creative duty on him, in that he has to shape it with maximal imagination, which the temporary 'leader' will do good to heed and, where necessary, follow; infinitesimal rhythmic liberties on the first violin's part will have to be taken into playing account.

In any event, the second violinist's solo must not, of course, be a copy of the first's theme, with which it will establish continuity none the less, as a variation establishes continuity with the theme. Compositorially, the first variation is the first violin's; interpretatively, however, it is the second's!

In the 'early' movement (Haydn was 40!), the second variation was the cello's. In the present second variation, it is likewise, the cello which takes on the leading part – in the shape of the theme, of course. The variation is now the job of the other three instruments – though chiefly the first violin's. But interpretatively speaking, the cellist will, of course, submit a novel version of the theme, which, at the same time, will link up not only with the first violin's, but also with the subsequent second's.

It is the third variation which is radically, indeed historically different from what we may describe as the model's – and it was really Haydn who, together with Mozart, had meanwhile made such history as accounts for the difference. It will be remembered that in the model, the third variation is the first violin's; the leader blossoms forth in the kind of figuration which, in the present movement, he has enjoyed in the first variation – except that 'figuration' is not, perhaps, quite the word for a decorative flow which so clearly implies the theme that it needn't be stated at the same time! But in the present movement, the first violin has, in addition, done most of the varying in the second variation: it has had its fill. In the present third variation, in any case, it is the viola which takes on the 'solo', the theme itself – the one instrument, that is, which hadn't been allowed a variation in the model; at that time, the viola's role in the string quartet was still distinctly subordinate – more subordinate, in fact, than the other lower instruments'. Meanwhile, Haydn had promoted the viola, not only as an enthusiastic viola player himself but also, in part, under the influence of the viola-playing Mozart, Mozart's quartets and, above all, his string quintets, which he had indeed played with Haydn, both of them preferring the viola parts in which they alternated. The viola player will now in his turn heed what has happened to the theme not only in its statement, but also in its two variations – as well as what is happening to it during his own characterization of it, bearing in mind that up to, and including part of, the theme's climax, the texture varies between a Dvořák-like string trio (see pp.36f and 188) and a normal one.

The two recapitulations are, admittedly, strikingly different: *qua* recapitulation, the present movement's is immeasurably more climactic, for what it eventually loses in harmonic adventure it gains in harmonic enrichment; in the second bar, for instance, there even is a turn to the relative minor, which the interpretation will not, of course, leave unheeded – but won't rub in either ! Let us indeed be fair: this recapitulation is far more of a variation than was the model's recapitulatory part of the final section, whence Haydn does call it one. And it has to be played as one, not only in view of its enrichments, but also by way of the first violin's phrasing, which will climax on that of the theme: for the first time, it now is *the same player* who submits a different version of the theme – the climactic version, in fact.

There is another feature which this Quartet shares with Op.20, No.4 – the (sub-) thematic relation between movements. In the earlier work, it was the themes of the middle movements that were subthematically connected – serially, in precise fact (cf.p.56): the slow movement's harmonic adventure needed closer integration (which was also achieved homotonally). In the present Quartet, it is the last two movements that are overtly integrated thematically: compare Exs.60 and 61.

Ex.60

Ex.61

The reason for this downright cyclic build-up (another unobtrusive innovation here!) is no doubt the minor-mode *Finale*: its sensational key would otherwise endanger its unity with the rest of the work, whose *Trio*, too, departs from the first movement's and the minuet's key: it is in the relative minor, thus again meeting the requirements of my empirical theory about 'third-relationships'.

In respect of accentuation and its suppression, there is not the slightest difference between the minuet's crotchet upbeat and the following main beat: the initial, unaccompanied 1½-bar solo is a single upbeat phrase, which the *Trio* further prolongs: there, it even extends beyond the other instruments' entry. The minuet's *allegro* is enthusiastically meant: many are the unfortunate occasions when the movement slips back into a foreground minuet's *allegretto* rhythm – which, if it is to make itself felt at all, will have to be reserved for the *Trio*. On the basis of my eminently practical theory (see pp.154 and 206f.), the *Trio*'s relaxation is readily explicable; at the same time, however, this minor-mode relaxation acts as a structural warning of things to come – the minor-mode *Finale* which, in the event, isn't all that relaxing; the relaxation sets in with the change to the major which, yet again, makes life as difficult as possible for itself, in that it brings about a change of personality in the very theme. For the purpose of realizing it, a marginal *meno mosso* will again prove advisable, at any rate – as before (*cf.* p.215) – to begin with. The *Finale*'s original *presto* character must, of course, have been uncompromisingly established. And the *Finale*'s quasi-orchestral texture is no excuse for the marked roughness with which it is so often played; none of the chords can be 'attacked' orchestrally: each has to achieve a well-rounded blend.

Op.76, No.4, in B flat major
(Hoboken III:78)

On the other hand – if I may hold out another hand after a few thousand words – 'The Sunrise' (1797) certainly is amongst the greatest of the great. It is the last of the five great B♭ quartets (leaving out Op.33, No.4), and none of them is greater. The nickname is self-explanatory and meaningless, but quite practical as a short means of identification.

The first movement starts with a sustained, accompanimental tonic chord which has to enter from nowhere; with its gradual evolution, the structure foreshadows the first movement of Beethoven's first Rasumovsky Quartet. This gradual and, let's face it, slow evolution contradicts the movement's tempo marking, *Allegro con spirito*, which only becomes relevant as from the transition – the movement's first *forte* (bar 22) that suddenly shows the players what this structure is 'about': contrasting tempo characters, whose rhythmic contrasts have to be realized without mutual adjustment; if the opening does disclose any *allegro con spirito*, it is wrongly phrased and probably also wrongly paced. The principal accent of the first, extended phrase is unquestionably its last note in bar 6, just as the aim of the equally extended second phrase is its own last note in bar 12: any intervening, sharply articulating stresses would destroy both the character and indeed the logical evolution of the theme. Other destructive factors from my own experience of (of 'leading' quartets that played to me) are a slight rush of the concluding crotchet motif, bar accents as from the diminution of the theme (before the *crescendo*), and a translation of the *forte* into rough playing, not only of the semiquavers but also of the underlying quaver motifs. In the *fortissimo*, the balance becomes an easily solvable problem so long as it is realized that the principal part remains in the first violin. For some psychological rather than musical reason, the cello's crotchet upbeats in the ensuing *piano* are often subjected to accentuating attacks; I am not a cellist, but would suggest that in order to invest these crotchets with their proper upbeating significance, and assuming that the cellist does not, at this particular stage, suffer from nerves, the bow should lie on the string before the beginning of the upbeat is articulated – if 'articulated' is the word: ideally, these upbeats will again come out of nowhere.

The alternation between the *sforzatos* and the *pianos* has to be clearly defined, and the first violin's E♭ in bar 55 easily runs the risk of being flat – perhaps in anticipatory contrast to the forthcoming E♮ in bar 56. Another risk that has to be avoided at all costs is a codetta rush as from bar 60: it is interesting how difficult many people find this type of cross-rhythmic passage in respect of tempo character; such passages are often either dragged or rushed, and attempted corrections of one of these evils all too readily result in the other. In any case, as has frequently been pointed out, avoidance does not communicate.

Speaking of rushing risks, there is the viola's in bars 120ff. and 125ff.: it is often amusing to hear the first violin responding correctively on both occasions. Quarter-bar accents are frequent destroyers of bars 156–7, and the afore-mentioned codetta rush easily recurs before the coda, nor is there any need for a major, tautologizing *ritardando* before the pause.

The *Adagio*'s gravest interpretative risks are to be found right at the beginning and right at the end. I simply speak from experience, and on the highest level too; I must confess that I have no idea how and why the temptation arises to commit these idiocies, the first of which is a pleonastic accent before each pause. It is abundantly obvious that a modern composer would have notated the beginning in 4/4, in which case he would probably have prevented an accent on the last crotchet of the bar; there's no harm in thinking the opening in 4/4 anyhow. What is yet more baffling are the two unrelated tempos, fast and slow, which you often hear three and two bars from the end from, respectively, the second fiddle and the cello; far be it from me to suggest that the cello should imitate the second fiddle – but uninterrupted continuity there must be, as if the two strings of semiquaver triplets came from one player. For the rest, this *adagio*'s character will best be understood as the diametrical opposite of the preceding Quartet's *poco adagios*, whose tensity was established from the outset, from the moment one had been transported to the opening movement's dominant. In the present instance, on the contrary, a state of profound repose is reached almost immediately; to be sure, we have to hear a bit of the music in order to experience its profundity, but reposeful we feel from the moment we withdraw, or are withdrawn, into the subdominant. Within this framework of withdrawal, plenty of complicating, indeed tensing events are happening, whose discussion I am, however, postponing on this single occasion: as we come to discuss the *Adagio* of Op.76, No.6, we shall find, and every single reader will agree, that these two *Adagios* simply have to be discussed together: it would be a downright artificial undertaking to consider each structure, together with its interpretative implications, in isolation.

The minuet needs a broad approach notwithstanding its *Allegro*, which must not tempt the characterization in the direction of flippancy, or haste, or urgency; the *allegro* character will, nevertheless, immediately establish itself – as soon, that is, as the first $1\frac{1}{3}$ bars are played as an upbeat to the second bar.

For the first time since the first F minor Quartet a quarter of a century ago (Op.20, No.5: see p.60), Haydn creates an overlapping *Trio*: in the preceding quartet, too, we noted a backward glance or two to an Op.20 quartet. Did he, in his old age, resume, not thoughts of his youth, but thoughts from his early quartet mastery, *its* youth?

And though, inevitably, the *Trio* starts on the third beat of the bar as the minuet has done, its immediate syncopation makes it start, in effect, with a main beat, as distinct from the principal section's upbeat – though the *Trio*'s entire opening phrase is, of course, an extended upbeat phrase to bar 5, as which it must (yes, paradoxically) be played despite the equally extended *diminuendo*, which therefore has to be invested with upbeating significance, whereas most interpretations one hears allow their *diminuendo*, insofar as it is at all in evidence, to be interrupted by bar accents whose irrational cause is the opening syncopation with its *sforzato*: it seems that the players in question feel obliged, compelled, to explain the time signature by subsequently correcting, repairing the initial accent on the tied-over third beat of the bar. The first F minor Quartet's overlapping *Trio* had changed to the tonic major for relaxation, but since the present minuet is in the major mode anyway, the *Trio* can afford to retain the minuet's key – and the interpreter can afford to spring the *Trio*'s contrast on the listener out of the blue, as if nothing had happened; tonally, nothing has in fact happened.

As invariably with Haydn, the *ma non troppo* is a substantial, essential qualifiaction of the *Finale*'s *Allegro*: the tempo character, stress on 'character', is comfortable, and the slightest sign of haste would make any truly structural phrasing impossible. The crucial criterion is, I would suggest, the ornament that helps to articulate the opening phrase's last note: these grace-notes have to be so unhurried that the four quavers that open bar 4 can be experienced as their variation in augmentation; both the model and the variation succeed their respective phrase's main accent, which falls on the first beat of bar 2 and, in the responsive phrase, is displaced on to the fourth beat of bar 3 – anticipatorily displaced, therefore. The metre should not, in any circumstances, induce a thoughtless common-time accent on the third beat.

The last two crotchets before the double-bar are very often heard off the string from first violin and cello alike. They thus tend to lose their crotchet value and turn into weightless quavers; in the violin, at least, they ought to be simple *staccatos* on the string, naturally on the upper half of the bow.

The movement turns into one of Haydn's characteristic ternary forms: a B♭ minor middle section holds out the faint prospect of double variation form, in which case it would turn out to be the second theme – but in the event, what there is of variation in the modified recapitulation is confined to the theme that preceded the middle section. In Haydn's mind, ternary form and double variation form lie very close together, so that the second theme, in the tonic minor or major, may or may not belie its thematic function and simply prove a middle section; we have already drawn attention to a particularly drastic example, the *Andante* from the homotonal A major Piano Trio, Hoboken XV:18 (1794 or earlier), the expected first variation of whose apparent second theme is replaced, *attacca*, with the finale.

As the first movement disclosed, to begin with, dramatic acceleration, so the *Finale* turns out to be a steadily accelerating structure – which makes the comfortable initial tempo all the more important! The *Più allegro* and the *Più presto* have to follow the original tempo very naturally, as a process of ineluctable, yet dramatic and exciting acceleration. The three tempos are altogether the responsibility of the leader, who will, ideally, have a complete and continuous picture of the movement in his mind, or rather, a variety of such pictures, for nothing sounds more calcified than an unchanging, rigidly 'natural' process of acceleration, always repeated with conscientious exactitude. No, the many possible different types of accelerating tempos ought to delight the leader and indeed the entire quartet; why not accept the challenge to find yet another truly natural way of speeding up the movement in utterly organic stages? It is, incidentally, Haydn's only steadily accelerating quartet structure, the acceleration being achieved by successively faster paces.

Op.76, No.5, in D major
(Hoboken III:79)

With the first movement of the last (1797) of his six great D major quartets, Haydn harks back to the form of the slow first movement of his second F minor Quartet, Op.55, No.2; instead of sonata form, however, a combination of variation and ternary form will be remembered, with a variational middle section in the tonic major. Now we have the variational middle section in the tonic minor, but it isn't only variational: it is developmental too. Sonata, then, has been added to the combination of forms, and here as there, variation is, of course, employed in the service of recapitulation (*cf.* also p.214). The initial *allegretto* tempo moves the siciliana theme into the realm of the not so slow movement, from which the eventual *Allegro* frees it: the revolutionary total structure of the second F minor Quartet (see pp.130f.) is not pursued; development has lent the first movement too much normal first-movement significance.

The sound of this D major movement is, of course, rich and brilliant, while its sense is very clearly notated: the siciliana motif does turn the quaver upbeat into a real upbeat which has to be heard as such, but the phrase's strongest accent is, needless to add, the middle of bar 2, which is intriguingly anticipated by the accompanimental accents in the middle of bar 1; it is quite a joyful task, a musical challenge, to make this anticipation as audible as was the upbeating function of the initial upbeat. The entire movement lies extremely well, as do all its individual phrasings; it would need an exceptional degree of stupidity to give a stupid performance of it, since misphrasings would necessitate downright technical discomfort, whereas the most logical phrasings are, technically, the easiest.

Texturally, too, the movement is without problems, so long as everybody is clearly aware of what he and everybody else is doing. Discomfort, in short, is reserved for the *Largo* which, true to his recent passion for 'third-relationships', Haydn cast in F♯ major – an unprecedented quartet key outside Haydn's output, though not within: we last encountered it in the coda of the F♯ minor Quartet's first movement as well as in its minuet (see p.99). My theory about third-relationships receives further confirmation: according to it, the movement 'leads' home to the minuet and the *Finale*, as the slow, E major movement of Beethoven's C minor Concerto leads home to its finale. By far the most important thing to realize is that this profound and profoundly sad movement (*mesto* = sad) has to be, and can be, in tune. There are great composers' pieces which can't – an outstanding example being the greater part of Mozart's last E♭ String Quintet (the slow movement, of course, excepted).

In the preceding Quartet, we considered the advance and promotion of the viola in the course of Haydn's quartet development. But although we were concerned with an important viola solo in that Quartet's slow movement, it now has to be asserted that the present slow movement contains the deepest viola solo in all Haydn – which, I am sure, none other than Bruckner comprehensively assimilated. When the viola arrives at this point, the violins have to get ready for the most ethereal variety of Carmirelli bowing (cf. Op.20, No.2, p.42), in which the viola itself joins as the cello takes over.

There is no need for individual practice of the movement – practice as distinct from study: the players will find that what will prove extremely fruitful will be a little preparatory thought devoted to the question of how best to take certain passages, which fingerings to use for the purpose of instant adjustment, which alternative fingerings might be available for the purpose of responding to other players' variable phrasings . . . In short, as soon as one clearly knows, at any given point, how one might cope with the next stage, the afore-mentioned discomfort evaporates, for it is then that one discovers that *for F# major*, the movement is very carefully, indeed very well-lyingly written; it is, obviously, just because of its profoundity that Haydn wanted the *Largo* to be as playable as at all possible. As for its structure, in view of the movement's originality and the importance, for each player, of discovering for himself what he is interpreting, I will, for once on this carefully chosen occasion, allow myself not to digress analytically; suffice it to say that on the basis of the present book's analytical observations, the player-reader oughtn't to find the lonely discovery of the movement's precise structural evolution an insurmountable task; I'm giving little away when I claim that Haydn never created a subtler, or more complex monothematic ternary structure. For the rest, I regard this book's analytic insights until the present stage as a lesson which ought to empower the attentive reader to analyse this supreme, sublime movement without any outside help.

The minuet with its D minor *Trio* represents a late stage in the history of Haydn's anti-minuets; if, in his first great D major Quartet (see pp.55f.), he superimposed a gavotte on the minuet, his polyrhythmic inventions in his last D major minuet are of a much subtler nature, though he seems to be remembering that gavotte when, at the beginning and end of the principal section's second part, he once again superimposes quadruple metre with a heavy three-four upbeat upon the background of the minuet; but whereas in the earlier example, the minuet was permanently relegated to the background, triple and quadruple metre refinedly alternate in the foreground of the present minuet – and, needless to add, have to be realized as such, without the metrical pulse gaining the upper hand over the actual phrasing.

Despite the *Trio*'s minor mode and its modulation to the dominant minor, it still retains its relaxing function vis-à-vis the principal section, though this time, it has to be admitted that both sections show an ambiguous – a tensing *and* relaxing – attitude towards each other – a complex state of structural affairs which may well prompt the cellist-reader *not* to relax the tempo of the *Trio*, in which case I would suggest to him that he might actually take it infinitesimally faster. What I am saying is that total identity of tempo between the two sections would, in view of their contrasting characters, be misleading.

Don't I understand the opening of the last movement, which everybody else calls a 'joke' because it starts with a repeated perfect cadence (Ex.62, p. 226), with which pieces normally end, not start? I am fully aware of the paradoxical opening, but can't hear what is funny about it. Why does nobody call the opening of Op.33, No.5 (Ex.63) a joke?

What's the difference, so far as the presence or absence of a joke is concerned? To my mind, the opening to the present *Finale* is Haydn's latest

Ex.62

Ex.63

last-movement variation on the theme of the introduction, which he not only immediately integrates into the body of the movement, but also urgently needs later on, at the end of the exposition: before the expected double-bar, in order to play a little, or not so little serious joke (if you want to describe it

Ex.64

thus) on his players and his audience, he builds up a little climax (*a* in Ex.64) which creates the certain expectation of a repeat at *x* in Ex.64, without meeting this expectation and proceeding to *y* instead: what Beethoven did seriously in the first movement of his first Rasumovsky Quartet, i.e. the dropping of the repeat of the exposition by way of a composed, mental bridge between the expected repeat and the actually ensuing development section, which consisted of a short-term return to the first subject in the tonic as if the repeat was going to take place, Haydn anticipated wittily in this *presto Finale*, thus introducing yet another innovation, the ommission of the repeat, with which Beethoven is normally credited.

At the recapitulatory stage, moreover, the introduction becomes a subordinate part accompanying a brilliant, pseudo-virtuosic second fiddle solo in fast semiquavers, of which what I said about the lower parts' brilliant passages in the *Finale* of Op.74, No.1 (see p.195) is doubly true: if the listner or, for that matter, one's own quartet members only knew how easy this dazzling virtuoso display is! One of the most outstanding students at the Summer School of Music at Dartington duly (if jokingly) reproached me with giving away the secret.

Although, as is, for once, to be expected, the movement lies as beautifully within its well-lying key as does the first, though the risk of misphrasing is, perhaps, slightly greater; in particular, the phrases which contain strings of motifs each of which consists of two semiquavers and a quaver should reserve their accents for their aims, please, and not lose or squander any accent on the way, on one of the quavers.

A heavy task falls on the middle parts if the introduction does not form part of the tempo definition – which approach is conceivable and could be rendered rhythmically plausible: they – with the second violin leading – will have to get down to a proper tempo definition as from the upbeat to bar 7, and the trouble is that at that stage, they can't define any character, because there ain't any! Their definition will have to be one of sheer pace – the speed of the accompanimental quavers of unvarying pitch. What is needed at this point, therefore, is real, complete empathy with the forthcoming characterization of the theme – the first violin's above all, but also the cello's. If the movement has been played before, the task is surmountable; if it hasn't, the task may not be, unless first violin and cello are prepared to heed the string quartet's leading maxim – the other person is always right – even at this stage, where the other person can't prove the sense they'd make of the theme at their tempo. The rhythmic situation is, of course, amusingly similar to the one obtaining at the beginning of 'The Bird', Op.33, No.3 (see p.73) – but it will, by now, have been noticed that whenever the old Haydn reverts back to a creative situation of his quartet mastery's youth, he never repeats or re-lives anything he has done before, always fills the old situation with new invention which, if one did not know his age, one would have no hesitation in describing as youthful exuberance.

My knowledge of other geniuses in old age could be firmer: while I know their music well, I am not always sure what they – Bach, for instance, who died at Haydn's present age – wrote when, the renowned example of Verdi's *Falstaff* apart. It seems to me, however, that alone among geniuses, the old Haydn was in clear possession of the advantages of all his biographical stages – that, perhaps just because he matured so incomprehensibly late, he was the only composing genius who reached a prolonged, consistent, late climax during which he was, simultaneously, young, middle-aged, and old.

For demonstrably, the broad, simplifying wisdom of old age presided over the continuing, overflowing invention, over the impetuosity and the invariably rebellious creative attitude of youth as well as over the comprehensive complexities of middle age: in his extended, climactic final period he had it three ways – which makes his sudden shut-down after the two middle movements from what would have become another D minor quartet all the more baffling.

Op.76, No.6, In E flat major
(Hoboken III:80)

The last of Haydn's six great E♭ quartets (1797) is perhaps – dare one compare on this level? – the greatest of them all; in any case, it is amongst the greatest of his great quartets as well as being the very greatest of the 'celebrated', which status it no doubt again owes to its symmetrical themes – the only aspect of the work, one is tempted to suggest, which is not drastically innovatory. One hardly knows where to start when listing its lasting innovations – nor indeed are they an integral part of the subject of this book, but inasmuch as they affect one's performance of the work, one can concentrate on them with a quiet conscience.

In the preceding D major Quartet, we had noticed that Haydn had temporarily turned his back on conventional 'first-movement form', both as regards its formal (sonata) attributes and in respect of its tempo; the same tendency manifests itself more decidedly in the opening *allegretto* of the present work, in that it goes all the way in the direction of variation form and further, renouncing even Haydn's own double variation form, whose bi-thematicism, together with its structural consequences, would have moved the movement closer to conventional first-movement form than was Haydn's desire at this particular stage in the development of his last creative period; proper variation form it was going to be, thus harking back, as the most effective innovations often do, to an earlier historical stage, when variation movements quite often started what could not yet be described as symphonic build-ups. But, as we shall see in two paragraphs' time, there was another reason why Haydn went back to variation proper: it was going to be variation plus, for he was about to invent one of his new, lasting forms.

In double variation form as well as in ternary forms related to it or combined with it, Haydn tended to cast his basic thematic contrast in the tonic's two modes – but in these variations on a single theme, he goes to the other extreme and does without a minor-mode variation altogether. The interpreter had better be aware of this self-imposed restriction from the outset: all contrasts will have to be expressed within the confines of the tonic major and its consequences.

The tonic major? A slight over-simplification, this, for the theme does, of course, develop a quasi-developmental middle: it manifests modulatory urges, which even produce a turn to the supertonic minor. But the E♭ framework is never seriously endangered; truly unprecedented harmonic adventure is reserved for later. At the same time, even the variations evince structural innovation; we have noticed before (see p.95) that Haydn does not force them to retain the theme's harmonic structure, but will subject the harmony to variation too: warned by the first variation, the first part of the second variation, for example, already turns to F minor – a harmonic event underlined not only by the composer's *sforzato* on the relevant upbeat, but also, one hopes, by the ensemble's harmonic enthusiasm, which the first violin will have anticipated in the duo for two violins that is the first part of the first variation – and which, to be wise after the event, the theme itself admittedly foreshadows.

'As usual', I had almost begun this sentence – compare the variation movements of Op.20, No.4 of a quarter of a century ago and of the recent past's 'Emperor' – the fourth variation bears distinct recapitulatory traits; in the Op.20 work it was, in fact, an outspoken recapitulation. But just as Haydn there broadened out into an utterly unexpected, unprecedented and hence unforeseeable development, so he now broadens out, overlappingly, into an *allegro* fugue with which he, the sole individual inventor of forms, had invented another new form that was to survive all historical upheavals, right into the present day – the form of 'variations and fugue', originally a typically Haydnian paradox, in that it let what was, potentially, the most homophonic form end up in sheer counterpoint, not to speak of the developmental urges it lent to what had been a form consisting of statements and nothing else – the 'stating' form *par excellence*.[1] One wonders whether Haydn divined at this point that he had invented, not only a highly original structure, but simply, or rather, complexly, a new, enduring form. In the case of both double variation form and the scherzo, in any case, it seems to me that we have to assume such awareness, but variations and fugue may have seemed too naughty, too paradoxical, to last.

Whatever tempo is chosen for the original *allegretto*, the fugue's *allegro* contrast must not be underplayed, as it often is, probably because the interpreters in question can't get used to the feeling that the selfsame phrases are capable of contrasting tempo characterizations; in the present structural context, Haydn's invention must have proceeded very cautiously until it had found ideas that were – or rather, basically, an idea that was – ambiguous in its character. It would seem to me that this is one of the very few occasions when

---

[1] Passacaglia and fugue had existed, of course – but that was sheer counterpoint ending up in sheer counterpoint!

the interpreter actually has to identify, if possible to empathize, with the creative process, in order spontaneously to appreciate the paradox – the sharp contrast between identical shapes which, through the contrast, have ceased to be identical.

Identity of shapes in different works is another matter – total identity, where the question of a difference, let alone a contrast, does not even arise. And if these shapes are basic shapes, i.e. the same initial idea for two different movements, they certainly are compulsory food for thought. We are, by now, very concretely aware that Haydn never repeats himself – except on a single occasion which, to my knowledge, nobody has yet noted – that of the present work's slow movement, whose basic motif (Ex.66) is a literal trans-position, in all four parts, of the basic motif (Ex.65) of the *Adagio* of the B♭

Ex.65   Ex.66

Quartet, Op.76, No.4, composed in the same year. Personally, I am never-theless convinced that the self-quotation was unconscious – for the simple reason that consciously, it would not, could not, have happened: demon-strably from work to work, Haydn was far too passionately intent upon not repeating himself, upon new and unpredictable melodic and structural departures. The absence of a conscious creative intention does not, of course, release us from the critical duty to try and discover the unconscious motiva-tion of this singular identity, for there is, after all, such a thing as unconscious creativity.

The two movements do, in fact, pursue the same revolutionary aim, and Haydn could have called the earlier one 'Fantasia' with the same justification as, if not indeed with yet greater relevance than, obtained in the case of the later one: again after the event, it is obvious that for him, the semitonal basic motif was the springboard for a structure in which semitones would play an unprecedented thematic role, in that the entire build-up would largely consist of development (Haydn's characteristic field of invention!), with statements playing a relatively minor role. In the case of the earlier, E♭ movement, one can in fact go so far as to say that the initial statement *is no longer than two bars*; thenceforth, the movement is developmental all the way, with, admittedly, nine momentary recurrences of the tonic, but, at the same time, no fewer than thirty-three modulations and thirty-six changes of key, all of them on the flat side, ranging from one flat to six.

So far as its notation is concerned, however, it is the later, B major movement that presents an unheard-of, lasting innovation: Haydn does not introduce the movement with the key signature of its home key, B major, which he only inserts at the recapitulatory stage; by that time, he has gone through thirteen modulations, ranging from five sharps to four flats, with, however, only a single momentary recurrence of the tonic. But he has at least had a complete tonical statement to begin with – an eight-bar theme, whose restatement modulates to C♯ minor at the end of its consequent. All in all, he could just as well have left the E♭ movement without initial key signature; I feel it may have been the experience of that movement which prompted his notational innovation in the later case – a veritable declaration of war on home tonality and, hence, on tonality. It was at the same time that he composed *The Creation*'s similarly constructed *Representation of Chaos*: was it the concept of chaos that gave him the original idea of an anti-diatonic structure – as 'air from another planet' had inspired Schoenberg towards atonality? And in the case of the B major movement, we note that he did feel impelled to develop his revolutionary harmonic approach in, as it were, a proportionately remote key, which no Mozart movement would ever have chosen for its home.

For the interpreter, a clear realization of the unprecedentedly labile tonal structure of both these monothematic movements is of the utmost import-ance: any feeling of relaxed stability during their modulatory adventures would give rise to misleading rather than 'leading' phrasings – leading from one key to another, that is to say.[2] The profundity of either movement's new, unstable, incessantly endangered structure has only been noticed in the case of the B major movement, whose title, 'Fantasia', gave observers something extra-musical to work on; that both movements penetrate uncharted terri-tory, and that one of them is history's first which, though not in C major or A minor, bears no key signature because of its continual modulations, seems to have escaped notice altogether. In the B major movement, however, the interpreter can at least enjoy and express the theme's stability, whereas in the earlier movement, the opening stability in which he can indulge is confined to

---

[2] Relevantly enough, the German term for 'development' in the technical sense is '*Durchführung*', the literal translation of which is 'leading-through' (keys, of course).

those two opening bars which, strictly speaking, *are* the theme, if not the complete opening melody.

The non-minuet is another *Presto* (*cf.* the G major Quartet's from the present *opus*, p.210) and thus further contributes to the abolition of the minuet and Haydn's innovatory replacement – the scherzo. If, that is to say, its *presto* character is truthfully realized: its rhythmic structure, which does betray the minuet's background, misleads many ensembles into a minuet-like execution – into replacing foreground with background, a frequent course of action in all kinds of misinterpretation. Once again, the opening upbeat does not lead to what, in the notated background, is a main beat, but is merely the first note of an upbeat phrase; once this basic fact is genuinely realized, a real *presto* has every chance of emerging.

The tonical trio is called *Alternativo* this time, perhaps in order to banish the minuet thoughts which the title '*Menuetto*' had conjured up despite the '*Presto*'; in any case, the downright comfortable element which distinguishes the motivic model of the theme's sequences asks for a more relaxed tempo than is characteristic of the principal section; and this time, the crotchet upbeat *is* an upbeat, thereby establishing an immediate contrast with the principal section where, rhythmically speaking, none exists. The new title is bad luck for the extremely varying texture, wherein both the normal string trio and the Dvořák trio (*cf.*pp.36f. and 188) play an essential part; only the trio consisting of two violins and cello are excluded from it. The structural role of the contrasting textures is dynamically strengthened: solos, duos and trios all unfold on the *piano* level, and thus form the chief contrast as against the climactic full quartet texture, which invariably expresses itself *forte* and indeed concludes the entire section. It follows, of course, that each player has to be aware, throughout, of the particular ensemble he is a member of; the three solos are confined to the cello, which thus opens the section at the other end of the textural scale.

The structure of the *Finale*'s theme offers us an excellent opportunity to discuss, as a matter of concrete rather than abstract principle, the phrasing of structures, be they statements or developments, which are composed of identical, successive shapes – identical, that is to say, in respect of their rhythmic organization and perhaps also, as in the case of a sequential build-up, their melodic proportions, not to speak of the thus implied harmonic equivalencies. Illogical phrasings are one thing, sensible phrasings whose repetition makes the music fall to pieces another. On the way to the structure's disintegration, moreover, they bore the listener to death, in proportion to their ever-increasing predictability.

How does it all happen? Easily and, therefore, incessantly. Let us assume a structure consists of four identical shapes, as does the antecedent of the *Finale* theme. Many are the interpreters who automatically feel that identical shapes require identical phrasings: they will thus phrase each shape quite logically, articulating and defining it identically on each of the four occasions – at the expense of continuity. For as soon as a shape is not phrased in view of both its predecessor and its successor, the structure of which those identical shapes are components remains unphrased, unarticulated: the components become isolated pieces of music without any connection between them, for identical phrasings, far from establishing a connection, preclude it. The strongest accent of the model will, of course, be in the same place as the strongest accent of, say, the first sequence – *but it won't be equally strong*: in the service of continuity, a later strongest stress will usually be stronger than an earlier strongest stress; in the present instance, the strongest principal accent will be bar 4's, the weakest bar 1's, which will have to be weak enough for the listening ear to require a continuation that will contain a stronger accent. The relation between the successive principal accents, then, is not precisely predictable: the listening ear's attention is held.

The present *Finale*'s opening upbeat, however, will have to receive special treatment which does not apply to its successors; the phrase could even easily precede the tempo definition. This upbeat phrase, it must not be forgotten, takes the listener into the movement of which, as yet, he knows nothing: ideally, the phrase will, persuasively, draw his attention to what is going to happen; a witty approach to doing just that is certainly not out of the question. There is even the possibility of heralding forthcoming events by way of a stress on the opening B♭ – which will, however, be eminently distinguishable, through its tone quality, from the first 'proper', structural accent on the F of the model. At the same time, the stress could be a variation of the distinguishing, articulating *sforzato* at the recapitulatory stage as well as of the accent that happens eleven bars from the end – which would produce functional receptive amusement at those points!

As for the differences between the model and each of its 'heirs', we once again arrive at the conclusion (cf.pp.178f. and 181), if from a different point of view, that in meaningful music *and its meaningful performance*, there simply is no repetition. And though our present point of view is different, the ultimate reason why there cannot be any repetition will always remain the same: repetition is the paradigm of predictability, whereas musical meaning – all meaning except for that of the final cadence – stands or falls by the contradiction of expectation. We only know that 'this is the end' because for the first time in our experience of the music in question, our expectation after, say, the ultimate dominant seventh is fully met.

Contrast and continuity – this is the two-faced relation between one idea and the next. The interpreter has to express both; if, as so often happens, he expresses one at the expense of the other, musical meaning is either irreparably interrupted, or – if articulation is sacrificed to continuity – not communicated at all: there is, alas, continuity without it having become clear what is being continued.

Even the last movement, let it finally be said, is an innovation, albeit an unobtrusive one. For quite some time, that is to say, Haydn had been working at making the finale exclusively a matter of *character*, not of *form*, and at thus increasing its weight which, in the present instance, is that of a fully worked-out, monothematic sonata structure, without any *formal* finale characteristics: it is entirely the character of the theme itself that turns the movement from the outset into a recognizable finale, and it is, again, the theme's character alone which enables the structure to function as the work's final resolution. The consequences of this novel approach for the future of symphonic thought are obvious; less masterly hands than Haydn's turned the increased weight of the finale into what became known as 'the finale problem' – which he, Mozart and Beethoven solved at the time when they created it.

For the interpreters it is again of the utmost importance to be deeply aware of the increased substance of the last movement – of the fact that the times of the light-hearted finale are over, however light-hearted the character of its theme. Once the interpreter is really inside the Haydn quartets, he will realize that the increase of the finale's weight had been a preoccupation of Haydn's from the word go – from the finale fugues of his Op.20, whence it isn't a far cry to the finale of the 'Jupiter' Symphony.

Op.77, No.1, in G major
(Hoboken III:81)

The dance's, pre-eminently the minuet's, normal *musical* history in danceless, elevated art music, and eventually in symphonic music, is fairly straight-forward. As utility music, as dance music proper, it started musical life in the foreground and, gradually or abruptly, or – with different composers – either, it moved into the background, very much *against* which the great composers wrote their foregrounds; in the case of the minuet, we have been able to follow this process and progress in some considerable detail.

The march, however – not a dance but still, as music accompanying or even prompting physical motion, metric utility music of the same category – has had a more curious and complex history. It, too, started in the fore-ground, where the ceremonial, operatic marches of Lully and Handel can be found; in fact, one of them, from Handel's *Scipione*, has remained the parade march of the British Grenadier Guards. But while the *Magic Flute*'s March of the Priests is a foreground march too, Figaro's 'Non più andrai' reverses the normal history of composition in that in the course of this finale aria, the march moves ever more closely to the fore, until it decidedly finishes in the foreground.

Figaro's third-act finale, too, starts with a march – the greatest in all opera? – whose title, *Marcia*, should perhaps be understood in a sense similar to Haydn's or Mozart's *Menuettos*: though the piece is not anti-martial, its character, from the opening *pianissimo*, does push the utility form at least some way towards the background. But *Fidelio*'s march – another greatest? – is far more in the foreground than any minuet at that stage in the history of composition,[1] and the special category of funeral marches – the *Eroica*'s, *Götterdämmerung*'s – would, as anti-marches, be robbed of their meaning, nor indeed could the *Mastersinger*'s march be imagined without its fore-ground significance: the continued function of the march as march, as opposed to the discontinued function of, say, the minuet as minuet, explains at least part of its musical history, which still finds the march, both the ordinary march and the funeral march, in the foreground as late as Mahler – the first composer to introduce the unfunereal march into the foreground of symphonic thought.

[1] Though a little earlier, the *Don Giovanni* minuet emerged as musical history's sole musically great foreground example.

Now for the complication; at the same time, or rather, long before that time, Mozart and Haydn had introduced the ordinary march into the distant background of symphonic thought: a measure of the complexity of the march's musical history. The two had written anti-marches the way they had written anti-minuets – Mozart in the piano concerto, Haydn in the first movement of the present string quartet, which is quite often killed by means of a simple transfer of the march into the foreground: I would guess that it is because of the continuing foreground history of the elevated musical march, even the symphonic march, that these murders happen at all – which is why it is our duty to consider the musical march's foreground history.

In short, then: the first movement of Haydn's fifth and last great G major quartet (1799) is not a march, though it is firmly written against the background of a march. In view of some all too representative peformances I have heard, this initial observation is more important than anything else that can be said about the work and its interpretation.

Both Op.77 quartets are, of course, celebrated, the second in F major in more editions than the present work – without being greater than it, needless to add. For some reason or other, utterly incomprehensibly to me in any case, the F major has repeatedly been described as 'Haydn's most beautiful quartet': this is an actual quotation, whose source shall remain anonymous. It is, in fact, meaningless, though the work is certainly *inter primos inter pares*.

For the purpose of performance, it behoves us clearly to define the way in which Haydn achieves his anti-march in the opening movement – or, as I would prefer to call it, his spiritualized march. Upon reflection, the answer is simple. Both the texture and the short melodic motifs of the theme are essentially lyrical, despite their metrical impulse: it is when this unobtrusive, but nevertheless intrinsic lyrical character is ignored that the movement begins to be executed rather than interpreted.

Structurally, too, it has reached the characteristic culmination of Haydn's symphonic development: there are no more than two bars of new thematic material in the first movement's second subject! The character of this *Allegro moderato* is immediately implied by the *subito piano* on the work's second beat and presently defined by the first melodic motif after the brief introductory accompaniment to nothing which, at the same time, outlines the martial background; how, after all that, one can still think in terms of an overtly martial approach is beyond musical comprehension.

While the Quartet is not so difficult as it looks, both its extended, if often fast-moving structures and its utmost thematic economy ought to be concretely present in the interpreter's consciousness. To be brief and to the point is a conventional virtue; but what about being lengthy and sticking just as much to the point, as Haydn does throughout the three fully worked-out sonata movements of his penultimate complete quartet? For that, you need unremitting genius at its maturest stage of development – as was to be shown again, *mutatis mutandis*, by the late Beethoven.

For the *Adagio*, too, profound and improvisatory all the way, is at the same time as complex a sonata structure as the first movement. This richly reinvented sonata build-up is ultimately based on a single motif: 'mono-thematic' would be an understatement (or, if you like, an over-statement), 'mono-motivic' an absolutely realistic description, despite the movement's ever more deeply moving melodic variety. What is particularly fascinating is that notwithstanding the sonata scheme, Haydn contrives to imply, throughout, a downright opposite formal background, i.e. that of his beloved passacaglia – which, to be sure, he has so far confined to his variation forms.

Improvisatory freedom – and, in fact, truly ever-changing improvisation – is, of course, the basic condition for the interpretation of an *adagio* greater than which there is none in the composer's output. At the same time, there is no Haydn movement which, if I may so put it, requires a greater compositional contribution from the performers, amongst whom the leader will, of course, be the leading composer.

In a clearly demonstrable sense, the minuet is the most passionate anti-minuet of them all, and not only because of the mere speed of the movement, which, after all, is precedented, but also because of that which underlies its tempo, to wit, its rhythmic and melodic characters, in regard to which one can go so far as to say that whenever the movement is strongly rhythmical, it most emphatically contradicts its nominal dance rhythm – a contradiction which, in each such case, can be readily defined. More, I hope, one need not say to the performer, whose task it is to make the *presto* character oppose the minuet rhythm throughout. Wise before the event, the movement is amongst the founders of the Beethoven scherzo and its successors.

Through the third-relationship as explained by our theory, the principal section relaxes into the E♭ *Trio* which, proportionately as it were, will have to be taken a little more slowly. Have I said too much? The pronounced *forte* of the *Trio*'s bars 2–4 will, in any case, impose some restraint upon the tempo – if, that is, it is to be played in character.

There is all the difference in the world of fast motion between the *presto* of the minuet and the *presto* of the *Finale* – an object lesson in how little a mere tempo marking tells you so long as you don't know anything about the character of the movement in question. Although a virtuoso *presto*, the *Finale* is a complete and, once again, completely monothematic sonata form – without any desire to avail itself of a rondo's simplicity, monothematic notwithstanding its extended, if fast-moving structure. There is, in fact, no other quartet in which Haydn's very own sonata structures celebrate such a concentrated festival; his extensions don't reduce his concentration.

The usual *presto* advice, 'one in a bar' would be sheer nonsense here; at the beginning, for instance, it's one in four bars – and not in the expected fourth bar either, but in the third, on to whose first beat *both* the second and the fourth bar's accents are displaced: the usual, almost normal performing fallacy is to displace only one of them. Once the theme is thus sharply characterized, largely by de-accentuation, the definition of the tempo character won't present any problems, but bar 2 has to be really sufficiently de-accented to turn bars 10–11 into a major event: bar 11 craftily contradicts the expectation set up by what has become bar 10's contradicted expectation, in view of the contradicted expectation of bars 2–3 and bars 6–7! Thus, we are here confronted with no fewer than three interdependent levels of contradicted expectations, each of which has to be unambiguously defined not only for its own sake, but also in order to clarify the next one.

In any case, there will necessarily be a sharp difference between the opening unison and the first violin's continuation, though both of them will, of course, be heedful of what has been said about accentual displacements. The fact remains that the unison, though under the leadership of the first violin, will be more tutti-like, and will thus form the basis for the first violin's imaginative solo phrasing within the given framework, which we have closely defined. *Mutatis mutandis*, the same holds true for the subsequent unisons, i.e. not only the recapitulation's opening.

Op.77, No.2, in F major
(Hoboken III:82)

At my L.R.A.M. examination, I was given, as a reading test, the first-violin part of Haydn's last completed quartet (1799), at the same time the last of his surprisingly few – three – F major quartets. I remember being profoundly shocked by the assumption that I wouldn't know the work – and rightly so. I said immediately that I knew it intimately, whereupon Arthur Catterall, the chairman of the jury (and the leader of an imaginative quartet), found me another of the great quartets, I forget which. 'I'm afraid I know that one very well, too.' The jury members looked at each other in utter and contemptible surprise, and Catterall said: 'Well, if you know 'em all, let's pretend that you're reading this one'. Might he have mistrusted my confession? I got a round of applause after I'd played the exposition: evidently, at least some of them had thought, to begin with, that I had been lying, that I didn't like the look of what I had been asked to play. Today, matters are a little different, but no more than a little. I still encounter students, even alleged young masters, who know no more than one or two of the great Haydn quartets, and I wonder how the history of our young musicians' knowledge of them would have developed, or wouldn't, without my BBC endeavours on behalf of the string quartet in general, and Haydn and Mendelssohn in particular – which I had pursued constantly for twenty years.

It has to be admitted that in one or two respects Haydn's last finished quartet tops them all, in that it simply has everything one could wish for –

all-pervasive originality combined with comparatively easy accessibility, as well as great virtuosity combined with comparatively easy playability: Haydn had really reached the point where, without the slightest strain, he was having it both ways all the way. The work even constitutes a partial exception to our initial rule regarding the common characteristics of the 'celebrated' quartets, to wit, their symmetrical rhythmic structures. Both minuet and *Finale*, that is to say, contain far-reaching rhythmic complexities, however pleasantly concealed: more thereof when our more detailed examination reaches these movements. At this stage, it can certainly be said that an instinctive realization of these complexities would, of course, be entirely adequate, sufficient, and indeed conceivably preferable, in its naturalness, to an interpretation based on an intellectual recognition of the diverse and contradictory metres involved.

Player-readers will be conceitedly amused to learn that in the middle of the first movement's development section, where Haydn indulges in one of his most adventurous enharmonic changes – from $E\flat$ and $F\flat$ to $D\sharp$ and $E\natural$ – he felt the need to write some verbal help into the cello part: '*L'istesso tuono*' (the same sound). That was for players whose ears were less developed than are those of the present book's readers, the cellists amongst whom will be careful *not* to play the same sound, but immediately, as from bars 93/4, to imply, foreshadow, E minor: it is a sobering thought indeed to realize that Haydn had to make provisions for – none too metaphorically speaking – piano-playing string quartets!

Even in this particular spot, let alone the quartet's more easy-going passages, one soon realizes that the work represents the ultimate synthesis of sound and sense – or, if you like, of beauty and truth: gone is all the friction which Haydn (and, after him, Beethoven) often needed in order to make his sense as clear as possible; where previously he had pointed to the beauty of truth, he now expresses the truth of beauty without having to point to it.

In the opening *Allegro moderato*, the second subject, characteristically, proves its truthfulness by really being the first subject all over again, come to think of it; only, what was the theme in the first subject now becomes an all-important subordinate part on the second violin, with a new chromatic tune on top, on the first violin. The interpretation has to make this structural story and history quite clear even to the innocent ear – one that hears the movement for the very first time, whether as a player or a mere listener – for without a clear experience of this continuity, which clarity involves textural definition too, the movement's total meaning, as distinct from its local meanings, cannot begin to be grasped. Structurally, the second violin's version of the theme's basic phrase will be a variation of the first violin's model which, nevertheless, will make itself felt in its variations. The most usual playing fallacy in both versions is an accent on the least accented note – the first of the first bar's two crotchets, which is often produced for purely physical reasons, i.e. by the new bow.

Now, the very facts that the first violin's is a *forte* version, the second's a *sotto voce* version, imply, structurally as well as texturally, a varying approach. And so far as the texture itself is concerned, the second violin's subordinate part must not forget that once upon a time it was not only a principal part but the principal part's most important part, namely, its beginning. It will have to be played with sufficient self-importance without, however, endangering the yet greater importance of the new principal part: quite a task for the two violins, which the other two will help to solve, bearing in mind that the viola's accompaniment veers towards a subordinate part whose importance is as reduced as the second violin's is increased, whereas the cello's pedal simply doesn't veer anywhere. The fact that at this very point, the quartet texture is full on the one hand and subdued, contained, on the other imposes heavy responsibilities of balance and blend upon the ensemble; the principal part and the viola's subordinate part, in particular, will have to achieve simultaneous balance and blend, with the subordinate part retiring behind the tune. In the latest Eulenberg edition, incidentally, there is a misprint here, as if there weren't enough requirements demanding attention without it: there's no note missing in the viola part, whose crotchet *d* should be a minim.

Not since the C major and G major Quartets from Op.64 of nine years before have we encountered the anti-minuet in second place, but the 'return' to the old order is violently outbalanced by a D♭ major *Trio* which, yet again, confirms our theory about third-relationships, in that the principal section thus relaxes into the *Trio* even more emphatically and unambiguously than it would, could have done in an old-fashioned minuet and trio!

The principal section's *presto* contradicts not only the minuet's tempo, but even, in part, its metre, in that it goes so far as to imply duple rather than triple time – the triple background being, of course, retained (if very far back), as in the case of the quadruple foreground of the principal section in the minuet of Op.20, No.4 (see pp.55f.). The duple foreground will have to be played with absolute conviction: the background implications can look after themselves – as, in a well-defined background, they always can.

Even though the minuet's is a restrained *presto*, the *Trio*'s tempo asks for further relaxation, which will have to take the *Coda* into account – not, however, as an immediate re-establishment of the *tempo primo*, but, on the contrary, as a tempo transition which does not redefine the principal section's tempo character before its actual recapitulation; the *Coda* itself is constructed in a way which not only permits, but resolutely requires the freest possible tempo approach, whose two extraneous determinants are the tempo of the *Trio* at one end, and the tempo of the principal section at the other – which definitely doesn't mean that what is logically desirable is a gradual metamorphosis of tempo from one to the other. Many an opposite approach will make far clearer sense – such as a pronounced slowing up towards the end of the *Coda*, where the temporal relation between the first violin's final two crotchets and the cello's can, again, be of diverse kinds; all that is required is the cello's decided answer to the first violin – which might, preferably, be witty, but which, at the same time, has to offer the leader a solid basis for the resumption of the principal section's tempo, a resumption which, through the cello's wit, can itself have an amusing effect to begin with: the very juxtaposition of this *tempo giusto* with the preceding, utterly free tempo will easily produce an amusing effect, which first violin and cello had better forehear in order to make their concluding crotchets a perfect and perfectly free springboard for a resumed strictness whose *presto* character will make the resumption quite easy.

The *Trio*'s and *Coda*'s *pianissimo* is part and parcel of the *Trio*'s own character and should never be abandoned or departed from; at the same time, it is a grave and common mistake to exclude dynamic shading from a section which bears a single dynamic direction; quite especially if it is an unusual one, many interpreters pride themselves on adhering to it unvaringly throughout the section, and thus on altogether robbing phrasing itself of one of its dimensions. There are lots of *pianissimo*s in this world, and even from the sheer textural point of view, the direction means different things according to changing circumstances in what we might describe as the diagonal sound picture. So far as this *Trio* is concerned, it is entirely possible – indeed, I would suggest, downright necessary – to make dynamic shadings within the range of what is experienced as *pianissimo* a normal part of every player's phrasing; to give just one example, the last four bars of the first part will naturally be yet softer than the rest. Any other approach to what we might call this mini-codetta on the dominant level would not only be artificial, but actually confusing – concealing, that is to say, an important articulation point in the section's build-up (or, if you like, hiding the fact that with the upbeat to bar 90, a build-down sets in).

According to our theory of third-relationships (see p.199), the slow movement's key, far from tensing up the total structure by moving up the circle of fifths as far as the dominant of the dominant's dominant, follows the more usual principle of relaxing into the slow movement (prototypically, of course, by way of the subdominant): the minuet's tonical F 'leads' into D major, as it had led into the *Trio*'s D♭ major. In fact, one or the other player-reader may agree with me when I suggest that at the beginning of the *Andante*, the *Trio*'s D♭ major is still experientially remembered, with the result that the experience of the *Andante*'s key is not one of simple repose due to the F's leading function, but that one feels a tensing process at the same time: the progress to the Neapolitan sixth is experienced as one to a closely related key, but it is the Neapolitan sixth that is felt to lead to, resolve into the tonic, so that the reverse process is experienced as one of accumulating tension. Music is indeed capable of expressing and inducing simultaneous relaxation and tension, and there may be player-readers who even feel the tension produced by D major's ascent to the dominant of the dominant's dominant, though I personally take leave to doubt it: I would suspect that in such a case, it is theoretical considerations which deceive the individual in question into the belief that he has this spontaneous tensing experience.

As players, we have to decide what is the stronger element in the relation of the *Andante*'s key to the tonic, and the answer to this question is, in my firm submission, unambiguous, not merely because of F's leading and D major's resolving function, but also because the character of both the theme and indeed the entire movement is palpably intended to relax: if my submission is true, it inevitably lends further support to my theory of third-relationships.

The very fact that what, structurally, is a combination of variation and sonata form starts with a theme whose structural relaxation is reinforced by the textural ease of the violin-cello duo seems to support the thesis of relaxation here advanced: what we are confronted with is an easy-going, well nigh playful *andante*, the walking tempo of whose theme is downright tangible, rather than one of Haydn's characteristic, weighty *adagios*. If walking, like marching or waltzing or hopping, were a metrically recognized, stylized and formalized bodily motion, the *Andante*'s theme could be described as a foreground dance, a foreground walk whose dotted march motifs are used in the service of walking relaxation rather than martial tension: could one describe the movement as *a walk composed against the background of a march*? If this description clicks with any player-reader, he will pursue the interpretation thus characterized; perhaps I may add from experience that it is likely to develop into a cogent and convincing structure.

The *mezza voce* of the duo as against the *subito piano* of the theme's last, recapitulatory section is a major inspiration which shows what happens if from the outset, the dynamic dimension is included in the composer's invention; many were and are the composers, then as now, whose dynamics are superimposed on, rather than an intrinsic element in, their thematic invention. And as an intrinsic element the dynamics have to be played: after the duo, none too obtrusive in its tone production on the one hand and not at all shy or embarrassed on the other, the expressive *piano* of the brim-full, totally rest-less quartet texture (*cf.* the theme of another, eminently comparable combination of variation and sonata – the slow movement of Op.42: see p.84) has to make an overwhelming impression, not only on any eaves-droppers, but on the tone-producers themselves.

At this final stage in the present book, it should no longer be necessary to warn the leader that in no circumstances should he phrase the first four bars of the 'tutti' identically with his opening four bars (his own part being identical): nothing short of a drastic, intensively imaginative variation will do in this radically contrasting context! And our two-dimensional and hence analytic description of the walk composed against the background of a march seems confirmed by the eventual *forte* and *fortissimo* contrast at the end of the theme, where the background comes to the fore: ends are recognizable as ends in proportion as the background, the form, the sum total of expectations, comes to the fore, so that the end of a work is its only point at which expectation is fully met – by the tonical perfect cadence's resolution.

The single-chord introduction of the *Finale*, Haydn's last variation on this theme, shows how wrong are the commentators who interpret his introductions as calls to a concert audience's attention. We have seen that in any case, Haydn was preoccupied with beginnings before the beginning long before he wrote for performance in bigger rooms; we now have to add that by the time of the finale, the concert audience's attention must be assumed to have been with the work for quite some time – so much so that the return from D major to F major is in need of an opening chordal warning, for while F led to D, D doesn't in any way lead to F! This, then, is the sole function of the present, exceptional introduction, which, for once, doesn't play any further role in the structure of the movement, though the last chords integrate it, and the layout of the very last chord even alludes to it.

A contemporary composer would have written the opening of the body of the movement thus: $^4/_4$, $^2/_4$, $^4/_4$, $^2/_4$, $^4/_4$, $^2/_4$ (one bar of each), followed by $^3/_4$ – and there are cross accents into this particular bargain too (Ex.67):

Ex.67

Any sensible interpretation will certainly follow this implied scheme, on whose instinctive recognition Haydn relied: it is only nowadays that we have to notate the metric foreground in order to make players understand. In any case, the emotional enjoyment which this repeated – and, proportionately, forefeelable – metric polarity yields should, its own playing definition apart, be conveyed to the listener (including, again, the playing listener) in so direct a fashion that it immediately becomes his enjoyment too; it is, after all, part of the communication, so much so that without it, the movement's truth-finding and/or its understanding would be gravely impeded. As we reach the end of this book on interpretation, we have to grasp *the* indispensable truth about musical truth: without a continuous, all-embracing and all-pervasive emotional experience, all musical truth – as opposed to musico-intellectual truisms and platitudes, however pseudo-complex – remains incomprehensible.

Consciously or (more likely) not, the *Finale*'s sonata from crowns Haydn's achievement in this, his most personal type of structure: yes, if anything, his sonata structures are yet more personal than the structures in the forms he personally invented, for he lets what seems sonata form's most distinguishing characteristic stand on its head – its polythematicism which, in Haydn's hands, becomes the most insistent monothematicism. The present last movement is the quartet's strictest monothematic structure, for the *Finale* is, simply, based on one theme, and on one theme only. A truly understanding and characterizing interpretation will convey this fundamental fact to the listener's instinctive ear.

The rhythmic complexities of the movement must never be allowed to overshadowed or indeed conceal its characteristic playfulness; I don't know enough about the Croatian folk style to be able to say whether it is as emphatic an element of this last movement as most commentators say (do *they* know enough?). What, however, is glaringly obvious on purely intra-musical evidence is that the entire structure has been thrown into relief against the background of a polonaise, whose cross-accented rhythmic pattern accompanies the theme in the cello from the moment the musical foreground settles down in ³/₄ (Ex.68):

Ex.68

The polonaise background does, in fact, make itself far more distinctly felt (and should, needless to add, make itself clearly felt in performance) than does the minuet background in most of Haydn's minuets. Its definition will help to retain the movement's playfulness on which Haydn insists, despite the music's complex substance; it is only on the very highest level of inspiration that playful complexity succeeds. Haydn apart, its only masters are Mozart, Beethoven, and Schoenberg.

Epilogue: Op.103, in prospective D minor
(Hoboken III:83)

The final fragment is most moving, especially the *Andante grazioso*, but it cannot possibly be adequately appreciated before Haydn's development as a quartet-composing genius – and never mind what happened before Op.9, No.4 and indeed immediately after – has been fully understood; I think its interpretation might profitably be postponed until then. 'Full understanding', to be sure, leaves much un-understood; I am sure we all agree with Tovey[1] that 'we may be satisfied to seek out what Haydn has done for us without more than a mystic notion of how he did it' – except that Tovey's phrase, 'more than a mystic notion' seems to imply that a mystic notion is a poor substitute for clear verbal knowledge.

I would submit, on the contrary, that ultimately and from the conceptual and hence verbal standpoint, a mystic notion is not only all we can have about great music, but also *clarity itself* so long as we needn't translate it into words, so long as the intrinsic mysticism of music in general and the string quartet in particular is allowed to have its clear say, occasionally aided, but never either supported by, or, heaven beware, replaced with, words.

I would go even further and suggest that upon inspection and reflection (both of which I have carefully undertaken before sitting down to write this epilogue), it may be conceded that the present book contains everything that can be said for the purpose of promoting a clear and natural interpretation of Op.103; any additional word would inevitably repeat one or the other point that has already been made. If, in other words, the present book's guide-lines have been fully and practically absorbed, towards which end all great Haydn quartets will have had to be understandingly played, the present middle movements will not pose any insoluble problems; at the same time, the solutions to any problems they may pose can, moreover, be concretely and specifically pin-pointed in this book. I could therefore conclude thus: 'As for Op.103, see pp.1–246'.

It remains to draw attention to a frequent near-miss translation of what Haydn called his 'visiting card', which he instructed the publisher to print at the end of each part after the minuet, and whose musical line is a quotation from one of his four-part songs (see Ex.69 overleaf).

---

[1] *Op.cit.*

Only the other night, I heard a Radio 3 announcer offer us the usual 'free' translation: 'All my strength is gone; I am old and frail.' Nothing is lost in the literal translation: 'Gone is all my strength, old and weak am I. *Fine.*'

For musical purposes, I suggest:

Ex.69

Molto Adagio

Hin ist al- le mei-ne Kraft, alt und schwach bin ich.
Gone is eve-ry ounce of strength; old and weak am I.

Fine.

Index of Names

Index of Names

Adler, Oskar 1, 2, 13, 14, 94, 139, 168

Bach, Johann Sebastian 60, 69, 108f., 227
  Chromatic Fantasy and Fugue 197
  Concerto for Violin in E major 61, 101
Bard, Raimund 213, 213n
Bärenreiter 213
Barret-Ayres, Reginald 36n
Bartók, Béla
  String Quartets 2
BBC 138, 238
Beethoven, Ludwig van 16, 28, 70, 73,
    143f., 144, 147, 163, 199, 214
  adagio composer 26
  Cello Sonatas, Op. 5 102
  and C minor 59, 136
  credited with *Terzverwandtschaft* 199
  deafness 26
  development 30
  difficulties, as part of composition, *see*
    Subjects Index
  early 210
  Fidelio, march 235
  and finale problem 234
  friction 239
  and homotonality 135
  jokes 179, 182
  late 236
  master of playful complexity 244
  monothematicism 237
  Piano Concertos
    No. 3 in C minor, Op. 37 224
    No. 4 in G major, Op. 58 27
  Piano Sonata No. 1 in F minor, Op.
    2 58f., 210
  Piano Trios, Op. 1 210
  problematic Grand Fugue 3, 17, 100
  quartet fugues 5, 30

  quartet textures, typical, *see* Subjects
    Index
  and rondo 133
  scherzo 210, 237
  second repeats in 76ff.
  slowing up before the end 174
  and sonata 133
  String Quartets 2, 7, 17
    Op. 18
      No. 4 in C minor 14, 39, 147f.,
        198
      No. 6 in B flat 34
    Op. 59 (Rasumovsky)
      No. 1 in F major 220, 226
      No. 3 in C major 195
    Op. 95 in F minor 58f.
    Op. 130 in B flat 33, 34, 100
      second finale for 68, 135
    Op. 135 in F 17, 76
  Symphonies
    No. 3 in E flat, Op.55 (*Eroica*) 175,
      190
      Funeral march 72, 235
      finale 134
    No. 5 in C minor, Op. 67 215
    No. 8 in F major, Op. 93 198
    No. 9 in D minor, Op. 125 24, 27,
      39, 72, 80, 136
  third-relationship 237
'Bird, The', Haydn's String Quartet Op.
    33, No. 3 72ff., 78, 87, 143, 218,
    227
Bland 137
Boccherini, Luigi 158
  metre, *see* 'Boccherini metre' in
    Subjects Index
Brahms, Johannes 46, 147
  Clarinet Quintet 68, 121

Index of Subjects

Index of Subjects

accent, one main per phrase 73
accents, three prominent, in phrase 193
accompaniment, to nothing 72f., 87, 236
adagio composers, *see* Beethoven, Bruckner, Haydn in Names Index
antecedents, postponed, *see* principle
anthem, national, *see* national anthem
anti-minuet 237
asymmetry
  Haydn's natural inclination towards 161f.
  and popularity 156
'atonality', *see* Haydn in Names Index
attack, orchestral 220, 221
authenticity and style 158
avoidance, does not communicate 21, 25, 167, 194, 221

background and foreground 22f., 153, 166, 240f.
  autobiographical 182, 189
balance, and blend 2f., 4, 33, 161, 240
beginning before the beginning 72f., 87, 175ff., 190ff., 201ff., 205, 242
B flat minor 170
B flat Quartets 175, 220
bi-thematicism 154
blend, *see* balance
'Boccherini metre', 20, 22, 23, 39f., 64
'bridge passage' 23, 23n

cadence, deceptive 79n
'call to attention' 201
'Carmirelli bowing' 42, 124f., 171, 224
'celebrated' quartets 170, 228ff.
chamber music 16
circle, vicious and virtuous 11f., 87
C major Quartets 164, 195, 216

colour melody, Haydn's 66, 110, 144f., 149
combined forms 74
  amalgam of variation and development 163
  monothematic ternary, variation, and monothematic sonata 124
  sonata and rondo 155
  ternary, sonata, variation 214, 224
  variation and sonata 242
  variation and ternary 223f.
comedy 187, 191
complementation, principal of 33, 38
conceptual
  logic *v.* musical logic 25
  thought, laws of 15
Concertante, see scordatura
contrast
  and continuity 234
  between one idea and the next 234
  between statement and development 216
craft of composition, the 16
critics 15

dance, in elevated art music 235
dance movements, within a symphonic work 198
deceptive cadence, *see* cadence
development, *see* contrast
developmental
  movements 231
  technique in variations, Haydn's 124
difficulties, as part of composition (Beethoven, Brahms) 67
D major 65
D major Quartets 164, 182, 223
  brilliance 182